D1607035

East of Paris

PROPERTY OF
ALPINE PUBLIC LIBRARY
805 W. AVE E
ALPINE, TX 79830

East of Paris

THE NEW CUISINES OF AUSTRIA AND THE DANUBE

DAVID BOULEY,
MARIO LOHNINGER, AND MELISSA CLARK

PHOTOGRAPHS BY THOMAS SCHAUER

An Imprint of HarperCollins*Publishers*

The cocktail glasses on pages 225 and 228 are manufactured by
   J. & L. Lobmeyr, Vienna, www.lobmeyr.at
The coffeehouse pictured on page 289 is Café Sperl, Vienna

EAST OF PARIS: THE NEW CUISINES OF AUSTRIA AND THE DANUBE. Copyright © 2003
by David Bouley. All rights reserved. Manufactured in China. No part of this
book may be used or reproduced in any manner whatsoever without written
permission except in the case of brief quotations embodied in critical
articles and reviews. For information, address HarperCollins Publishers Inc.,
10 East 53rd Street, New York, NY 10022.

HarperCollins books may be purchased for educational, business, or sales
promotional use. For information, please write: Special Markets Department,
HarperCollins Publishers Inc., 10 East 53rd Street, New York, NY 10022.

FIRST EDITION

Designed by Douglas Riccardi/Memo Productions, NY

Printed on acid-free paper

Library of Congress Cataloging-in-Publication Data
Bouley, David.
East of Paris : the new cuisines of Austria and the Danube / by David Bouley,
Mario Lohninger, and Melissa Clark.
   p. cm.
ISBN 0-06-621449-1 (alk. paper)
1. Cookery, Austrian. I. Lohninger, Mario. II. Clark, Melissa. III. Title.

TX721.B67 2003
641.59436—dc21   2003044956

03 04 05 06 07 ❖/SC 10 9 8 7 6 5 4 3 2 1

Acknowledgments

Writing a book is a team effort, and there are always so many people
to thank, people whose wonderful work and creativity have contributed
significantly to this project.

First, of course, we must thank everyone at the Danube, especially manager Walter Krajnc, recipe tester and developer Amy Theilen, bar chef
Albert Trummer, sous chefs Thomas Mayr and Thomas Kahl, and pastry
chef Alex Grunert.

This book would certainly not exist without the loyalty, support, and vision
of our publisher, Daniel Halpern, editorial director of Ecco. And we could
not be more pleased with the beautiful photography of Thomas Schauer
and the design efforts of Douglas Riccardi.

We are also grateful to Karen Rush and Zoe Singer, for their help in testing
and editing these recipes.

Finally, we must thank Hans Hass, whose inspiration and mentorship has
been felt throughout our work on this book.

David Bouley
Mario Lohninger
Melissa Clark

Contents

INTRODUCTION BY DAVID BOULEY (left) One of the first questions I am always asked about the Danube is why I opened a Viennese restaurant. What is the connection that makes Austrian cuisine such an important part of my life?

The answer goes back to my childhood. But it wasn't that I was exposed to Austrian food at a young age. Though I was brought up in Connecticut, my family is French, and I grew up in the embrace of French food and culture. My happiest memories are of the days at my grandmother's house in Rhode Island. It was a magical place for a kid. She raised chickens and pheasants and goats, and grew her own vegetables. She was a wonderful cook, and my family would spend Sundays at her house, helping her prepare amazing multicourse meals.

It was from her that I learned to appreciate the true, basic flavors of ingredients. I remember the moment when I realized the power of a fresh, perfectly cooked vegetable. I was a young boy, maybe nine or ten, and we were all helping with the harvest on a neighbor's farm. It was at the end of the season and we were gathering up the vegetables that hadn't been collected yet, the last of the beets, parsnips, onions, potatoes, green tomatoes, squash, and eggplant. Before the ground was turned and prepared for the winter, we pulled out all the dead plants and made them into a huge bonfire. Then we wrapped all the newly dug vegetables in aluminum foil and threw them in the fire. When the fire was dead we took out all the little wrapped packets and ate the vegetables. I was shocked by the flavors. They were unbelievable. There were onions so soft you could squeeze out the pulp, and squash with thickened juices that were transparent but so intense. Even the artichokes tasted amazing roasted like this.

When I became a cook after high school, these flavors stayed with me. I worked in many restaurants, a number of the top restaurants in France in fact. (I originally went to Paris to study business at the Sorbonne, but I was more interested in studying at the restaurants.) I worked for the best chefs around at the time, including Roger Vergé and Paul Bocuse. But I also worked at less exalted restaurants, and what I learned was that in many French restaurants, flavor isn't the primary objective. Service is getting the food out of the kitchen and into the dining room. That's in part why classic French food is so heavy and filled with cream and butter. It's all about executing the dish. It's nothing like my memories of my grandmother's cooking. She rarely made beurre blanc, that rich sauce that's the foundation of so many French dishes. If she did make it, she flavored it with orange and put it on asparagus. And then the dish was about the asparagus and not the sauce. That's the difference.

In the hands of masters like Vergé, French food became something that was at once refined and classic in technique but built on fresh ingredients. It had soul, like my grandmother's cooking. And it was a lot healthier than traditional "haute" fare. This was what I based my cuisine at Bouley restaurant on, this clean, healthful cooking that pays homage to the brilliance of a perfect ingredient. I built my repertoire around fruit and vegetable juices, pulps, and stocks instead of starches and cream. Adding these to an ingredient that is already sweet and clean tasting gives you a beautiful dish that is easy to digest.

After I returned to the United States, I worked my way around different restaurant kitchens to learn what I could. One of the places I cooked at was the then four-star Vienna 79 restaurant. Although I hadn't been exposed to Austrian cooking as a child, when I got to Vienna 79, it was already familiar. Here were some of the flavors and techniques of my grandmother's Sunday dinners. Here were the slowly braised meats that rendered all their fat and became tender and concentrated. Here were the vegetable salads and pickles, the bouillons, stuffed whole fish, and braised chickens. The ingredients might have been spiced differently than the French seasonings she used, but their soul was the same. This cuisine spoke to me.

Through my experience at Vienna 79 I met a lot of Austrian people and went on trips in their country—in the winter to ski, in the summer to hike and ride bikes, and any time of year just to be in Vienna. I fell in love with Austrian culture as well as the food.

But while I'm devoted to all the classic Austrian dishes, the goulashes and schnitzels and roasted ducks, there is also another side to the cooking, a more modern, innovative side. This movement toward "new Austrian" cuisine followed close on the heels of France's nouvelle cuisine and was based on many of the same philosophies, like lightening up the sauces and incorporating influences from different parts of the globe. A leader in this movement was Vic Sigmund at Tantris restaurant in Munich. Although Tantris is in Germany, Sigmund is Austrian. After he retired, another Austrian, Hans Hass, took over Tantris's kitchen and continued this legacy of fresh, ingredient-driven dishes that were both dependent on classic technique and intensely creative and contemporary. He was interpreting Austrian food in a way that was similar to the way I was interpreting French food at Bouley.

So I thought, what if I combined what I was doing at Bouley with the cuisine at Tantris? It would be a restaurant unlike any other. I decided to give it a shot. I opened the Danube in 1999, with Mario Lohninger as executive chef. I was lucky to have found Mario. Having worked at Tantris, in Paris, and in California, he shared my vision of what the Danube needed to be.

The food at the Danube has developed into something unique—not just contemporary Austrian food, nor Austrian-French-American fusion, but what I imagine the cuisine of Austria would be if the Austro-Hungarian Empire were still extant. What would the cuisine of an empire be like in the

modern world? I like to think it would resemble what Mario and I evolved–capturing the moment of peak flavor in our ingredients, combining classic technique and influences from around the world, and translating that into a culinary language with an Austrian gestalt.

This cuisine is what Mario and I hope to bring to you in this book. Some of the recipes here are for dishes that have been modified for the home cook. Some of the recipes are from my own repertoire, some are from Mario's, and some we worked on together over the years. There are some recipes we specifically created for the home cook, and there are some old-fashioned, traditional dishes that Austrian home cooks have been making for generations. I hope you will enjoy the recipes as much as Mario, Melissa, and I have enjoyed writing this book.

INTRODUCTION BY MARIO LOHNINGER (right) Like a lot of European chefs, I made the decision to start cooking at a very early age. In fact, since my father is a chef and my grandfather a baker, you could say it wasn't really a decision. It was in my blood when I was born.

I grew up in a small village in Austria near Salzburg. My grandfather owned the only bakery in town, and by the time I was four I was helping him shape the little white flour and poppy seed rolls he made every morning. It seemed only natural for my parents to go into the restaurant business, and they opened their restaurant near our home when I was nine, with my father in the kitchen and my mother in the dining room. My sister and I helped out, too. She helped my mother with the customers, and I worked in the kitchen with my dad.

So no one in my family was surprised when I chose cooking as my course of study in school. I was twelve years old, which seems young in the United States, but this is how things work back home in Austria. I went to restaurant and hotel management school in Tyrol and did my apprenticeship in Salzburg, then moved on, landing a job at a Michelin two-star restaurant called Obauer.

Obauer was my introduction to really fine cuisine. I spent eighteen months there in the one-thousand-year-old city of Werfen. I was part of a big team, and we all worked fifteen- to sixteen-hour days together. Obauer was an idyll for chefs in Austria: We cut our own fresh herbs and in the summer we picked our own salad greens from the garden. If we ran out of salad in the middle of service, we would just run outside and pick some more. It was all that fresh. Some afternoons, we'd hunt for wild ramps with the chef. And when lunch was slow, half the waitstaff came into the kitchen to help jar the honey.

We did a lot of things most restaurants had stopped doing, like making our own cured meat and sausage, muesli, cheeses, sour cream, and jams. We cooked with these ingredients and also packaged them to send home with guests. It was wonderful to have beautiful, fresh-tasting preserves to use in the middle of the snowy winter and thick sour cream to finish a sauce. It taught me a very important lesson, one that I think all good chefs learn early in their careers, that the quality and freshness of your raw ingredients make all the difference. Being at Obauer also taught me a respect for the cuisine of the region—for the local products and for the ways these products can best be employed, highlighted, and used efficiently in a restaurant kitchen.

I had to leave Obauer to do my military service. When I got out, I felt ready for some international cooking experience and I sent my résumé to all the biggest restaurants. I was barely twenty, with only one major work experience on my résumé, and I didn't hear back from anyone. So I called a

friend who knew Hans Hass, whose Austrian restaurant Tantris in Germany had received three Michelin stars. Hass hired me, and working there was really challenging—it would have been even if I hadn't been so young. Tantris was much more cosmopolitan than Obauer had been. It was more French-influenced and stylish, and people paid a lot of attention to the trends that began there. I spent a year and a half at Tantris, working in every station of the kitchen.

Although I left Tantris to work in Paris at Guy Savoy, in New York at San Domenico, and in Los Angeles with Wolfgang Puck, it was my experience with Hans Hass that eventually led me to David Bouley and the Danube restaurant.

David had already come up with the Danube project when he hired me. He had modeled it somewhat on Tantris and was looking for an Austrian chef who understood the kind of creative, contemporary cuisine Hans Hass was famous for, in addition to being comfortable cooking the classics like schnitzel.

It was and still is an excellent collaboration. David told me how New Yorkers like to eat and explained that he wanted his food to be "clean," without very much fat, cooked in vegetable oils whenever possible. We liked each other's styles. We both put ideas on the table and then met each other halfway. David really pushes his chefs and encourages them to revise until their ideas work. That gave me a feeling of security and confidence in the food we were making.

It's been really interesting to cook food from so many Eastern European countries, using so many ingredients, always looking back to that time two hundred years ago when such important and beautiful things were happening in Vienna. Working with David at the Danube has been a perfect way for me to draw on my cooking experiences in Austria, Germany, France, and America and also to grow and develop a more personal style. We've been able to bring a lot of the elements of Austrian cooking onto the menu and to show diners that there's another way of looking at this cuisine, while at the same time we're expanding horizons, serving food that's really new. That's been our goal in writing *East of Paris*—to introduce readers to a refined cuisine that draws on Austrian cooking, is prepared with really high standards, and that goes beyond the culinary canon.

ALONG THE DANUBE: A BRIEF HISTORY OF AUSTRIAN CUISINE

Modern-day Austria covers only a fraction of the territory that came under the rule of the Austrian and then the Austro-Hungarian empires. This goes far to explain why this tiny, mountain-hugged country has such a far-ranging cuisine, at once rustic, refined, exotic, and exalted.

To trace the diverse influences on Austrian cuisine, one may begin by following the wandering Danube. Commerce and culture have long flowed along the river's 1,771 miles, as it wends through current Germany, Austria, Slovenia, Slovakia, Hungary, the Czech Republic, Yugoslavia, Bulgaria, and Romania. At times during the period from the late thirteenth to the early twentieth century, the Austrian and Austro-Hungarian empire's borders stretched from czarist Russia to the Adriatic and encompassed people of over ten different nationalities and four major religions. During this time Vienna, with its prime seat on the Danube, served as a cultural center in many ways, and often the food preferences of the emperor in Vienna set the vogue throughout the empire. Today Austria is bordered by Switzerland, Germany, the Czech Republic, Slovakia, Hungary, Slovenia, and Italy. These neighboring cultures added their culinary traditions to the melting pot of Austrian cuisine, but they were not the only ones. Other influences include Turkish, Alsatian, French, Spanish, Dutch, Bohemian-Moravian, Polish, Croatian, Serbian, and Jewish cuisines. While Hungarian paprika is perhaps the best known of these contributions, the Turkish legacy of coffee is at least as important, not to mention the dumplings and sauerkraut of Bohemia, the pasta of Italy, and the fish cookery found all along the Danube. The Baroque Period, which spanned about 100 years beginning in 1600, saw the rise of an opulent style of eating and entertaining that still leaves us in awe. The aristocracy of the Old Empire did much to further the art of Austrian cooking with their multicourse feasts. This was the period that cemented the supremacy of Austrian pastry. Diplomats from all parts returned to their countries to broadcast the splendor of Austrian confections.

While this grand style of living is no more, and the Empire itself has been divided and redivided since, Vienna's splendid coffeehouses display dizzying arrays of pastries as wonderful to look at as they are to eat, and the Austrian love for food, and the wide range of influences encompassed by Austrian cuisine, remain a matter of pride to Austrians and a delight to all others.

Fall

Liptauer

SPREAD

1 cup QUARK CHEESE (see page 14)

$1/2$ cup GOAT CHEESE

$1/2$ cup RICOTTA SALATA, finely grated

1 SHALLOT, minced

$1/2$ GARLIC CLOVE, mashed to a paste

1 tablespoon plus 1 teaspoon finely chopped CORNICHONS

1 tablespoon finely chopped FRESH CHIVES

1 tablespoon finely chopped FRESH PARSLEY

1 tablespoon finely chopped CAPERS

2 teaspoons fresh LEMON JUICE

$1 1/2$ teaspoons SWEET HUNGARIAN PAPRIKA (see page 275)

Fine SEA SALT and freshly ground BLACK PEPPER, to taste

FOR SERVING

Sliced PROSCIUTTO (optional)

Finely chopped CHIVES (optional)

Finely chopped FRESH PARSLEY (optional)

CAPERS, whole (optional)

SWEET HUNGARIAN PAPRIKA (optional)

SLICED BREAD, preferably wheat, pumpernickel, or rye

SERVES 8 AS AN HORS D'OEUVRE

Liptauer is a traditional Austro-Hungarian dish that varies from cook to cook and region to region. Named for the formerly Hungarian town of Lipto, it is essentially a tangy, full-flavored cheese spread made with a combination of cheeses, including goat cheese and Quark. Some recipes call for the addition of herbs, paprika, and pickles; others for onions, garlic, and beer. In Austrian restaurants Liptauer is served as an hors d'oeuvre, piled onto a cheese board and garnished with crudités, bread, pickles, and prosciutto. You'll often find it served with another popular spread called *Grammelschmalz*, a heady, slippery-textured mix of freshly rendered pork fat seasoned with pumpkin seed oil, marjoram, and shallots and mixed with crunchy bits of fried pork skin. This is the kind of rustic food you'd find at a *Heurigen*, a Viennese wine restaurant.

NOTES FROM THE KITCHEN This spread is what we hand out when we overbook the restaurant, the bar gets crowded, and Walter Krajnc, the manager, begins to wave his hands frantically around the kitchen: "Get them something to eat in the bar, get them something to eat in the bar." Originally we began this concept of "bar food," or little complimentary snacks for those sipping aperitifs in the bar, when one of the Austrian sous-chefs began whipping up gargantuan vats of green Grammelschmalz. We in the kitchen loved the concept of thin, hip New Yorkers eating pure fat. But the waitstaff became tired of explaining what that peculiar mouthfeel was, so we changed to Liptauer, which is also a traditional Austrian pre-dinner snack.

1. Combine all the ingredients for the spread in a bowl, and stir together with a wooden spoon until smooth; or use a food processor, pulsing until just combined.

2. Mound the Liptauer on a platter, and if desired, surround it with prosciutto and additional chives, parsley, capers, and paprika. Serve with the bread.

QUARK *Quark*, as it is called in German (and commonly referred to in the U.S.), or Topfen, as it is known in Austria, is a soft, fresh white curd cheese, similar to pot cheese. It is made from whole or low-fat cow's milk, or sometimes buttermilk. The word *Quark* means "curd," and this simple cheese is said to have been made in Germany since the Iron Age. Mild and light, Quark is used in ravioli, cheesecake, spreads, and many other preparations both sweet and savory. It is increasingly available at specialty cheese stores and by mail order (see Sources, page 337). If you can't find it, substitute farmer's cheese, first processing it in a blender or food processor until it is very smooth.

HEURIGEN *Heurigen* is the Austrian word for the year's new wine, and for the vineyard wine gardens where the proprietors serve this wine. Viennese vintners have been selling their wines this way since a 1784 edict from Emperor Franz Josef II allowed the wineries on the outskirts of Vienna to sell new wines without paying a tariff (to this day, the proprietors must sell only their own wines). Since then, vintners have indicated they have wine to serve by hanging a pine branch in front of their Heurigen. And the tradition of making a trip to these establishments has been firmly in place ever since.

At the Heurigens, wood tables are set up, outside whenever possible, and pitchers of the new wine are poured, to be drunk from glass mugs. While it was once customary to bring a picnic—often a meal of bread, meats, and cheeses, and perhaps a jar of potato salad—this began to change when boys started to sell bread and bakery items at the wine gardens, and sausage vendors made their rounds of the tables. These snacks were so popular that now most Heurigens function as restaurants as well as wineries, so customers no longer need to provision themselves for a visit.

Liptauer and other spreads, breads, pretzels, cured and hot cooked meats, and hot and cold vegetables and salads are standard fare at many Heurigens now, as are musicians, who add to the mood with sentimental tunes played on violin, accordion, harmonica, or perhaps zither. While this tradition was at first limited to the late-summer nights when the days were long, now many Heurigens are open almost year-round, one year's wine merging into the next.

Liptauer-Stuffed Peppers

8 small RED BELL PEPPERS

3 large RED BELL PEPPERS

1 tablespoon fresh LEMON JUICE,
   or to taste

1 tablespoon extra-virgin OLIVE OIL

Fine SEA SALT and freshly ground
   BLACK PEPPER

1 recipe LIPTAUER (see page 12)

PARMIGIANO-REGGIANO CHEESE,
   shaved with a vegetable peeler,
   for garnish

FRESH PARSLEY LEAVES, for
   garnish

SERVES 4 AS AN APPETIZER

Stuffing Liptauer into vegetables such as roasted peppers or hollowed-out cucumbers, or even using it to fill hollowed-out soft pretzels, is a fun and classic presentation. A red pepper vinaigrette intensifies the color and sweetness of the roasted peppers.

1. Roast the 8 small peppers over the open flame of a gas burner or under the broiler, turning them frequently, until the skin is charred all over, about 5 minutes. Immediately transfer the peppers to a deep bowl and cover with a plate to trap the steam. Let sit until cool, about 5 minutes, then carefully rub the peel off the peppers, using your hands or a metal spoon and keeping the peppers intact. Cut out the stems and inside ribs, and discard the seeds. Place the peppers in a bowl.

2. If you have a juicer, juice the 3 large peppers and skim the foam. You should have 1 1/2 cups juice. Alternatively, puree the peppers in a blender with just enough water to allow them to move around. Strain the juice.

3. Place the pepper juice in a small saucepan over medium heat and bring it to a simmer. Cook gently until reduced to 1/2 cup, 15 to 20 minutes. Let cool. Transfer the juice to a bowl, whisk in the lemon juice and olive oil, and season with salt and pepper. Pour this dressing over the peeled peppers and let marinate in the refrigerator, turning occasionally, for at least 1 hour or overnight.

4. Drain the peppers and stuff them with the Liptauer. Set 2 peppers on each plate, and spoon some of the marinade around them. Garnish with the Parmigiano-Reggiano and parsley leaves.

Kumamoto Oysters
WITH APPLE GELÉE

5 grams (about 2 sheets) LEAF
   GELATIN (see Sources, page 337)

1 tablespoon fresh LIME JUICE,
   or more to taste

Pinch of ASCORBIC ACID (see Note)

4 GRANNY SMITH APPLES

5 sprigs FRESH MINT, leaves
   stripped from the stems

1 tablespoon CHAMPAGNE

24 KUMAMOTO OYSTERS

SERVES 12 AS AN HORS
D'OEUVRE

*Note: Ascorbic acid, also sold as
granular vitamin C, is available in
health food stores. It keeps fresh
fruit and vegetable mixtures from
oxidizing and turning brown.*

NOTES FROM THE KITCHEN If you don't have a juicer at home, bring your ascorbic acid and mint to a juice bar and ask them to make some apple juice with mint. As soon as you have it, stir in a pinch of ascorbic acid.

1. Soak the gelatin sheets in cold water until softened, about 5 minutes. Squeeze out the excess water and pat dry with a paper towel. Set them aside.

2. Put the lime juice in a small bowl. Add the ascorbic acid and whisk to dissolve. Place the bowl under the spout of a juicer.

3. Wash the apples and quarter them. Cut out the stems and seeds, and then cut the quarters in half lengthwise into pieces that will fit in the juicer. Feed the apples and mint leaves through the juicer, then skim the foam from the juice.

4. Bring a small pot of water to a simmer. Place the gelatin sheets in a small metal bowl and moisten them with a few tablespoons of the apple juice. Set the bowl over the simmering water and heat gently, whisking, until the gelatin dissolves completely. Pour it through a fine-mesh strainer into the remaining apple juice. Whisk until combined. Taste for acidity, and add more lime juice if desired. Refrigerate until set, about 3 hours. (This is a loose gel and will never set up solidly.)

5. About 1 hour before serving, scrub and refrigerate the oysters (see page 231).

6. Stir the Champagne into the apple gelée.

7. Open the oysters with an oyster knife. Pour off the excess liquid, and make sure the oysters are clear of bits of shell (see page 231). Spoon a small dollop of the gelée on top of each oyster in its shell. It should spread and cloak the oyster in translucent green. Serve immediately.

DAVID BOULEY Kumamoto oysters have a sweet, clean, meaty flavor. Here, the apple gelée brings out their salt and minerals, and the two marry really well. But it's not only about the flavor—the mouthfeel is just as important. The gelée has almost the same texture as the oyster, so when you put one of these hors d'oeuvres in your mouth, you can't tell them apart. Both the gelée and the oyster seem to float across the palate, spreading their very different flavors but also melding together.

Hot-Smoked Salmon

WITH APPLE SALAD, SALMON CAVIAR, AND SHERRY DRESSING

MARIO LOHNINGER In Austria hot-smoking is much more popular than cold-smoking, especially for fish. It gives the fish a light smoky flavor and cooks it at the same time. But you have to be careful not to overdo it because it cooks quickly. You want the fish to still taste fresh and have a soft texture without drying out, so watch it closely. I like the way salmon works in this salad. It has a richness that's nice with the crisp fennel and apples.

1. Fill a bowl with water and ice. Bring a pot of water to a boil and salt it until it tastes like seawater (about 2 teaspoons per quart). Blanch the fennel slices in the salted water for 3 minutes, then drain and transfer them to the ice water to cool.

2. Drain the cooled fennel. In a small bowl, toss the fennel with salt and pepper to taste and the chive oil. Cover and refrigerate.

3. Combine the sour cream, crème fraîche, and shallots in a small bowl. Whisk in the vinegar, chives, and orange zest, and season with salt and pepper. Refrigerate until serving time.

4. Lightly brush both sides of the salmon fillet with olive oil, and season it with salt and pepper on both sides. Slice off the thinnest third of the fillet and cut that piece in half lengthwise. Quarter the thicker piece lengthwise.

5. Line a wok with aluminum foil and place it over high heat for several minutes. Add the wood chips and drizzle them with 2 tablespoons water, tossing the chips until they are dry and burned at the edges. Lightly oil a rack and place it over the wood chips.

6. Lay the salmon on the rack and cover the wok. Let the fish cook, opening the wok every few minutes to release some of the smoke and to monitor the cooking process. Reduce the heat if the chips begin to smoke profusely—the smoke should just curl gently around the lid of the wok when it is covered. Turn the pieces of fish as soon as the first side begins

1 large FENNEL BULB, trimmed and thinly sliced

Fine SEA SALT and freshly ground BLACK PEPPER

2 tablespoons CHIVE OIL, plus additional for garnish (see page 330)

1/3 cup SOUR CREAM

1/3 cup CRÈME FRAÎCHE

3 tablespoons diced SHALLOTS

2 teaspoons SHERRY VINEGAR

1 tablespoon chopped FRESH CHIVES

1/8 teaspoon grated ORANGE ZEST

1 pound SALMON FILLET

2 tablespoons extra-virgin OLIVE OIL, plus additional for brushing the salmon

1/2 cup HARDWOOD CHIPS, for smoking (see Note)

1/4 cup fresh LEMON JUICE

2 GRANNY SMITH APPLES

1 1/2 cups mixed MICRO GREENS or baby lettuces

1/4 cup SALMON ROE

SERVES 4 TO 6 AS AN APPETIZER

to cook, about 3 minutes. Continue to smoke, turning it again if the fish is cooking unevenly, until it is done on the outside but tender and rare on the inside. The thin pieces of salmon will take 5 to 8 minutes, and the thicker pieces will take 10 to 12 minutes. Transfer the fish pieces to a plate as they are cooked.

7. Place the lemon juice in a small bowl and season it with salt and pepper. Whisking constantly, drizzle in the remaining 2 tablespoons olive oil. Peel and dice the apples and place them in a bowl. Dress the apples with 2 tablespoons of the vinaigrette. Place the salad greens in another bowl and lightly dress them with some of the vinaigrette. Gently fold half of the salmon roe into the reserved sour cream mixture.

8. Lay pieces of salmon in the center of salad plates. Garnish with the apple salad and the fennel salad, and top the fish with some of the sour cream mixture. Place a dollop of the remaining salmon roe on top of each piece of fish. Scatter the green salad around the salmon, and dot the plate with chive oil.

Note: Wood chips for smoking are sold at gourmet and kitchenware stores, or by mail order (see Sources, page 337). If you do not purchase wood chips specifically packaged for the purpose, be sure the ones you're using are made from hardwood. Hickory, grapevine, and fruitwoods such as apple or cherry impart a particularly nice flavor. Don't use pine, because it will give the food a resiny taste.

Rösti Potatoes

WITH SMOKED SALMON AND MUSTARD VINAIGRETTE

MUSTARD VINAIGRETTE AND LEMON CRÈME FRAÎCHE

2 1/2 teaspoons German sweet WHOLE-GRAIN MUSTARD or whole-grain honey mustard

1 teaspoon DIJON MUSTARD

3 tablespoons fresh LEMON JUICE

Fine SEA SALT and freshly ground WHITE PEPPER

2 tablespoons extra-virgin OLIVE OIL

2 tablespoons CANOLA OIL

3 tablespoons chopped FRESH CHIVES

1/4 cup CRÈME FRAÎCHE or sour cream

RÖSTI POTATOES

4 tablespoons UNSALTED BUTTER

3 large or 6 small YUKON GOLD POTATOES (about 1 pound), peeled and grated

2 tablespoons CANOLA OIL, plus additional if needed

Fine SEA SALT and freshly ground BLACK PEPPER

MARIO LOHNINGER There are two ways to make rösti potatoes. The first is my favorite. It's like a hash brown: You julienne the raw potato and season it with salt, pepper, and melted butter. Then you cook it in a cast-iron pan until golden brown, pressing down with the spatula to compress the potatoes into a cake. The idea is to have caramelization and crunch on the outside while the inside remains moist. You have to cook it slowly, though, so the inside cooks all the way through before it gets too brown on the surface. The other way to make rösti is to use grated cooked potatoes. The result is a little chewier and softer, and there's not as much contrast of texture. But it's good too, and a great way to use up leftover potatoes.

Here I put smoked salmon on top of the potatoes for a brunch or lunch dish; it's also good as an appetizer. You can use any smoked fish—sturgeon is popular in Austria. The caviar is nice with it, but you don't absolutely need it.

1. Prepare the mustard vinaigrette: In a small bowl, whisk together the mustards, 1 1/2 tablespoons of the lemon juice, and salt and white pepper to taste. Gradually drizzle the olive oil, then the canola oil, into the mustard mixture, whisking constantly until well combined. Stir in the chives and add up to 3 tablespoons water, 1/2 tablespoon at a time, until thinned to the desired consistency (you should be able to drizzle the dressing). Set it aside.

2. In another small bowl, combine the crème fraîche with the remaining 1 1/2 tablespoons lemon juice. Season with salt and white pepper, and set aside.

3. Prepare the potatoes: Melt the butter in an 11-inch cast-iron skillet over medium heat (see Note). Place the grated potatoes in a large bowl and pour the melted butter over them. Toss to coat.

FOR SERVING

2 cups mixed MICRO GREENS or
   baby lettuces

3/4 pound COLD-SMOKED SALMON,
   thinly sliced

SALMON ROE or CAVIAR (see
   page 259) (optional)

SERVES 4 AS AN APPETIZER OR
LIGHT MAIN COURSE

4. Add enough canola oil to the same pan to coat the bottom well (1 to 2 tablespoons), and warm it over medium heat. Add the potatoes and press them down to form a 1/2-inch-thick cake. Season well with salt and pepper, and cook until brown on the underside, 12 to 15 minutes—reduce the heat if the potatoes are browning too quickly. Slide the cake out onto a plate and flip it over back into the pan. Cook until brown on the other side, 8 to 10 minutes, adding another 1/2 tablespoon oil if necessary to keep the potatoes from sticking.

5. Gently toss the micro greens with 2 tablespoons of the mustard vinaigrette.

6. To serve, divide the rösti potatoes into 4 portions and place a portion on each plate. Spread a thin layer of lemon crème fraîche over the potatoes. Pile 3 or 4 slices of salmon on each piece. Arrange a few of the dressed greens on top, and scatter the rest around the potatoes. Drizzle the salmon and potatoes with mustard vinaigrette, and sprinkle a few beads of salmon roe or caviar over the top if desired. Serve at once.

Note: This recipe calls for an 11-inch cast-iron pan. If you don't have one, use a 10-inch pan, decreasing the heat and increasing the cooking time slightly. Or use an 8-inch pan to make 2 smaller röstis: Decrease the cooking time; transfer the first rösti to an ovenproof plate lined with paper towels and keep it warm in a 200°F oven; and add more oil to coat the bottom of the pan before cooking the second rösti.

Duck and Cabbage Sausages

SAUSAGES

2 tablespoons GARLIC OIL (see page 330) or extra-virgin olive oil

1 pound CABBAGE (about 1/2 large head), cored, quartered, and thinly sliced

Fine SEA SALT and freshly ground BLACK PEPPER

2 teaspoons BLACK SESAME SEEDS (see Sources, page 337)

2 teaspoons WHITE SESAME SEEDS

1 teaspoon CARAWAY SEEDS

2 teaspoons POPPY SEEDS

1 teaspoon chopped FRESH ROSEMARY

1/2 teaspoon chopped FRESH THYME

1/2 teaspoon chopped FRESH MARJORAM

SAUSAGE CASINGS (see Sources, page 337)

3/4 cup (5 ounces) RENDERED DUCK FAT (see page 335)

3/4 cup (7 ounces) LEAN DUCK MEAT, ground (see Note)

DAVID BOULEY I learned the technique for making these sausages during an apprenticeship in Alsace, at the Auberge de l'Ile in Strasbourg. After you grind the meat and sauté the cabbage, you need to have a certain amount of fat to hold it together. Since it's duck sausage, we use duck fat. If you whip the fat until it puffs up, the sausages will be lighter. But you have to whip the fat without letting it melt, which would make it heavy. The trick I learned is to add ice cubes to the food processor when whipping the fat. These sausages melt in the mouth

NOTES FROM THE KITCHEN We use lamb casings for these sausages, but you can also form them into little patties without the casings and fry them up like hamburgers. Just make sure to cook them all the way through. It's a great way to cook them, in fact, because the patties get very crunchy on the outside. And it's easier!

1. Heat the garlic oil in a large skillet. Add the cabbage and season well with salt and pepper. Add all the seeds and herbs, and cook until the cabbage is crisp-tender, about 5 minutes. Let cool.

2. Pick out a long strand of sausage casing and soak it in cold water for 30 minutes.

3. Place the duck fat in a food processor with 2 ice cubes. Process until it is light and fluffy. In a bowl, combine 1 3/4 cups of the cooked cabbage with the duck fat and the duck meat (reserve any extra cabbage for another use). Season with salt and pepper.

4. Brown a spoonful of the sausage mixture in a small pan and taste it for seasoning. Add additional salt and pepper to the rest of the sausage mixture if necessary.

HORSERADISH CREAM

¹/₂ cup SOUR CREAM or crème fraîche

¹/₄ cup YOGURT

¹/₄ cup prepared HORSERADISH

Fresh LEMON JUICE, to taste

Fine SEA SALT and freshly ground BLACK PEPPER, to taste

2 tablespoons UNSALTED BUTTER

¹/₄ cup minced FRESH CHIVES

SERVES 12 TO 15 AS AN HORS D'OEUVRE

5. Bring a large pot of water to a simmer and salt it moderately. While the water is heating, open one end of the soaked casing and run cold water all the way through it. Use a pastry bag fitted with a ¹/₂-inch plain tip to fill the casing (or use a sausage-stuffing machine). Thread as much of the casing as possible onto the tip, bunching it around the top of the pastry tip. Pipe the sausage meat into the casing and tie off each sausage with kitchen string at 2-inch lengths.

6. Lower the sausages into the simmering water and poach gently for 5 minutes. Drain and let cool. Then cut the sausage links apart and remove the strings.

7. Whisk together all the ingredients for the horseradish cream, and set aside.

8. Melt the butter in a small saucepan. Add the sausages to the pan and cook them over medium-high heat, turning them until they are nicely browned, about 10 minutes. Place the chives in a shallow bowl and roll the sausages in the chives. Serve with the horseradish cream. (Alternatively, form the sausage mixture into 2-inch patties ¹/₂ inch thick and fry them in the butter until well browned on both sides and cooked through, about 10 to 15 minutes. Serve garnished with the chives and horseradish cream.)

Note: Unless you have a meat grinder and a supply of lean duck meat, you'll probably have to order this from a butcher.

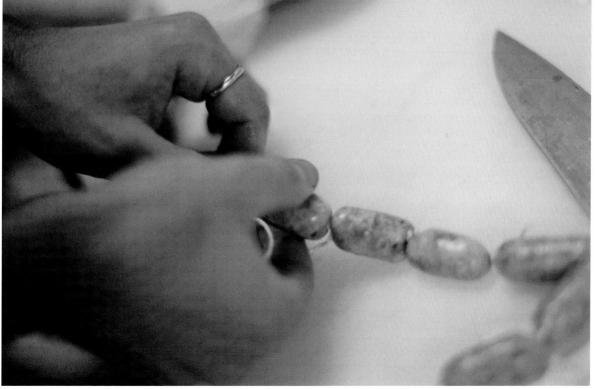

Krautwickler

CABBAGE ROLLS STUFFED WITH DUCK, DATES, AND FOIE GRAS

Wherever cabbage is part of the cuisine, you usually find stuffed cabbage rolls of some kind, and Austria is no exception. But with a filling of foie gras, truffles, and dates, these are an unusual and upscale version.

1. Preheat the oven to 400°F.

2. Bring a large pot of water to a boil, and salt it until it tastes like seawater (about 2 teaspoons per quart). Fill a large bowl with water and ice. Blanch the cabbage leaves in the salted water until tender, about 2 minutes, then drain them and transfer to the ice water to cool. Drain the cooled cabbage leaves on paper towels.

3. Place the bread in a bowl and soak it in the milk until soft, about 15 minutes. Drain the bread and squeeze out the excess milk with your hands. If you are grinding the duck meat yourself, put it through the grinder and feed the bread through afterward, to push through all the meat. Otherwise, chop the bread finely with a knife. In a large bowl, combine the ground duck meat with the bread, dates, black truffle, parsley, and egg. Season generously with salt and pepper. Fold in the cream.

4. Season both slabs of foie gras with salt and pepper, and dust one side with flour. Heat a heavy sauté pan until it is extremely hot, about 5 minutes. Add a film of canola oil and then the foie gras, floured side down. Cook until dark brown on the bottom and then flip it over, about 2 minutes. Tip the pan and continue to cook for 1 minute while spooning the collected fat over the foie gras. Transfer the foie gras to a plate and let it cool. Then cut it into 10 equal cubes.

Fine SEA SALT

10 large green outer leaves SAVOY CABBAGE (from 2 heads)

3 slices (about 1 1/2 ounces) white SANDWICH BREAD, cubed

1 1/2 cups MILK, or to cover

11 ounces DUCK LEG MEAT (trimmed of bone and sinew), ground (see Note, page 30)

6 PITTED DATES, sliced crosswise

2 tablespoons chopped FRESH BLACK TRUFFLE

2 tablespoons roughly chopped FRESH PARSLEY

1 EGG

Freshly ground BLACK PEPPER

2 tablespoons HEAVY CREAM

7 ounces FOIE GRAS, sliced 1 1/2 inches thick

WONDRA FLOUR (see Note, page 250), for dusting

CANOLA OIL, for searing the foie gras

1 cup thinly sliced ONION

1 medium RED BELL PEPPER, trimmed, seeded, and thinly sliced

2 sprigs FRESH THYME

SERVES 4 TO 6 AS AN APPETIZER

5. Dry the cabbage leaves and halve them along the ribs. Discard the ribs. Lay 1 piece of cabbage inside the bowl of a 2-ounce ladle 1 1/2 inches in diameter, and then lay another piece of cabbage across it so that about 2 inches of excess hangs over on all sides. Trim the leaves if necessary. Place about 1 1/2 tablespoons of the duck filling in the ladle and top it with a cube of foie gras. Fill the ladle with another 1 1/2 tablespoons of duck filling, and fold the excess cabbage over the filling, packing the roll down with your palm. Upend the ladle to release the cabbage roll. (Alternatively, to form the rolls without using a ladle, place the overlapping cabbage leaves on a board, place the filling in the center, and fold in all sides to secure.)

6. Scatter the onion, bell pepper, and thyme in the bottom of a wide ceramic casserole. Place the cabbage rolls on top, and carefully pour 1/4 cup water around them. Transfer the casserole to the oven and bake for 15 minutes. Continue baking, basting the rolls with the liquid in the pan every 5 minutes, until the meat firms up and the onions and peppers are cooked, another 30 to 35 minutes.

7. Serve hot, with some of the vegetables and their juices.

Chestnut Agnolotti
WITH FRESH WHITE TRUFFLES

CHESTNUT FILLING

1/2 pound FRESH CHESTNUTS, shells scored with an X

1 1/2 cups WHOLE MILK

Fine SEA SALT and freshly ground BLACK PEPPER

PASTA

CORNMEAL, for dusting the pans

1 recipe EGG PASTA DOUGH (see page 328)

1 EGG WHITE, beaten

TRUFFLE SAUCE

2 tablespoons UNSALTED BUTTER

3 SHALLOTS, thinly sliced lengthwise

Fine SEA SALT and freshly ground BLACK PEPPER

1 1/2 cups MADEIRA

1 3/4 cups MUSHROOM STOCK or vegetable stock (see page 332)

1 1/2 cups CHICKEN STOCK (see page 333) or canned low-sodium chicken broth

MARIO LOHNINGER If you work with white truffles, you need to let the truffle speak—you don't want to overpower it. Chestnuts are good because they have a gentle sweet taste that complements the truffle flavor. They also make this dish Austrian instead of purely Italian. We don't have white truffles in Austria, but we do have chestnuts. In the fall you can buy roasted ones on the street in Vienna or Salzburg, the way we buy hot dogs and pretzels here. You eat them as you walk along, dropping the peels as you go. You always know when there's a chestnut seller nearby because you can smell that burning aroma, and the peels others have scattered crunch underfoot. It's one of the best things for me about the fall, an intense childhood memory.

1. Bring a large pot of water to a boil and salt it until it tastes like seawater (about 2 teaspoons per quart). Blanch the chestnuts in the boiling water for 3 to 4 minutes. Drain. When the chestnuts are just cool enough to handle, pull off and discard their shells. Place them in a pot and cover them with the milk. Bring to a simmer and cook until tender, about 35 minutes.

2. Drain the chestnuts, reserving the milk. Season the chestnuts with salt and pepper, and place them in a blender or food processor. Add 1/2 cup of the milk and puree until smooth. Transfer the puree to a pastry bag or to a resealable plastic bag with one corner cut off.

3. To form the agnolotti, dust two baking sheets with cornmeal. Spread out the rolled pasta dough, and cut 2-inch rounds from the dough using a cookie cutter or an empty can. Spoon a quarter-size dollop of chestnut puree onto the center of each round, and brush the perimeter of each round with egg white. Fold each round in half, sealing it around the filling, making sure there are no air bubbles. Transfer the agnolotti to the prepared baking sheets as they are done, keeping them covered with a clean dish towel as you work. Cover the pans with plastic wrap and refrigerate until ready to use. The agnolotti can be made up to 12 hours in advance.

1 cup HEAVY CREAM

3/4 teaspoon WHITE TRUFFLE OIL,
    or to taste

FOR SERVING
Fine SEA SALT

2 tablespoons UNSALTED BUTTER

6 tablespoons CHICKEN STOCK (see
    page 333) or canned low-sodium
    chicken broth

Freshly ground BLACK PEPPER

2 tablespoons CRÈME FRAÎCHE

1/4 cup PARMIGIANO-REGGIANO
    CHEESE, or to taste

FRESH WHITE TRUFFLE, sliced

SERVES 8 TO 10 AS AN APPETIZER

4. To prepare the truffle sauce, melt the butter in a saucepan over medium-low heat. When the butter foams, add the shallots, season them with salt and pepper, and cook gently, stirring occasionally, until golden brown and very tender, 30 minutes. Pour in the Madeira and bring to a simmer. Simmer until the liquid has been reduced to about 1/4 cup, about 30 minutes. Add the mushroom stock, bring to a simmer, and cook until reduced to 1 1/2 cups, about 15 minutes. Add the chicken stock and continue to simmer until the mixture is reduced to 1 1/4 cups, about 15 minutes. Add the cream, bring to a boil, and then remove from the heat. Strain the liquid, discarding the solids, and transfer it to a blender (or use an immersion blender). Blend on low speed until the mixture is well combined and emulsified. Season with salt and pepper. Just before serving, add the white truffle oil and run the blender to foam the sauce.

5. Bring a large pot of water to a boil and salt it until it tastes like seawater (about 2 teaspoons per quart). Melt the butter in a pan over medium heat. Let the butter cook until the white milk solids fall to the bottom and turn nut-brown, about 5 minutes. Add the 6 tablespoons chicken stock and simmer until the sauce is syrupy, about 5 minutes.

6. Meanwhile, add the agnolotti to the boiling water and cook until tender, 1 to 2 minutes. Drain, and add them to the pan with the butter sauce. Season with salt and pepper. Add the crème fraîche and Parmigiano-Reggiano, and toss well. Place the agnolotti on plates, and spoon the foamy truffle sauce on and around them. Garnish with the sliced truffle, and serve hot.

Gently Heated Salmon

WITH A JULIENNE OF STYRIAN WURZELGEMÜSE AND CHIVE-HORSERADISH SAUCE

APPLE-ROSEMARY PUREE

1/2 CINNAMON STICK, about
    3 inches long

1 WHOLE CLOVE

3 GRANNY SMITH APPLES, peeled,
    cored, and thinly sliced

2/3 cup DRY WHITE WINE

1 tablespoon SUGAR

1 tablespoon UNSALTED BUTTER

1 sprig FRESH ROSEMARY

STYRIAN WURZELGEMÜSE

3 cups VEGETABLE STOCK
    (see page 332) or water

1 CARROT, peeled and cut into
    matchsticks

1 YELLOW BEET, peeled and cut into
    matchsticks

1 KOHLRABI, peeled and cut into
    matchsticks

1 TURNIP, peeled and cut into
    matchsticks

1 SMALL ZUCCHINI, peeled and cut
    into matchsticks

NOTES FROM THE KITCHEN The apple-rosemary puree is a hidden jewel in this recipe. It has incredible flavor from heating the fresh rosemary sprigs in brown butter before adding the apples. No matter how many times we make it, we never get tired of the moment when the rosemary hits the butter in the pan and releases its scent; it smells so good, you just have to stop for a second and breathe it in. The recipe makes plenty, and the leftovers are divine.

1. Prepare the apple-rosemary puree: Wrap the cinnamon stick and clove in a piece of cheesecloth and tie it with kitchen string. Place it in a large saucepan along with the apples, wine, and sugar, and stir. Cover and cook over medium heat for 10 minutes. Remove the cover and cook, stirring frequently, until the liquid has been absorbed and the apples are very soft, about 30 minutes.

2. Meanwhile, melt the butter in a small saucepan over medium heat. Let it cook until the white milk solids fall to the bottom and turn nut-brown, about 5 minutes. Add the rosemary and shake the pan so that the butter foams up around it. Remove from the heat and let steep for at least 5 minutes.

3. When the apples have finished cooking, remove and discard the cheesecloth-wrapped spices. Remove the rosemary from the butter and discard the sprig. Place the apple mixture and the butter in a food processor or blender, and puree until completely smooth. (The puree can be made 1 day ahead and refrigerated.)

4. Prepare the Wurzelgemüse: Bring the vegetable stock to a boil in a medium saucepan, and blanch each vegetable separately until crisp-tender (about 2 minutes for the carrot and beet, 1 1/2 minutes for the kohlrabi, 1 minute for the turnip, 20 seconds for the zucchini). Remove each vegetable with a slotted spoon as it is done. (The vegetables can be blanched 1 day ahead and refrigerated.)

SALMON

8 skinless SALMON FILLETS (about 3 ounces each)

Fine SEA SALT and freshly ground BLACK PEPPER

2 tablespoons UNSALTED BUTTER, softened

1 tablespoon UNSALTED BUTTER

Fine SEA SALT and freshly ground BLACK PEPPER

3/4 cup CHIVE OIL (see page 330)

1 tablespoon fresh LEMON JUICE, or to taste

One 2-inch-long knob FRESH HORSERADISH, peeled

SERVES 4 AS A MAIN COURSE

5. To prepare the salmon, preheat the oven to 250°F. Season both sides of the salmon fillets with salt and pepper. Spread 1/2 tablespoon of the softened butter over each of two large ovenproof plates. Lay 4 fillets on each plate, and top the fillets with the remaining 1 tablespoon butter. Wrap the plates in plastic wrap to form a tight seal. Place them on the middle rack in the oven and cook for 10 minutes. The fish will still look raw but it will have taken on a silky, firm texture and will be heated through.

6. While the salmon is cooking, reheat the Wurzelgemüse: Melt the 1 tablespoon butter in a saucepan over moderate heat. Add the vegetables, tossing to coat them in the butter. Cook until they are heated through, about 4 minutes. Season to taste with salt and pepper.

7. Season the chive oil with 1/4 teaspoon salt and the lemon juice. Gently reheat the apple puree.

8. To serve, put 1 tablespoon of the apple puree in the center of each plate. Arrange 2 salmon fillets over the puree, and top with 1/4 cup of the Wurzelgemüse. Spoon the chive oil around the salmon, and grate a dusting of fresh horseradish over all.

DAVID BOULEY I first learned about this technique for cooking salmon from Hans Hass, the chef at Tantris in Munich. He is one of the most creative chefs cooking in that part of the world today. Like many innovations, it was the result of an accident. Hans put a plate of seasoned salmon covered in plastic wrap in the plate warmer and forgot about it. (He was about to cook it but got distracted.) When he finally pulled it out and touched it, it fell apart. The color hadn't really changed, but the salmon was cooked through, and it was soft and buttery, really amazing. What happens is that the fish cooks almost like it's in a *sous-vide*, or vacuum. At such a low temperature, about 250°F, the plate gets hot and the air around the salmon heats up, but the fish never gets hot enough to brown or even turn opaque. It stays pink and is like velvet in the mouth; it just melts.

We pair it with *Wurzelgemüse*, a modern rendition of a classic vegetable mixture that's usually served with pork shoulder. The vegetables are julienned and topped with freshly grated horseradish. I was amazed the first time I saw Hans grate fresh horseradish over vegetables—it's so pungent your eyes tear up immediately. But it adds incredible flavor.

Roasted Duck

WITH POTATO DUMPLINGS AND RED CABBAGE

MARIO LOHNINGER This is a homey Sunday-dinner dish. Since it is such a traditional recipe, I like to stuff it with traditional ingredients like apples, chestnuts, and onions. Long Island duck is the type to use here—it is very tender and succulent, and when it cooks it braises in its own fat, almost like a confit. The cabbage garnish is lovely and its acidity cuts the richness of the duck. The potato dumplings are everyone's favorite, very light and fluffy. One of the sous-chefs, Thomas Mayr, added the carob powder (that's the way his mother does it), which makes the dumplings a little richer and earthier—but you can leave it out.

1. Place the red cabbage in a large bowl and salt it well. Add the lemon and orange juices, and use your hands to squeeze and toss the cabbage in the juices. Let marinate until ready to use.

2. Heat a large stockpot over medium heat, and add the sugar. Cook without stirring until it melts and turns into a brown caramel (swirl the pan if the caramel darkens unevenly), about 7 minutes. Add the onions and the duck fat, reduce the heat, and cook until the onions are soft and brown, about 10 minutes. Pour in the red wine and port, raise the heat, and bring the liquid to a simmer. Cook at a gentle simmer until very reduced, about 1 hour: The wines should bubble on the surface and should have concentrated into a thick, syrupy mass beneath the layer of clear duck fat.

3. Stir in the cabbage and citrus juices, preserves, and 2 1/2 tablespoons of the vinegar. Cook until the cabbage begins to soften, about 20 minutes. Then add the grated apple and continue to cook until the cabbage is soft, 10 minutes. Season to taste with honey, the remaining 1/2 tablespoon vinegar, and salt and pepper. The cabbage should be tangy, sweet, and sour, complemented and balanced by the richness of the duck fat. Set it aside.

4. Preheat the oven to 500°F.

5. Wash the duck and pat it dry. Cut off the wing tips and the entire neck. Cut out the wishbone, and trim the excess skin and fat from around the neck opening. Sprinkle some salt and pepper in the bird's cavity.

RED CABBAGE

1 small RED CABBAGE (about 2 1/2 pounds), quartered, cored, and thinly sliced

Fine SEA SALT

1 cup fresh LEMON JUICE

3/4 cup fresh ORANGE JUICE

2 tablespoons SUGAR

2 cups diced ONION

1/3 cup rendered DUCK or CHICKEN FAT (see page 335) or canola oil

1/2 cup DRY RED WINE

1/2 cup PORT WINE

1/4 cup LINGONBERRY or RED CURRANT PRESERVES

3 tablespoons CHAMPAGNE VINEGAR

1/4 cup grated GRANNY SMITH APPLE

1 tablespoon HONEY, or to taste

Freshly ground BLACK PEPPER

DUCK

1 LONG ISLAND DUCK (about 5 pounds)

Fine SEA SALT and freshly ground BLACK PEPPER

2 cups chopped GRANNY SMITH APPLE

3 cups chopped ONION

Approximately 15 roasted and
    peeled CHESTNUTS (see Note)

6 sprigs FRESH MARJORAM

5 sprigs FRESH THYME

1 sprig FRESH ROSEMARY

4 tablespoons UNSALTED BUTTER,
    softened

2 sprigs FRESH SAGE

POTATO DUMPLINGS

1 1/4 pounds YUKON GOLD
    POTATOES

1 BAY LEAF, preferably fresh

Fine SEA SALT

1 1/2 teaspoons CAROB POWDER
    (optional; see Sources, page 337)

Freshly grated NUTMEG

Freshly ground BLACK PEPPER

3 EGG YOLKS

3/4 cup ALL-PURPOSE FLOUR

4 tablespoons UNSALTED BUTTER,
    melted and cooled

1/4 cup DRY WHITE WINE

1 cup CHICKEN STOCK (see
    page 333) or canned low-sodium
    chicken broth

SERVES 6 AS A MAIN COURSE

6. Combine the apples, onions, chestnuts, marjoram, 3 sprigs of the thyme, and the rosemary in a bowl. Add the softened butter and combine, using your hands. (Reserve the sage sprigs for Step 9.) Stuff the duck with as much of this mixture as fits, and set aside the remaining stuffing. Use a needle and heavy thread or kitchen string to sew or tie up the cavity. Truss the bird with string, tying the wings together behind its back. Place the duck in a roasting pan, breast side down, and roast it for 30 minutes.

7. Meanwhile, prick the potatoes with a fork and wrap them individually in aluminum foil.

8. Reduce the oven heat to 350°F, and place the potatoes in the oven with the duck. Bake until they are very soft, about 1 hour. Remove the potatoes from the oven and set them aside.

9. At this point a lot of fat will have been rendered from the duck's breast. Turn the duck over and carefully remove the fat from the pan. Add the reserved stuffing mixture, the remaining 2 thyme sprigs, and the sage sprigs to the pan. Roast for another 45 minutes. Then raise the oven temperature to 500°F and roast the duck until the internal temperature of the thigh is 160°F and the juices run clear, about 15 minutes. Transfer the roasted stuffing mixture (minus the thyme and sage sprigs) and the duck to a serving dish, cover with foil, and let the duck rest for 15 minutes before carving.

10. Meanwhile, prepare the potato dumplings: Bring a large pot of water to a boil, and add the bay leaf and enough salt so it tastes like seawater (about 2 teaspoons per quart). Scoop out the flesh from the baked potatoes and push it through a ricer or a coarse sieve. Place 2 loosely packed cups of potatoes in a large bowl. Season the potatoes with 1 teaspoon of the carob powder (if desired), nutmeg, salt, and pepper. Add the egg yolks and mix well to combine. Sprinkle in the flour and knead with your hands to make a soft dough that just barely holds together. Pour 2 tablespoons of the butter over the dough and mix to combine. Gently form the dough into balls about 2 inches in diameter. Poach them in the simmering water until they are cooked through, 15 to 20 minutes. Drain.

11. Pour the excess fat from the duck roasting pan, then place the pan on the stovetop over medium-high heat and pour in the white wine. Bring to a simmer and cook, scraping the bottom and sides of the pan with a wooden spoon, until the liquid is thickened and reduced, about 5 minutes. Add the chicken stock and continue to simmer until slightly thickened. Strain the contents of the pan into a glass measuring cup; you should have about 1 cup of duck *jus*. Keep warm.

12. To reheat the potato dumplings, place the remaining 2 tablespoons butter in a wide sauté pan and cook over medium heat until the milk solids have fallen to the bottom and the butter is nut-brown, about 5 minutes. Add the remaining 1/2 teaspoon carob powder (if using), toss to coat, and season with salt and pepper. Add the drained dumplings to the butter and warm them.

13. Reheat the cabbage, covered, over medium heat, 5 minutes. Carve the duck and serve with the stuffing, the red cabbage, the potato dumplings, and the duck *jus*.

Note: To roast and peel fresh chestnuts, preheat the oven to 375°F. Score an X in each chestnut shell and place the nuts in a single layer on a baking sheet. Roast for 15 minutes, shaking the pan halfway through. Let rest until just cool enough to handle, then pull their shells off immediately (rewarm them in the oven or for 30 seconds in the microwave if they become too difficult to peel as they cool).

Kavalierspitz

TRADITIONAL BOILED BEEF WITH SPINACH PUREE, APPLE HORSERADISH SAUCE, AND BABY VEGETABLES

KAVALIERSPITZ

1 large ONION, halved crosswise

Fine SEA SALT

1 large or 2 small "CHICKEN STEAKS," from the chuck (about 4½ pounds total), trimmed

5 VEAL MARROWBONES

6 baby CARROTS

4 baby TURNIPS

4 small KOHLRABI

1 CELERY ROOT, quartered

1 tablespoon JUNIPER BERRIES

1 teaspoon ALLSPICE BERRIES

Freshly ground BLACK PEPPER

1 BAY LEAF, preferably fresh, cut in half

1 sprig FRESH THYME

1 GARLIC CLOVE

SPINACH PUREE

6 tablespoons UNSALTED BUTTER

3 SHALLOTS, diced

1 teaspoon fine SEA SALT

2 large GARLIC CLOVES, minced

½ cup HEAVY CREAM

1 sprig FRESH THYME

¾ cup VEGETABLE STOCK (see page 332) or canned low-sodium vegetable broth

¾ pound SPINACH, stems removed

Freshly ground WHITE PEPPER

CAYENNE PEPPER

Freshly grated NUTMEG

Boiled beef is an institution in Austria, and this is a fairly classic rendition. There are a lot of different garnishes you can serve with it, but these are David and Mario's favorites.

1. Heat a heavy sauté pan over high heat and add the onion halves, cut side down. Cook until they blacken on their cut sides, about 10 minutes.

2. Fill a stockpot halfway with water and set it over high heat. When the water boils, salt it well, then add the meat, onions, and 2 of the marrowbones. Reduce the heat to medium-low. Partially cover the pot and bring the water to a very low simmer; it should bubble only slightly for the duration of the cooking time. Simmer for 3 hours, checking on the meat periodically, turning it occasionally and adding a little more water if necessary to keep the meat covered.

3. Add the carrots, turnips, kohlrabi, celery root, juniper berries, allspice berries, pepper, and bay leaf. Simmer until the vegetables are cooked, 20 to 30 minutes. Use a slotted spoon to transfer the vegetables to a platter as they become tender. Continue to cook the meat until there is no resistance when it is pierced in its center with a long fork yet it still retains its shape, another 30 minutes.

4. Place the remaining 3 marrowbones, marrow sides up, in a saucepan. Cover with cold water, and add the thyme and garlic. Bring to a simmer, then remove from the heat and let the bones poach until the marrow is translucent and soft, about 5 minutes. Drain the bones. Slide a paring knife around the inside of the hole to gently push the marrow free, and cut the marrow into ½-inch slices. Reheat the marrow in a 250°F oven or at a low setting in a microwave just before serving.

5. Meanwhile, prepare the spinach puree: In a wide saucepan or sauté pan, melt 3 tablespoons of the butter over medium heat. Let it cook until the white milk solids fall to the bottom and turn nut-brown, 2 to 3 minutes. Add the shallots and ½ teaspoon of the salt, and cook, stirring, until the shallots soften, 5 minutes. Add the garlic and continue to cook for 2 more minutes.

APPLE HORSERADISH SAUCE

3 GOLDEN DELICIOUS APPLES
   (1 1/2 pounds)

JUICE of 1 LEMON

2 tablespoons SUGAR

1/2 CINNAMON STICK, about 3 inches

1 WHOLE CLOVE

2 tablespoons prepared
   HORSERADISH, or more to taste

CHIVE MAYONNAISE

1 cup cubed WHITE BREAD, crusts
   removed

3/4 cup WHOLE MILK

2 extra-large EGG YOLKS

8 small CORNICHONS, chopped

1 heaping tablespoon CRÈME
   FRAÎCHE

1 heaping tablespoon SOUR CREAM

1/4 cup CHAMPAGNE VINEGAR

1 1/2 cups CANOLA OIL

Fine SEA SALT and freshly ground
   WHITE PEPPER

1 HARD-COOKED EGG, finely diced

3 tablespoons finely chopped FRESH
   CHIVES

OPTIONAL GARNISH

Freshly grated HORSERADISH

Sliced FRESH LOVAGE LEAVES

Freshly grated NUTMEG

FLEUR DE SEL (see Note)

Finely chopped FRESH CHIVES

SERVES 4 TO 6 AS A MAIN COURSE

6. Add the cream and thyme to the pan and bring the liquid to a boil. Simmer until reduced by one third, 3 to 4 minutes. Pour in the vegetable stock and let the liquid return to a boil. Add the spinach and cook gently, stirring and tossing, until it is tender, about 2 minutes.

7. Remove the thyme. Use a slotted spoon to transfer the spinach to a blender or food processor, reserving 1/2 cup of the cooking liquid. Puree the spinach, and season it with the remaining 1/2 teaspoon salt, white pepper, a pinch of cayenne, and nutmeg to taste. If necessary, add some of the reserved cooking liquid so the puree is just loose enough to pour. Keep warm (or reheat gently before serving).

8. Prepare the apple horseradish sauce: Peel the apples, reserving the peels and submerging the apples in a bowl of water acidulated with the lemon juice.

9. Place the apple peels in a small saucepan. Cover with 3/4 cup water and add the sugar, cinnamon stick, and clove. Bring to a boil and let simmer, stirring, until the sugar dissolves, about 5 minutes. Turn off the heat and let the peels steep in the liquid until cool.

10. Place the horseradish in a large bowl and grate the apples finely over it. Strain the apple-peel liquid, and pour 1/2 cup of the liquid over the grated apple. Toss to combine, and add more horseradish if desired. Set aside.

11. To prepare the chive mayonnaise, place the bread cubes in a bowl and cover with the milk. Let soak until soft, about 20 minutes.

12. Use your hands to squeeze the milk from the bread cubes, and place them in a blender with the egg yolks, 1/4 cup broth taken from the Kavalierspitz, chopped cornichons, crème fraîche, and sour cream. Blend to combine. With the motor running, add a few drops of Champagne vinegar, then drizzle in a small amount of the canola oil in a very thin stream, processing until the oil is absorbed before adding a little more vinegar. Continue alternating vinegar and oil until you have used it all. The mixture should be of a thick but pourable consistency, and just slightly piquant. Season it to taste with salt and white pepper, and set it aside. Just before serving, stir in the hard-cooked egg and chives.

13. When the beef is tender, transfer it to a platter and cover it with plastic wrap. Strain the broth through a fine-mesh strainer. If you're not going to serve it immediately, place the beef in a clean pot, cover with the strained broth, and surround with the baby vegetables. Heat gently just before serving.

14. To serve, slice the beef across the grain into 2-inch-wide pieces. Lay them in the center of each soup plate, and garnish with the baby vegetables. Ladle the cooking liquid on top of and around the meat. Garnish with a slice of bone marrow, and any or all of the garnishes (freshly grated horseradish, lovage, grated nutmeg, a sprinkle of fleur de sel, chopped chives). Serve with the spinach puree, apple horseradish sauce, and chive mayonnaise on the side.

Note: Fleur de sel is a sea salt skimmed from the surface of French Mediterranean seawater that has been allowed to evaporate naturally in shallow, sun-warmed basins. The crystals from this top layer are pure white, with a more delicate, nuanced flavor than table salt and other evaporated sea salts. This salt is widely available in gourmet food stores.

BOILED BEEF Boiled beef is a simple-sounding, fundamentally Viennese dish with a long list of traditional variations in both cut of meat and accompaniments. Restaurants specializing in the dish have been known to list as many as twenty-four different varieties of beef! *Kavalierspitz* is a cut from the shoulder, while the best-known cut, *Tafelspitz*, comes from the upper leg.

Whatever the cut is, it should be somewhat tough and gelatinous yet full of flavor. It is given a long, gentle simmer until the meat is fork-tender and the gelatin has melted, adding a luxurious mouthfeel. The meat is then sliced across the grain and served with a little of the clear cooking broth (or sometimes the broth is served as a separate course before the meat). Slices of marrow, cooked in the bone, make a rich side to the meat, while several sauces add variety and panache. The most common of these include a horseradish sauce, sometimes combined with apples or folded into whipped cream, and a chive sauce. Other cold sauces feature pungent, fat-cutting ingredients like gherkins or anchovies. Potatoes, beets, and pickles are common additions to the meal.

While boiled beef consumption reached its heyday during the Austro-Hungarian Empire, when it was rumored to be a favorite of Emperor Franz Josef I, it is still a fixture on Viennese menus, and there still exist restaurants that serve it exclusively. All in all, it's not hard to understand how nineteenth-century Austrians could eat this basic, yet varied, meal nearly daily.

Whole Roast Suckling Pig

WITH WHITE WINE-BRAISED CABBAGE

DAVID BOULEY In every culture where pork is eaten—from New England to Austria—suckling pig is served as a celebratory dish during the fall harvest and the holiday season. It is also the time of year when there are plenty of root vegetables and cabbages, so serving it all together makes sense.

MARIO LOHNINGER I like to do a suckling pig every New Year's Eve. My father always does one too, in his restaurant near Salzburg, where I grew up, and I learned it from him. In Austria we say a pig brings you luck, so it's traditional to kill a suckling pig and eat it on New Year's. In New York people have heard about the meal, and now customers always want to celebrate New Year's Eve with us at the Danube. Everyone loves it.

1. Preheat the oven to 500°F.

2. Rinse the pig with cold water and pat it dry with paper towels. Season the inside with salt and pepper, and rub the skin with canola oil. Place the pig in a roasting pan and roast for 20 minutes. Reduce the oven temperature to 400°F and continue roasting for 1¼ hours. When the ears and tail begin to brown, cover the pig with aluminum foil, about 45 minutes.

3. While the pig is roasting, prepare the cabbage: Bring the chicken stock to a boil in a wide saucepan, and simmer until reduced to 2 cups, 20 minutes.

4. While the stock is reducing, toss the cabbage with the caraway seeds and 1 teaspoon salt in a large bowl. Let marinate at room temperature while the stock simmers.

5. Heat a large stockpot over medium heat and add the sugar. Cook without stirring until it melts and turns into a golden caramel (swirl the pan if the caramel darkens unevenly), about 3 minutes. Stir in the onions and duck fat, and season to taste with salt and pepper. Cook over medium-low heat until the onions are soft and brown, 20 to 30 minutes.

SUCKLING PIG

1 small SUCKLING PIG (about 16 pounds)

Fine SEA SALT and freshly ground BLACK PEPPER

CANOLA OIL

WHITE WINE-BRAISED CABBAGE

6 cups CHICKEN STOCK (see page 333)

2 pounds GREEN CABBAGE, trimmed and shredded

1½ teaspoons CARAWAY SEEDS

1 teaspoon fine SEA SALT, plus additional to taste

2 tablespoons SUGAR

2 cups diced ONION

¼ cup RENDERED DUCK or POULTRY FAT (see page 335) or canola oil

Freshly ground BLACK PEPPER

10 WHITE PEPPERCORNS

4 JUNIPER BERRIES

1 WHOLE CLOVE

1 sprig FRESH THYME

½ BAY LEAF, preferably fresh

1¼ cups RIESLING or other white wine

⅓ cup CHAMPAGNE VINEGAR

1 thick slice BACON, or 2 thin slices

½ GARLIC CLOVE, smashed

ROASTED VEGETABLES

15 small FINGERLING POTATOES

12 SCALLIONS, white and light green parts only

12 CIPOLLINI ONIONS, blanched and peeled (see Note)

10 SHALLOTS, halved if large

1 bunch BABY CARROTS, trimmed, or 4 regular carrots, cut into 2-inch lengths

4 CELERY STALKS, cut into 2-inch lengths

2 whole bulbs GARLIC, halved crosswise

2 large ONIONS, sliced crosswise into 1/2-inch-thick rings

Fine SEA SALT and freshly ground BLACK PEPPER

14 ounces (1 3/4 cups) LAGER or ALE

SERVES 12 TO 16 AS A MAIN COURSE

6. While the onions are cooking, cut a 6-inch square of cheesecloth and use it to wrap up the white peppercorns, juniper berries, clove, thyme sprig, and bay leaf. Tie the sachet closed securely with a piece of kitchen string.

7. Stir the wine and vinegar into the onions and simmer for 5 minutes. Add the reduced chicken stock, cabbage, bacon, garlic, and sachet, and simmer until the liquid has reduced and the cabbage has softened, 20 to 30 minutes. Season with salt and pepper, and set aside.

8. When the pig has been cooking for a total of 1 1/2 hours, add all the vegetables to the pan and season them with salt and pepper. Continue roasting for another hour, basting the pig now and then with the accumulated juices.

9. Pour the lager on and around the pig, and roast until the leg joints are loose and tender when you move the leg back and forth, about 20 minutes. Remove it from the oven and let it rest for 30 minutes before carving. To serve, cut the pig in pieces (shoulder, belly, loin, ham . . .) and pile the roasted vegetables beside it. Serve with the braised cabbage.

Note: To peel cipollini or other small onions, bring a large pot of water to a boil. Blanch the onions in the boiling water for 30 seconds, then drain. When they are cool enough to handle, cut off the root ends and slip off their skins.

Pear Caramel Strudel

CARAMEL CUSTARD

1 teaspoon powdered UNFLAVORED GELATIN

2 large EGG YOLKS

1 large EGG

1/3 cup LIGHT CORN SYRUP

6 tablespoons SUGAR

1 tablespoon UNSALTED BUTTER

1 1/2 cups HEAVY CREAM

1/2 VANILLA BEAN, split lengthwise, seeds scraped out with a knife

PEAR COMPOTE

3 PEARS, peeled, cored, and diced

6 tablespoons SUGAR

Grated ZEST of 1 ORANGE

JUICE of 1 LEMON

1 VANILLA BEAN, split lengthwise, seeds scraped out with a knife

STRUDEL LAYERS

1/4 cup SUGAR

1/2 teaspoon GROUND CINNAMON

9 sheets PHYLLO DOUGH (about 8 ounces; see Note)

8 tablespoons (1 stick) UNSALTED BUTTER, melted and cooled

1/3 cup CONFECTIONERS' SUGAR

1/2 cup BALSAMIC VINEGAR

FRESH MINT LEAVES

VANILLA ICE CREAM

SERVES 9 AS DESSERT

In Vienna, winter is the season of extravagant balls, when the cream of society spend their nights dancing until all hours and their days sleeping it off. This is a busy time for pastry chefs, who are kept occupied stretching, filling, and baking millions of pieces of apple strudel, the traditional dessert at these parties. In between dancing, everybody eats apple strudel and sips little cups of coffee. Then they get up and dance some more.

This strudel is different—it's made with phyllo instead of strudel dough. The pastry is baked separately so it retains its crispness and is then layered with caramel custard. Alex Grunert, the pastry chef at the Danube, prefers this version to the classic recipe—but, then again, that might be because he has baked his way through too many ball seasons!

1. Prepare the caramel custard: Line a 9-by-9-inch baking pan with parchment paper. Place 2 tablespoons cold water in a small bowl, sprinkle the gelatin over the water, and set it aside. In another small bowl, lightly beat the egg yolks and whole egg together; set it aside.

2. Place 3 tablespoons water in a medium saucepan, and add the corn syrup and sugar. Cook, stirring, over medium heat until the sugar dissolves. Raise the heat to high and cook without stirring until the caramel turns very dark amber (swirl the pan if the caramel colors unevenly), about 7 minutes. When the caramel begins to smell like it's toasting (just before it begins to burn), add the butter (stand back—it will spatter and boil up). Stir in 1/2 cup of the heavy cream and bring the mixture to a boil.

3. Transfer the mixture to a blender (or use an immersion blender), and pulse several times to ensure that the custard is smooth and to lighten the cream (be careful not to splash the hot caramel). Let it cool slightly, then stir in the remaining 1 cup cream and the vanilla bean seeds and pod. Return the mixture to the saucepan and bring it to a simmer over medium heat.

4. Whisking constantly, pour a little of the hot mixture into the eggs to warm them. Whisk the warmed eggs into the caramel-cream mixture, and cook over medium heat, stirring constantly, until the mixture thickens enough to coat the back of a spoon and reaches 185°F on an instant-read thermometer. Add the gelatin and water, and whisk until the gelatin has dissolved. Pour the caramel custard through a fine-mesh strainer into the prepared baking pan. Let cool, then freeze for 1 hour or overnight.

5. Prepare the compote: Place the pears in a saucepan. Place 1 cup water in another saucepan, and add the sugar, orange zest, lemon juice, and vanilla bean seeds and pod. Bring to a boil, and let the mixture simmer for 2 minutes. Then strain the syrup through a fine-mesh sieve set over the pears. Cook the pears gently over medium-low heat until tender, about 10 minutes. Let cool.

6. Prepare the strudel layers: Preheat the oven to 400°F, and line two baking sheets with parchment paper.

7. Combine the sugar and cinnamon in a small bowl. Lay out a sheet of phyllo dough on a dry surface, brush it with melted butter, and sprinkle it with confectioners' sugar. Repeat the layers of phyllo, butter, and confectioners' sugar. Place a third sheet of phyllo on top, brush it with butter, and sprinkle with the cinnamon sugar. Cut the layered phyllo into 3-inch squares. Repeat this process with the remaining phyllo sheets, butter, and sugars. Lay the squares out on the prepared baking sheets, and bake until crisp and golden brown, 8 to 10 minutes.

8. Place the balsamic vinegar in a small saucepan and bring it to a simmer. Simmer until it is as thick as maple syrup, 8 to 10 minutes.

9. To assemble the strudels, if the custard has been frozen overnight, remove it from the freezer 10 minutes before serving. Cut the caramel custard into 3-inch squares. Place a square of custard on a square of phyllo. Top with another phyllo square. Spoon pear compote on top of the second phyllo square. Balance another square of phyllo on top of the pears. Garnish each plate with balsamic sauce and a sprig of fresh mint, and serve immediately with vanilla ice cream.

Note: Phyllo (or filo) dough is a leaf-thin Middle Eastern pastry that is sold refrigerated or frozen, usually in 1-pound boxes (for convenience, look for ones that contain two separately wrapped 8-ounce rolls of dough). Allow the frozen dough to thaw completely before using it, then tightly wrap any extra dough in plastic and refrigerate or refreeze. Look for phyllo dough at Middle Eastern or specialty food stores, or order it by mail (see Sources, page 337). Many good supermarkets carry it today as well.

Bohemian Plum Pancakes

BATTER

1 cup WHOLE MILK

¹/₄ teaspoon ACTIVE DRY YEAST

1¹/₄ cups ALL-PURPOSE FLOUR

1 large EGG YOLK

2 tablespoons UNSALTED BUTTER, melted and cooled

1 teaspoon STROH RUM (see Note, page 298) or dark rum

¹/₈ teaspoon grated LEMON ZEST

Pinch of SALT

QUARK FILLING

¹/₂ cup QUARK CHEESE (see page 14)

1 tablespoon RAISINS

2 tablespoons STROH RUM (see Note, page 298) or dark rum

¹/₃ cup plus 2 tablespoons CONFECTIONERS' SUGAR

3 tablespoons SOUR CREAM

Grated ZEST of 1 LEMON

Grated ZEST of ¹/₂ ORANGE

Pinch of SALT

This is a traditional dish in the Czech Republic. It's a yeasted pancake lightened with meringue, and filled with a thickened plum paste called *Powidl* and a sweetened Quark cream studded with rum-soaked raisins. It's a pretty substantial dish and is best served after a light meal, or as a brunch dish on its own. Start this the night before you want to serve it.

NOTES FROM THE KITCHEN It's better to make the batter for this the day before you want to serve it and let it rise overnight in the refrigerator. It's good for the yeast to rise slowly, because it develops more flavor that way. Then you can fold in the meringue and fry the pancakes at the last minute.

1. Prepare the pancake batter: Gently warm the milk in a small saucepan. Place the yeast in a large mixing bowl and whisk in the milk. Stir in the flour, egg yolk, melted butter, rum, lemon zest, and salt. Cover tightly with plastic wrap and refrigerate overnight.

2. Prepare the Quark filling: Put the Quark in a cheesecloth-lined sieve set over a bowl and let it drain in the refrigerator overnight. Place the raisins in a dish and cover them with the 2 tablespoons rum. Let sit overnight.

3. Drain the rum raisins and put them in a bowl. Add the drained Quark, confectioners' sugar, sour cream, lemon and orange zests, and salt, and stir well. Set aside.

4. Prepare the Powidl filling: Pour the port into a saucepan and add the lemon and orange juices, zests, cinnamon stick, star anise, and vanilla bean pod and seeds. Bring to a simmer and cook until reduced by half, about 10 minutes. Strain into a bowl and stir in the Powidl.

5. Prepare the plum compote: In a small saucepan over low heat, combine the sugar with 2 tablespoons water and cook, stirring, until the sugar is dissolved. Raise the heat to high and cook without stirring until the syrup turns a light caramel color (swirl the pan if the caramel colors unevenly), about 5 minutes. Pour in the red wine (stand back—it may spatter and boil up), then stir in the plums, vanilla pod and seeds, cinnamon stick, and rum. Simmer until the plums are soft, about 15 minutes. Remove and discard the vanilla bean pod and cinnamon stick.

POWIDL FILLING

1/2 cup PORT WINE

2 tablespoons fresh LEMON JUICE

1 tablespoon fresh ORANGE JUICE

2 teaspoons grated ORANGE ZEST

1/2 teaspoon grated LEMON ZEST

1 CINNAMON STICK, 3 inches

1 whole STAR ANISE

1/4 VANILLA BEAN, split lengthwise,
   seeds scraped out with a knife

2 cups POWIDL (see page 67)

PLUM COMPOTE

1/2 cup SUGAR

1/4 cup DRY RED WINE

1 1/2 pounds (about 15) ITALIAN
   PRUNE PLUMS, pitted and
   quartered

1 VANILLA BEAN, split lengthwise,
   seeds scraped out with a knife

1 CINNAMON STICK, 3 inches

1 tablespoon STROH RUM (see Note,
   page 298) or dark rum

MERINGUE

2 large EGG WHITES

2 tablespoons SUGAR

UNSALTED BUTTER, for cooking the
   pancakes

SERVES 12 AS DESSERT

6. When you are ready to make the pancakes, let the batter come back to room temperature if it was refrigerated (about 30 minutes).

7. Prepare the meringue: Place the egg whites in a clean bowl of an electric mixer fitted with the whisk attachment, and whip until soft peaks form. Gradually add the sugar and whip until stiff, shiny peaks form. Use a rubber spatula to gently fold the egg whites into the batter.

8. Place a large nonstick skillet over medium heat for 3 minutes. Brush the pan with butter, and pour 3-inch rounds of batter onto the pan (or make the pancakes in cast-iron mini-pancake pans of this size). Cook for about 3 minutes, then turn and cook for another 1 to 2 minutes, until the pancakes are brown and crisp on both sides. Stack them three high, spreading the first layer with Powidl and the second with Quark filling. Top with plum compote, and serve.

POWIDL *Powidl* is the Austrian name for a thick, condensed plum jam. Traditionally, summer's plums were cooked in huge vats as a way to preserve them. This slow, labor-intensive process involved first simmering the whole fruits until softened, then straining out their pits and cooking the resulting puree for hours (even weeks!) while stirring it constantly to prevent burning. The finished Powidl, almost prunelike in color and consistency, was stored in earthenware jugs and used as a spread, dessert topping, or sweet pasta or pastry filling. Now Powidl is stirred by machine and sealed in glass jars, but the authentic product should still contain nothing but plums. Look for Powidl in gourmet markets and specialty stores, or purchase jars by mail order (see Sources, page 337).

Winter

Oxtail Strudel Canapés

OXTAIL FILLING

2 tablespoons CANOLA OIL

2 pounds OXTAILS, cut crosswise
 into 3-inch sections

Fine SEA SALT and freshly ground
 BLACK PEPPER

2 CARROTS

2 CELERY STALKS

1 tablespoon UNSALTED BUTTER

1/2 large ONION, sliced

1 teaspoon TOMATO PASTE

2/3 cup DRY RED WINE

2 1/2 cups VEAL STOCK
 (see page 335)

1 PARSNIP

5 WHITE PEPPERCORNS

3 ALLSPICE BERRIES

2 sprigs FRESH PARSLEY

1 sprig FRESH THYME

1 GARLIC CLOVE, smashed

1/2 BAY LEAF, preferably fresh

2 tablespoons finely chopped
 CELERY LEAVES

STRUDEL

12 sheets PHYLLO DOUGH
 (see Note, page 62)

4 tablespoons UNSALTED BUTTER,
 melted and cooled

1 EGG, beaten

CANOLA OIL, for deep-frying

SERVES 12 TO 15 AS AN
HORS D'OEUVRE

MARIO LOHNINGER Oxtail is one of the most delicious parts of the cow, and people should use it more than they do here in America. It's very popular in Austria. It has a lot of gelatin and some marrow from the bones, which makes the meat soft and tender and full of flavor. Here we pick it off the bone and chop it up with vegetables, then roll it in strudel pastry and deep-fry it. It's a nice little canapé.

1. Preheat the oven to 375°F.

2. In a large, heavy ovenproof saucepan or Dutch oven, heat the oil over high heat. Season the oxtails generously with salt and pepper, and sear them on all sides, about 20 minutes. Meanwhile, slice one of the carrots and one of the celery stalks. Transfer the oxtails to a plate and pour off the oil.

3. Add the butter to the pot and let it melt over medium heat, scraping up the cooked-on juices with a wooden spoon as the butter foams. Add the sliced onion, sliced carrot, and sliced celery. Cook, stirring, until soft and browned, about 15 minutes. Add the tomato paste and cook, stirring, until it has darkened, 2 minutes.

4. Pour in the wine and bring it to a simmer over high heat. Simmer until the mixture is reduced by half, about 10 minutes. Add the oxtails and the veal stock. When the liquid returns to a simmer, cover the pot and transfer it to the oven. Cook for 2 hours.

5. Stir in the remaining whole carrot and celery stalk, the parsnip, white peppercorns, allspice berries, parsley, thyme, garlic, and bay leaf. Continue cooking until the whole vegetables are tender, about 45 minutes. Using a slotted spoon, transfer the whole vegetables to a plate to cool; then cut them into very small cubes and refrigerate until ready to use. Continue to cook the oxtails until the meat is very tender, another 45 minutes or so. Remove the pot from the oven and let them cool in the cooking liquid for about 1 hour.

6. Pick the meat from the oxtails and pack it into a bowl, pressing down to compact it. Cover the bowl with plastic wrap and weight it down with a small saucer or plate topped with a heavy can. Refrigerate overnight. Strain the braising liquid remaining in the pot and refrigerate it, covered.

7. The next day, unmold the oxtail and cut it into very small cubes. Combine the cubed oxtail, the reserved cubed carrot, celery, and parsnip, and the celery leaves in a bowl. Season with salt and pepper.

8. Place the braising liquid in a saucepan and bring it to a simmer over medium-high heat. Let the liquid reduce slightly, 5 to 10 minutes, skimming off any foam. Add $1/2$ cup of this liquid to the oxtail mixture and toss to combine. Refrigerate for at least 1 hour.

9. Cut the phyllo into 4-inch-wide strips. Scoop out 2 teaspoons of the filling and mold it into an oblong shape. Lightly brush a phyllo strip with melted butter. Lay the filling at the bottom of the strip and roll it up, pinching the sides as you go, making sure not to create any air bubbles. Brush the ends with a little of the beaten egg to seal them. Continue with the remaining filling and phyllo. (The strudels may be formed in advance and then refrigerated for up to 4 hours before frying.)

10. Fill a saucepan or deep-fryer halfway with oil, and heat it to 375°F. Fry the strudels in the canola oil until golden brown, about 1 minute. Drain on paper towels and serve while hot.

Oxtail Consommé

WITH BONE MARROW DUMPLINGS

CONSOMMÉ

1 ONION, halved

3 ¼ pounds OXTAILS

Fine SEA SALT and freshly ground BLACK PEPPER

3 tablespoons CANOLA OIL

4 pieces MARROWBONE (½ to ¾ pound each)

10 cups WHITE BEEF STOCK (see page 333) or canned low-sodium beef broth

6 JUNIPER BERRIES

2 sprigs FRESH THYME

12 WHITE PEPPERCORNS

1 BAY LEAF, preferably fresh

1 CARROT, chopped

1 CELERY STALK, chopped

½ NUTMEG, freshly grated

GARNISHES

BONE MARROW DUMPLINGS (recipe follows)

FRESH LOVAGE LEAVES, sliced (optional)

FRESH BLACK TRUFFLE, thinly sliced (optional; see page 136)

SERVES 6 AS A SOUP COURSE

NOTES FROM THE KITCHEN Some chefs add egg whites to clarify their consommés. Ours is clear because we keep it at a perfect simmer the entire time and never stir or disturb it. Then we ladle it out through cheesecloth. Mario likes it to have just a glimmer of fat on the surface—it gives it good flavor. In the wintertime, Mario will often get a phone call from David, across the street in the office, and he'll make a consommé for him and bring it over. It's David's favorite lunch on the days he doesn't cook.

1. Heat a heavy pan over high heat. Place the onion halves cut side down in the dry pan and let the cut sides blacken completely, about 10 minutes. Set aside.

2. Season the oxtails with salt and pepper. Heat a large heavy stockpot over high heat. Add the canola oil and let it heat for 30 seconds. Add the oxtails and sear them on all sides until they are dark brown, about 20 minutes. Transfer the oxtails to a plate. Discard the oil and wipe out the pot.

3. Return the oxtails to the pot and add the marrowbones and blackened onion. Pour in the beef stock. Bring to a simmer and skim off any foam that forms on the surface. Let the liquid simmer gently for 2 hours without stirring.

4. Place the juniper berries, thyme, white peppercorns, and bay leaf in a 6-inch square of cheesecloth. Tie it securely with kitchen string. Add the sachet to the pot along with the carrot, celery, and nutmeg. Simmer until the broth is concentrated, about 2 more hours.

5. Strain the liquid into a saucepan through a sieve lined with three layers of cheesecloth. Discard all the solids.

6. Just before serving, cook the dumplings: Bring the consommé to a simmer and drop in the dumplings a few at a time. (Do not let the soup come to a boil while cooking the dumplings or it may cloud up.) Cook until they float to the surface, 3 to 5 minutes; then use a slotted spoon to transfer them to a platter. When they are all cooked, return them to the soup, and heat through if necessary. Serve the consommé garnished with the lovage leaves and sliced truffle, if desired.

Bone Marrow Dumplings

NOTES FROM THE KITCHEN Marrow bones need to be soaked in salted water in the refrigerator for 2 days, so be sure to plan in advance.

DUMPLINGS IN AUSTRIA Large or small, heavy or light, yeasted, fruit-filled, meat-filled, or plain, dumplings are a major Austrian comfort food. They are often made from a base of stale bread bound with eggs, both of which are almost always available. Along with bread dumplings, those made with regular or semolina flour, and sometimes Quark cheese or pureed potatoes, are also very common. Other additions run the gamut from apricots to cabbage, and more often than not, leftovers find their way into dumplings. Cooks will grind leftover meat from a roast to mix into their bread dumplings, perhaps adding herbs, then cook the dumplings in stock or serve them in a sauce. Fried onions are also popular, and in the Tyrolean region dumplings are filled with bacon. Liver dumplings are a favorite, as are other organ meats and most pork products. Many cooks keep clean white cloth napkins to use for napkin dumplings, which are wrapped in the cloth and then steamed. Platters of dumplings are usually drizzled with melted butter and topped with poppy seeds, nuts, cheese, or sugar. Dumplings are a warm, rustic, sustaining food, clearly developed over the generations when people worked outside, even on the coldest days.

1/4 pound MARROWBONE

Fine SEA SALT

1 tablespoon UNSALTED BUTTER

1 tablespoon extra-virgin OLIVE OIL

10 ounces diced BRIOCHE or white bread (about 6 1/2 cups)

2 large EGGS

1 tablespoon chopped FRESH PARSLEY

Freshly grated NUTMEG

1/8 teaspoon freshly ground BLACK PEPPER

MAKES ABOUT 50 DUMPLINGS

1. Place the marrowbones in a bowl and cover with cold water. Salt the water heavily, and refrigerate for 2 days, stirring and agitating the water occasionally.

2. Drain and rinse the marrowbones, and pat them dry with paper towels. Use a small knife to pick out the marrow. Wrap the marrow in plastic and freeze it for at least 2 hours.

3. Warm the butter and olive oil in a large skillet over medium-high heat. Add the diced bread and fry, stirring, until golden, about 10 minutes. Drain on paper towels. Place the bread in a food processor and pulse until it is reduced to crumbs. Transfer the crumbs to a bowl.

4. Let the marrow thaw slightly, then place it in a food processor and pulse until ground. Add the eggs, parsley, nutmeg, 1/4 teaspoon salt, and the pepper, and process to combine.

5. Transfer the marrow mixture to the bowl with the bread crumbs and mix with your hands until smooth. Working with about 2 teaspoons of the mixture at a time, form round dumplings. These can be made about 4 hours ahead. Cover with plastic and refrigerate.

Austrian Potato Salad

WITH FRESH BLACK TRUFFLES

FRESH BLACK TRUFFLE OIL

1 whole FRESH BLACK PÉRIGORD TRUFFLE (about 1 3/4 ounces)

1/2 cup GRAPESEED OIL

Fine SEA SALT and freshly ground BLACK PEPPER

PORCINI PUREE

2 tablespoons extra-virgin OLIVE OIL

1 GARLIC CLOVE, smashed

1 sprig FRESH THYME

1/4 pound FRESH PORCINI MUSHROOMS, sliced 1/4 inch thick

Fine SEA SALT and freshly ground BLACK PEPPER

1/2 cup WHOLE MILK

POTATO SALAD AND PUREE

1 1/2 pounds (about 16) FINGERLING POTATOES

2 cups OXTAIL CONSOMMÉ (see page 74) or beef stock or broth (see page 333)

1 1/2 cups CHICKEN STOCK (see page 333) or canned low-sodium chicken broth or water

1 tablespoon CHAMPAGNE VINEGAR

5 tablespoons grated BRIN D'AMOUR CHEESE (see Note)

Fine SEA SALT and freshly ground BLACK PEPPER

MARIO LOHNINGER This is something we created when we were cooking at a skiing event in the Austrian mountains. We had plenty of truffles because we had stopped in Paris on the way and picked up a big bag to bring with us. We made this salad at the end of the trip, when we needed to use up the last of the truffles. Potato salad is a big thing in Austria—we make it with a special yellow potato, but you can use fingerlings. What we did differently from the standard Austrian recipe was to marinate the potatoes with fresh truffle oil. Then we made a potato puree with cheese, and a porcini mushroom puree, and covered it all up with a mâche salad and more black truffles. It was a greatly successful dish. When you're making it, you just love digging your hands in there and tasting it over and over.

1. Prepare the truffle oil: Use a truffle shaver or a mandoline to shave off 12 very thin slices of truffle. Arrange the slices between two sheets of plastic wrap on a plate, and set it aside. Pound the remaining truffle with a mortar and pestle to crush it (or roughly chop it). Place the crushed truffle in a blender with the grapeseed oil and process until smooth. Season with a little salt and pepper, and set aside.

2. Prepare the porcini puree: Heat the olive oil in a sauté pan over medium-high heat. Add the garlic and thyme, stir to coat, and then add the sliced porcini. Season with salt and pepper. Cook, stirring, until the mushrooms are tender, about 7 minutes. Add the milk, reduce the heat, and let simmer until the mushrooms are very soft and the milk is reduced by half, 5 minutes. Drain, reserving the milk. Remove and discard the garlic and thyme. Transfer the mushrooms to a blender and process, adding some of the reserved milk as needed to make a smooth puree. Set it aside.

3. Place the potatoes in a small saucepan and pour the consommé and chicken stock over them. Bring to a boil, then reduce the heat and simmer until the potatoes are just tender, about 12 minutes. Drain the potatoes, reserving the cooking liquid. Keep the cooking liquid warm.

FOR SERVING

1 1/2 cups (3/4 ounce) mixed FRISÉE
   and MÂCHE, torn into small
   pieces

2 tablespoons extra-virgin
   OLIVE OIL, plus additional for
   the truffles

1 teaspoon aged BALSAMIC VINE-
   GAR, plus additional for garnish

Fine SEA SALT and freshly ground
   BLACK PEPPER

FLEUR DE SEL, for garnish
   (see Note, page 53)

SERVES 4 AS AN APPETIZER

4. When the potatoes are cool enough to handle, cut 3 of them into 1/4-inch-thick slices. Toss the slices with the Champagne vinegar and 1/4 cup of the truffle oil. Cover to keep warm.

5. Push the remaining potatoes through a fine-mesh sieve into a bowl. Stir in the cheese, 1/3 cup of the warm potato cooking liquid, the remaining 1/4 cup truffle oil, and 3 tablespoons of the porcini puree. Season with salt and pepper. Keep warm.

6. In a bowl, toss the greens with the olive oil and balsamic vinegar, and season with salt and pepper.

7. To serve, season the reserved sliced truffles with salt and pepper to taste, and rub them lightly with olive oil. Place a spoonful of potato-cheese puree in the center of each plate. Neatly pile the potato salad over the puree. Top the potatoes with a layer of greens. Finally, lay the fresh truffle slices on top like shingles, covering up the greens completely. Garnish the plate with drops of balsamic vinegar and a few more sprigs of salad greens. Sprinkle the truffles with a few grains of fleur de sel, and serve.

Note: Brin d'Amour is a semisoft raw-milk cheese produced in Corsica from ewes or goats that have a lot of herbs in their diet. The creamy, flavorful cheese is formed into square blocks and covered with herbs. Look for Brin d'Amour at fine cheese stores or purchase it by mail order (see Sources, page 337).

Cured Mahimahi

WITH BEET-FENNEL SALAD AND BLOOD ORANGE VINAIGRETTE

Mahimahi is a dense, sweet fish. Curing it in citrus juices and gin firms it up just enough without making it tough. Translucent slices of the cured fish atop a blood orange and fennel salad are a bright update of the pickled fish and red sauerkraut of traditional Eastern European cuisine. If you want to, you can skip the blood orange vinaigrette—the dish will be good without it.

1. Combine the coriander seeds, juniper berries, and peppercorns in a mortar or in a spice grinder and crush slightly. Transfer to a bowl and add the dill, zests, juices, gin, salt, and sugar. Whisk to dissolve the sugar and salt. Place the fish in a deep bowl and add the curing ingredients, making sure the fish is completely submerged in the liquid. Cover with plastic wrap and refrigerate. Check after 16 hours, and every 4 hours thereafter, until the fish is slightly firmed throughout, even at the center. This should take 20 to 24 hours.

2. Prepare the beet-fennel salad: Put the beet juice in a small saucepan and bring to a boil over medium-high heat. Simmer until the juice has reduced by one third, about 15 minutes. Then measure out 1/2 cup juice and set it aside for the blood orange vinaigrette. Continue to simmer the remaining beet juice until it is reduced to 1/4 cup, about 10 more minutes. Strain into a large bowl. Whisk in the vinegars, oils, salt, and pepper. Add the fennel and toss well. Let marinate at room temperature for 30 minutes.

CURED MAHIMAHI

1/2 cup CORIANDER SEEDS

1/3 cup JUNIPER BERRIES

3 1/2 tablespoons WHITE PEPPER-
CORNS

1 1/2 cups packed chopped FRESH
DILL FRONDS and stems

Grated ZEST and fresh JUICE of
5 ORANGES (1 1/2 cups juice)

Grated ZEST and fresh JUICE of
5 LEMONS (3/4 cup juice)

1 cup GIN

7 tablespoons FINE SEA SALT

1 cup SUGAR

1 1/3 pounds sashimi-quality
MAHIMAHI

BEET-FENNEL SALAD

1 2/3 cups BEET JUICE (see Note,
page 230)

2 teaspoons RASPBERRY VINEGAR

2 teaspoons CHAMPAGNE VINEGAR

2 teaspoons CANOLA OIL

2 teaspoons OLIVE OIL

3/4 teaspoon FINE SEA SALT, or to
taste

1/4 teaspoon freshly ground BLACK
PEPPER, or to taste

1 FENNEL BULB, shredded (about
2 cups)

3. Prepare the blood orange vinaigrette: Place the blood orange juice in a shallow saucepan over medium-high heat. Bring it to a boil, then let it simmer rapidly until the juice becomes syrupy, about 5 minutes. Transfer the juice to a heatproof glass measuring cup—you should have about $1/4$ cup juice (if you have too much juice, return it to the saucepan and simmer for another minute, then measure again). Strain the reserved $1/2$ cup beet juice into a bowl. Whisk in the reduced blood orange juice, the canola and olive oils, and the vinegar. Set the vinaigrette aside. The vinaigrette can be made 1 day ahead.

4. When the fish has cured, rinse it thoroughly under cold water and use it immediately or refrigerate for up to 24 hours. Before serving, use a long, sharp knife to slice the fish into thin sheets.

5. To serve, place a small pile of beet-fennel salad on each plate and top with a thin slice of fish. Spoon a little vinaigrette over and around the fish and salad, and garnish with the scallion slices.

BLOOD ORANGE VINAIGRETTE
Fresh JUICE of 3 to 4 BLOOD
 ORANGES ($3/4$ cup juice)
2 tablespoons CANOLA OIL
2 tablespoons extra-virgin OLIVE OIL
2 tablespoons CHAMPAGNE VINEGAR

SLICED SCALLIONS, green part only,
 for garnish

SERVES 6 TO 8 AS AN APPETIZER

Shrimp

WITH SWEET AND SOUR SQUASH AND PUMPKIN SEED SAUCE

PUMPKIN SEED DRESSING

1 EGG YOLK

1/2 SHALLOT, roughly chopped

2 tablespoons SHERRY VINEGAR

1 GARLIC CLOVE, smashed

1 teaspoon SUGAR

1 teaspoon DIJON MUSTARD

1/2 cup extra-virgin OLIVE OIL

1/3 cup VEGETABLE STOCK (see
   page 332) or canned low-sodium
   vegetable broth

Fine SEA SALT and freshly ground
   BLACK PEPPER

1 tablespoon plus 1 teaspoon PUMPKIN
   SEED OIL (see page 247)

1 tablespoon DRY VERMOUTH

1 tablespoon aged BALSAMIC
   VINEGAR

2/3 cup SOUR CREAM

NOTES FROM THE KITCHEN The Danube has two sous-chefs named Thomas, both from Austria. So for ease, we call them T1 and T2. T1 is Thomas Mayr; T2 is Thomas Kahl. This dish is T1's brainstorm. He experimented with many different kinds of winter squash to find something dense and sturdy but still sweet and delicate in flavor. Buttercup was the best, but a combination of red kuri or kabocha and butternut was also great. You can use any one of them, though.

Poaching the shrimp in oil, a classic technique, cooks them through without making them rubbery.

1. Prepare the dressing: Place the egg yolk, shallot, sherry vinegar, garlic, sugar, and mustard in a food processor, and pulse to combine. With the motor running, gradually drizzle in the olive oil, and then the vegetable stock, until the mixture is smoothly combined and as thick as honey. Season with salt and pepper.

2. Transfer the dressing to a bowl and fold in all the remaining ingredients, whisking in the sour cream last. Cover and refrigerate until ready to use.

3. To prepare the sweet and sour squash, place the coriander in a large, heavy skillet over medium heat. Toast, stirring, until fragrant, 1 to 2 minutes. Transfer the seeds to a plate to stop the cooking, and wipe out the pan. Sprinkle the sugar in the pan in an even layer. Heat without stirring until it melts and turns into a medium-dark amber caramel (swirl the pan if it colors unevenly), 6 minutes. Pour in the orange juice and the Champagne vinegar (stand back—it will spatter), and cook slowly, stirring, until the caramel dissolves.

4. Add the grated squash, ginger juice, toasted coriander seeds, salt, and pepper to the pan and cook over medium heat, stirring occasionally, for 10 minutes. Add the grated apple and continue to cook until the apple and squash are just barely tender, about 10 minutes longer. Stir in the honey as needed to achieve a sweet-sour effect. Keep warm.

SWEET AND SOUR SQUASH

1/2 teaspoon GROUND CORIANDER

3 tablespoons SUGAR

1/2 cup fresh ORANGE JUICE

1/2 cup CHAMPAGNE VINEGAR

1 3/4 cups grated WINTER SQUASH
(about 1 small squash), such as
buttercup, kabocha, or butternut

1 1/2 teaspoons GINGER JUICE
(see Note)

Fine SEA SALT and freshly ground
BLACK PEPPER, to taste

1/2 GREEN APPLE, grated

1 to 2 teaspoons HONEY

SHRIMP

4 cups CANOLA OIL

2 GARLIC CLOVES

2 sprigs FRESH THYME

1 sprig FRESH ROSEMARY

1/2 pound (about 12) large SHRIMP,
shelled and deveined, tails on

Fine SEA SALT and freshly ground
BLACK PEPPER

SERVES 4 AS AN APPETIZER

5. Cook the shrimp: Place the oil, garlic, thyme, and rosemary in a 2-quart saucepan over medium heat. Place a thermometer in the oil, add the shrimp, and slowly heat until the oil reaches 150°F. Remove the pan from the heat and let the shrimp cook until just the tails begin to curl and the flesh feels firm, about 10 minutes. Use a slotted spoon to transfer the shrimp to a paper towel–lined plate, and season with salt and pepper.

6. Strain the pumpkin seed dressing through a fine-mesh sieve into a bowl, and dip the shrimp in the dressing to coat each one. To serve, make a small bed of the sweet and sour squash on each plate and arrange the shrimp on top.

Note: To make ginger juice without a juicer, grate peeled fresh ginger into a fine-mesh sieve set over a bowl (or use a piece of cheesecloth). Press down on the ginger (or squeeze the cheesecloth) to extract all the juice.

Roasted Prosciutto-Wrapped Striped Bass

WITH SZEGEDINER SAUERKRAUT

MARIO LOHNINGER Szeged is a town in Hungary that is famous for its paprika. So calling a dish Szegediner means it has a lot of paprika and fresh sweet peppers in it. The cabbage is a great recipe on its own if you don't want to stuff it into the fish, or you can serve it with roasted chicken or duck. This is a perfect dish to make at home, especially for a dinner party. You can prepare the fish in advance, wrap it up in the prosciutto, and then put it in the oven at the last minute.

1. Heat two skillets over medium heat (one of them should be large enough to eventually accommodate all the sauerkraut). Add 1 tablespoon butter to each pan and heat until foaming. Place the onion in one pan and the bell peppers in the other. Season both pans well with salt and pepper. Gently fry the onions and the peppers until the vegetables are soft, 7 to 10 minutes. Do not let either of the vegetables brown. (Alternatively, fry the onions and peppers separately in one large pan, combining them when they are cooked.)

2. While the vegetables are cooking, place the garlic, rosemary, thyme, and bay leaf in a 6-inch square of cheesecloth, and tie the sachet securely with kitchen string.

3. Combine the onions and peppers in the larger pan. Stir in the paprika, including the hot paprika, if using, and cook for 5 seconds. Immediately stir in the sauerkraut, tomato water, beef stock, bacon, and the sachet. Simmer until the sauerkraut is soft and the flavors have melded, 45 minutes to 1 hour. Add the grated potato and cook until the liquid has thickened and you can no longer taste raw potato, 5 to 10 minutes. Season to taste with salt and pepper. Let cool.

SZEGEDINER CABBAGE

2 tablespoons UNSALTED BUTTER

1 large ONION, halved and thinly sliced

1 large YELLOW BELL PEPPER, trimmed, seeded, and cut into very thin strips

1 large RED BELL PEPPER, trimmed, seeded, and cut into very thin strips

Fine SEA SALT and freshly ground BLACK PEPPER

1 GARLIC CLOVE, smashed

1 sprig FRESH ROSEMARY

1 small sprig FRESH THYME

1 fresh BAY LEAF, or 2 dried

1 tablespoon SWEET PAPRIKA

Pinch of HOT PAPRIKA (optional)

2 cups packed drained SAUER-KRAUT, thoroughly rinsed (see page 94)

1 1/2 cups TOMATO WATER (see page 329) or water

1 cup WHITE BEEF STOCK (preferably homemade, see page 333)

1 thick slice BACON, or 2 thin slices

1 tablespoon finely grated POTATO

STRIPED BASS

1 STRIPED bass (about 3 pounds),
  boned and cut into 2 fillets

Fine SEA SALT and freshly ground
  BLACK PEPPER

1/3 pound sliced PROSCIUTTO

2 tablespoons CANOLA OIL

6 cipollini or PEARL ONIONS,
  peeled (see Note, page 58)

2 SHALLOTS, sliced

3 GARLIC CLOVES, sliced

1 small bunch FRESH THYME

1 small bunch FRESH SAGE

2 sprigs FRESH ROSEMARY

SERVES 6 AS A MAIN COURSE

4. Preheat the oven to 425°F.

5. Season the bass fillets on both sides with salt and pepper. Arrange overlapping slices of prosciutto crosswise on a platter that is the length of the fish. Lay one fillet skin side down on the prosciutto, and spoon a thick layer of sauerkraut over it. Top with the other fillet, skin side up, and fold the prosciutto over the fish to wrap it (the prosciutto may not reach all the way around the fish). Use kitchen string to tie the fish together at 2-inch intervals.

6. Heat a large ovenproof sauté pan over high heat for 3 minutes, and add the canola oil. When the oil is very hot, place the prosciutto-wrapped fish in the pan. Sear the fish on both sides, about 3 minutes per side.

7. Add the onions, shallots, garlic, and herbs to the pan, and transfer it to the oven. Roast until the fish is just cooked through, about 18 minutes.

8. Meanwhile, warm the remaining sauerkraut. When the fish is cooked, transfer it to a serving platter and it let rest for 3 to 4 minutes. Then use scissors to cut the string, and discard it. Slice the fish and serve it with the remaining Szegediner cabbage and the roasted onions, shallots, and garlic.

SAUERKRAUT The making of sauerkraut is an age-old tradition in Austria and many neighboring countries. Authentic sauerkraut relies on nothing more than salt and time to render sliced or whole white cabbage leaves tangy and softened yet still crisp. The pickling is done in wooden barrels. The cabbage is salted and seasoned with bay leaves, chiles, peppercorns, and sometimes caraway seeds, then weighted and left undisturbed for about 2 weeks while lactic fermentation takes place. The fermentation lends the cabbage a gentle sour flavor, yet it retains a freshness that is usually lacking in the highly seasoned and acidic packages of sauerkraut available in American supermarkets. While imported sauerkraut is preferable, even a pouch of sauerkraut can be turned into a delicious condiment or side dish by rinsing the cabbage, then simmering it in stock and/or wine and adding sautéed onions, apples, caraway seeds, or other shredded vegetables as desired.

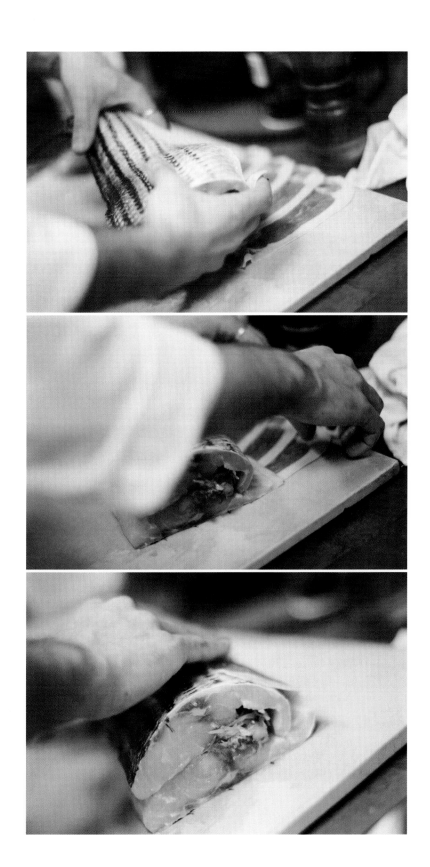

Beef Cheek Goulash
WITH POTATO PUREE

1/3 cup RENDERED DUCK FAT (see page 335) or canola oil

5 large (2 pounds) ONIONS, sliced

5 RED BELL PEPPERS, trimmed, seeded, and roughly chopped

3/4 cup TOMATO PASTE

1 tablespoon plus 2 teaspoons SWEET HUNGARIAN PAPRIKA (see page 275)

1 1/2 teaspoons HOT PAPRIKA (see page 275)

2 tablespoons RED WINE VINEGAR

2 tablespoons DRIED MARJORAM

1 tablespoon chopped GARLIC

2 teaspoons toasted CARAWAY SEEDS, freshly ground (see Note, page 100)

1/8 teaspoon grated LEMON ZEST

2 teaspoons finely chopped FRESH MARJORAM, plus additional for garnish

1 1/2 teaspoons finely chopped FRESH THYME

1/4 teaspoon finely chopped FRESH ROSEMARY

3 1/2 pounds BEEF CHEEKS, trimmed and halved

Fine SEA SALT and freshly ground BLACK PEPPER

2 tablespoons CORNICHON JUICE (see Note)

Potato Puree (recipe follows)

SERVES 6 TO 8 AS A MAIN COURSE

DAVID BOULEY When we opened the Danube, we knew we needed to develop an exceptional recipe for goulash. We wanted its flavors to be classic because they are so good—I love the way the onions melt into a sweet sauce, and the piquant taste of the paprika. But the challenge was finding the right cut of beef. Austrians butcher their cows differently than we do in the U.S., and differently than the French too. So using the traditional Austrian cuts wasn't a practical option. After a lot of experimentation, we tried beef cheeks, and they turned out to be the best. They have a very tender texture that won't dry out, even if you make them ahead and reheat them. Beef cheeks can be a little challenging to find, but a good butcher will order them for you.

1. Melt the duck fat in a large heavy pot over medium-low heat, and add the onions. Cook them very slowly and evenly, stirring occasionally, until they are very dark brown, about 2 hours.

2. Meanwhile, place the bell peppers in a steamer set over boiling water, and steam until very soft, 15 to 20 minutes. Transfer the peppers to a food mill or blender and puree (straining afterward if you use a blender). You should have 3/4 cup red pepper puree.

3. Add the tomato paste to the onions and cook until it darkens, about 5 minutes. Add the sweet and hot paprikas, and mix well. Add 7 cups water, the red pepper puree, vinegar, dried marjoram, garlic, ground caraway seeds, and lemon zest. Add half of the fresh marjoram, thyme, and rosemary.

4. Season the beef cheeks with salt and pepper, and add them to the pot. Bring the liquid to a bare simmer and keep it there, stirring only three or four times, for 3 hours. Add the rest of the fresh herbs and begin to check the tenderness of the cheeks with a fork. They are done when they fall easily from the fork, after about 4 hours total cooking time. They should be meltingly tender, but not so soft as to fall apart. Some pieces of meat will take longer than others; pull them from the liquid as they are done. Spread the cooked beef cheeks in a single layer in a pan.

5. When all the cheeks are cooked, pass the cooking liquid through a colander. (Don't use a sieve, as you want to push tiny bits of onion through to make a slightly chunky sauce.)

6. Pour the sauce over the cheeks and season to taste with salt, pepper, additional fresh marjoram, and the cornichon juice. Serve immediately, very hot, or reheat by covering the pan and baking at 350°F until hot. Serve with the potato puree.

Note: Cornichons are tiny gherkin pickles, classically served with charcuterie. For cornichon juice, buy good-quality jarred cornichons at a gourmet food store and drain the desired amount of vinegary pickling liquid from the jar.

Potato Puree

This simple puree is more French than Austrian. As rich and smooth as possible, its excellence lies in the perfect balance of potato, salt, butter, milk, and cream.

1 3/4 pounds (about 20 small) FINGERLING POTATOES, peeled, eyes removed, cut into 1-inch lengths
1 1/2 teaspoons fine SEA SALT, plus additional to taste
3/4 cup WHOLE MILK
3/4 cup HEAVY CREAM
6 tablespoons UNSALTED BUTTER, cut into 1/2-inch cubes, softened
Freshly ground BLACK PEPPER

SERVES 6 TO 8 AS A SIDE DISH

1. Put the potatoes in a saucepan with 1 teaspoon of the salt and cold water to cover. Bring the water to a boil, then reduce the heat and simmer, uncovered, until the potatoes are very tender, about 20 minutes.
2. When the potatoes are almost cooked, combine the milk and cream in a microwave-safe container. Microwave on medium power until hot, about 2 minutes. (Or heat in a small saucepan on the stove over medium heat for 2 to 3 minutes.)
3. When the potatoes are cooked, drain them well and return them to the pot. Cook them over medium heat for another 1 to 2 minutes to dry them. Transfer the potatoes to a food mill or coarse-mesh strainer set over the cooking pot or a bowl, and stir in the butter; then push the mixture through. Add about two thirds of the hot milk mixture to the pureed potatoes and stir well. Gradually stir in more of the milk until the puree is the consistency of a thick pudding—it should not be soupy. Discard any remaining milk.
4. Use a rubber spatula to push the puree through a fine-mesh sieve set over a heated serving bowl, working quickly so the potatoes do not cool. Season with black pepper and the remaining 1/2 teaspoon salt, or to taste, and serve immediately.

GOULASH

Goulash, the Austrian version of Hungary's most widespread dish, can be a soup or stew depending on how much liquid it contains. It is usually made of beef, with a sweet base of slow-cooked onions, and flavored with garlic, paprika, caraway, and marjoram. Tough cuts of beef are often used here, since they are tenderized through the long, gentle cooking. Austrian goulash contains larger pieces of meat than its Hungarian namesake, and the meat should be soft in texture while the stew is hearty in flavor. Though the thickness of the sauce is a desirable trait, this should come from the paprika, potatoes, or perhaps some tomato paste, but never from the addition of flour or cornstarch, which is considered a goulash taboo. Goulash soup makes a great lunch, and it is also a favorite dish for the midmorning second breakfast, or "fork-breakfast," that occurs around 10 A.M. (The first breakfast is a much lighter meal, usually coffee and a roll, eaten first thing.)

Goulash Soup

6 tablespoons RENDERED DUCK FAT (see page 335) or canola oil

5 large ONIONS (2 pounds)

Fine SEA SALT and freshly ground BLACK PEPPER

10 cups WHITE BEEF STOCK (see page 333) or low-sodium canned beef broth

1/3 cup CHAMPAGNE VINEGAR

4 GARLIC CLOVES, minced

2 tablespoons TOMATO PASTE

1 teaspoon ALL-PURPOSE FLOUR

3 teaspoons HOT PAPRIKA (see page 275)

1/4 cup SWEET HUNGARIAN PAPRIKA

1/4 cup DRIED MARJORAM

1 teaspoon finely chopped FRESH LEMON THYME or regular thyme

1 teaspoon finely chopped FRESH ROSEMARY

2 tablespoons CARAWAY SEEDS, toasted and ground (see Note)

1 1/2 teaspoons grated LEMON ZEST

1 JALAPEÑO PEPPER, halved lengthwise, seeds removed

3 pounds boneless BEEF SHANK or beef shoulder, cut into 1-inch cubes

2 RED BELL PEPPERS, trimmed, seeded, and diced

2 YELLOW BELL PEPPERS, trimmed, seeded, and diced

2 pounds FINGERLING POTATOES, diced

SERVES 8 AS AN APPETIZER OR LIGHT MAIN COURSE

MARIO LOHNINGER This is a really good dish to have around the house. If I had any time to spend at my house, I would regularly make a pot of goulash soup and keep it in the refrigerator. It's one of those things that gets better when it sits. You can eat it for breakfast, especially if you have a hangover. But it's also good for lunch or supper. It will last for 10 days if you make enough.

1. Heat 4 tablespoons duck fat in a large pot over medium heat. Chop 4 of the onions very fine, add them to the pot, and season with salt and pepper. Reduce the heat to medium-low and cook, covered, stirring occasionally, until the onions are caramelized and very soft, about 45 minutes.

2. In a separate pot, combine the stock and vinegar and warm over medium heat.

3. When the onions are done, raise the heat to medium, add the garlic, and cook, stirring, for 2 minutes. Then add the tomato paste, flour, and paprikas, and stir for 3 to 4 seconds (any longer will turn the paprika bitter). Add the warm stock mixture. Add the marjoram, thyme, rosemary, ground caraway seeds, lemon zest, jalapeño, and beef. Bring the soup to a steady simmer and let it cook, uncovered, until the meat begins to soften, about 2 hours.

4. Meanwhile, heat the remaining 2 tablespoons duck fat in a sauté pan over high heat. Dice the remaining onion and add it along with the bell peppers. Sauté until golden and tender, 1 minute.

5. When the beef is just tender, add the potatoes to the pot and simmer for 10 minutes. Then add the sautéed peppers and onion. When the vegetables are soft and the meat is tender, the soup is done. Remove the jalapeño before serving.

Note: To toast caraway seeds, place them in a small pan over medium heat and cook, tossing and stirring, until they are fragrant, about 2 minutes. Transfer the seeds to a plate and let cool. Grind them in a spice grinder or using a mortar and pestle.

Wiener Schnitzel

WITH AUSTRIAN CRESCENT POTATOES, CUCUMBERS, AND LINGONBERRIES

CUCUMBER SALAD

3 large (about 3 pounds) HOTHOUSE CUCUMBERS, peeled, sliced lengthwise, and seeded

2 1/2 teaspoons fine SEA SALT

1 cup SOUR CREAM

1/3 cup CRÈME FRAÎCHE

2 GARLIC CLOVES, mashed to a paste with a mortar and pestle

1 tablespoon prepared HORSERADISH

1 tablespoon CHAMPAGNE VINEGAR

1/2 teaspoon CARAWAY SEEDS, toasted and ground (see page 100)

2 teaspoons finely chopped FRESH DILL

Freshly ground WHITE PEPPER

POTATO SALAD

12 AUSTRIAN CRESCENT or other fingerling POTATOES (about 2 1/2 pounds)

2 teaspoons CARAWAY SEEDS

2 tablespoons plus 1 teaspoon fine SEA SALT

1 1/2 cups WHITE BEEF STOCK (see page 333) or low-sodium canned beef broth

1 tablespoon plus 1 teaspoon CHAMPAGNE VINEGAR

1 tablespoon plus 1 teaspoon SUGAR

1 tablespoon DIJON-STYLE MUSTARD

1/4 cup CANOLA OIL

NOTES FROM THE KITCHEN Oh, it's so hard to make a perfect schnitzel. Some people just have the knack, like the sous-chef Thomas Kahl. His just puff, puff, and keep on puffing. There are a lot of ways schnitzel can be bad, but only one way it is good. The bad ones can be cooked too quickly (medium-rare meat and a blackened crust), cooked too slowly (dry inside and pale outside), breaded sloppily (they fry up as flat as pancakes), or cooked without enough heat and too much oil (which makes them greasy). By contrast, the perfect schnitzel seems to have been blown up like a balloon; the crust shatters at the touch of the fork, and the veal inside is tender.

To achieve the "puff" so desirable in schnitzel, first, you must bread the veal correctly. Do not overhandle it as you bread it, and be sure to remove all excess flour and egg. Try not to directly touch the veal when it is coated in the bread crumbs; instead, reach way beneath it and flip it over, so that the crumbs are between your hand and the meat. Do not fry too many schnitzel in one pan; they must have room to slide around. Shake the pan so that the oil constantly flows over the schnitzel. And monitor the temperature of the oil when frying. The pan and the oil should be extremely hot when you begin, but it should take 30 seconds to a minute for the first side to properly brown. So if it burns right away, the oil is too hot.

1. Prepare the cucumber salad: Using a mandoline or a sharp knife, slice the cucumbers very thin. Sprinkle with 1 1/2 teaspoons of the salt, and let sit for 30 minutes.

2. Whisk the sour cream and crème fraîche together in a bowl. Add the garlic, horseradish, vinegar, caraway seeds, dill, the remaining 1 teaspoon salt, and white pepper to taste. Drain the cucumbers, pressing down on them to extract as much liquid as possible, and place them in a bowl. Gradually stir in some of the sour cream mixture, adding just enough to coat the cucumbers. Set the cucumber salad aside, cover, and refrigerate. Reserve any unused dressing.

1 cup diced RED ONION

2 tablespoons finely CHOPPED CORNICHONS

Freshly ground WHITE PEPPER

2 tablespoons chopped FRESH CHIVES

WINE DRESSING
1/2 cup PORT WINE

1/2 cup MADEIRA

1/4 cup plus 1 tablespoon aged BALSAMIC VINEGAR

1 teaspoon DIJON MUSTARD

3/4 cup extra-virgin OLIVE OIL

1/2 cup CANOLA OIL

FRIED PARSLEY
CANOLA OIL, for frying

1/2 small bunch FLAT-LEAF PARSLEY, stems discarded, leaves rinsed and dried completely

Fine SEA SALT

3. Prepare the potato salad: Place the potatoes in a saucepan and add water to cover by 2 inches. Add the caraway seeds and 1 tablespoon of the salt, and bring to a boil. Cook until tender, 20 minutes.

4. While the potatoes are cooking, prepare the vinaigrette: Bring the beef stock to a boil, then remove the pan from the heat and whisk in the vinegar, sugar, mustard, and the remaining 4 teaspoons salt. Whisk in the canola oil.

5. When the potatoes are tender, drain them well. As soon as they are cool enough to handle, peel them and slice them crosswise into 1/2-inch-thick slices. If the vinaigrette has cooled, reheat it. Drizzle some of the hot vinaigrette over the warm potatoes, mixing well. You may not need all of the vinaigrette—the potatoes should slide loosely over each other, but they should not be soupy. Add the red onion and chopped cornichons, and season with white pepper. Sprinkle with the chopped chives and cover to keep warm.

6. Next, prepare the wine dressing: Combine the Port and Madeira in a saucepan, and bring to a boil. Simmer until reduced to 1/4 cup, about 7 minutes. Pour into a large bowl and add the vinegar and mustard. Whisk to combine, and continue whisking while you slowly pour in the oils. Set the dressing aside. Whisk it well before using.

DAVID BOULEY   There's an art to cooking schnitzel, and there are a lot of variables that make the difference between a great schnitzel and a good one. One important part of the puzzle is the technique when you fry it. You need the crust to puff like a soufflé, and to do that you have to trap the air inside the crust. Moving and shaking the veal while it's cooking in the oil creates steam that lifts the crust away from the meat. That way you don't get a damp crust stuck next to gummy veal. Your aim is for the oil to continually roll over the top of the cutlet like waves, so you have to use enough oil in the pan.

Another important element is the bread crumbs. The best bread crumbs are from simple country bread or a baguette—not sandwich bread or other processed breads, and not any fancy bread that has fennel or onion or dried apricots in it. It's easy to make your own crumbs in a food processor (see Notes), and it makes all the difference. If you're using top-quality ingredients, they don't require so much manipulation and talent. They do some of the work for you.

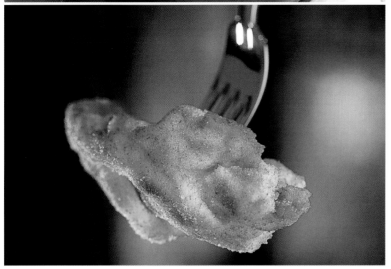

VEAL

1 ½ cups ALL-PURPOSE FLOUR

3 large EGGS

2 cups plain dried BREAD CRUMBS,
preferably homemade
(see Notes)

1 pound VEAL EYE LOIN, cut into
eight 2-ounce medallions

Fine SEA SALT and freshly ground
BLACK PEPPER

CANOLA OIL, for frying

GARNISH

½ pound mixed SALAD GREENS
(such as frisée, Boston lettuce,
mustard greens, baby arugula,
lolla rossa, and watercress)

Fine SEA SALT and freshly ground
BLACK PEPPER

1 SHALLOT, minced

2 teaspoons finely chopped FRESH
FINES HERBES (a mix of chervil,
parsley, chives, and tarragon, if
possible)

PUMPKIN SEED OIL, for drizzling
(see page 247)

2 LEMONS, halved

LINGONBERRY COMPOTE
(see Notes)

SERVES 4 AS A MAIN COURSE

SCHNITZEL

Viennese schnitzel is a dish with counterparts in other cuisines. Schnitzel is the German word for cutlet, and Wiener Schnitzel is essentially a pounded, breaded, and fried cutlet. It is typically made with scallops of veal in restaurants, though pork is often used in Austrian homes. Schnitzel is often likened to the Italian veal dish Cotoletta alla Milanese. Certainly the ingredients and presentation are similar—the meat pounded thin and dredged in flour, egg, then bread crumbs—yet most Austrian cooks would take offense at the comparison, pointing out the critical difference in technique and the rich array of traditional accompaniments. Viennese schnitzel is cooked in undulating oil or lard. This encourages a slight separation between the crust and the meat, which makes for a distinctly delightful contrast between the crisp breading and the tender meat. The dish can be served with nothing more than a wedge of lemon and perhaps some fried parsley, but often it arrives with a battery of salads, including a green salad and a warm potato salad, perhaps a cabbage salad, and in some parts of Austria, lingonberry compote.

7. To fry the parsley, heat 2 inches of canola oil in a saucepan over high heat. The parsley leaves must be completely dry before frying. Test the temperature of the oil with 1 parsley leaf—it should sizzle right away. Fry the parsley in small batches, 30 seconds, scooping out the leaves with a spider or a fine-mesh strainer as soon as they are dark green (do not let them brown). Drain on paper towels and sprinkle with salt.

8. Now make the schnitzel: Place the flour on a plate. Beat the eggs in a shallow bowl. Place the bread crumbs on another plate, and arrange the plates on the counter.

9. Preheat the oven to 300°F.

10. Use a meat pounder or rolling pin to pound the veal medallions until they are $1/8$ inch thick. Season them on both sides with salt and pepper. Dip a medallion in the flour and pat off the excess. Next, dip it into the egg and let the excess drip off the bottom. Finally, lay the medallion on the bread crumbs and pile more crumbs on the top; pat it lightly. Scoop your hand under the schnitzel, turn it over, and add more bread crumbs on top. Shake off the excess crumbs. Lay the breaded meat flat on a cookie sheet, and repeat with the other pieces.

11. Heat a large, high-sided sauté pan over high heat for 4 or 5 minutes, until it is nearly smoking. Add canola oil to a depth of $1/4$ inch. When the oil is hot, gently lay as many schnitzel in the oil as will fit comfortably without crowding. Actively shake the pan back and forth on the burner, bathing the veal in oil. The schnitzel should begin to puff up. Cook until golden brown on the bottom, then turn the schnitzel over and continue to cook, shaking the pan, 3 minutes on each side. When the schnitzel are golden brown and puffed on both sides, transfer them to paper towel-lined plates. Keep warm in the oven while you fry the remaining schnitzel.

12. Just before serving, place the salad greens in a bowl and season them to taste with salt and pepper. Sprinkle the shallots and fines herbes over them, toss with some of the wine dressing, and drizzle with a little pumpkin seed oil.

13. On each large dinner plate, arrange a lemon half, a spoonful of lingon-berry compote, a pile of cucumber salad, a mound of potato salad, a little of the green salad, and 2 schnitzel pieces. Garnish the schnitzel with the fried parsley, and serve immediately.

Notes: Tart little red lingonberries are like tiny cranberries (in fact, they are a relative of the cranberry) and are cultivated mostly in northern Europe, although they also grow in Maine. Lingonberry compote resembles cran-berry sauce and is used in similar ways, to accompany game or fowl, or as an off-sweet topping for puddings, pancakes, and crêpes. You can purchase lingonberry compote or jam at specialty food shops, or by mail order (see Sources, page 337).

To make homemade bread crumbs, bake bread slices in a 250°F oven until they are hard and dry. This could take over an hour or even several hours, depending upon the moisture content in the bread. If you start with old, stale bread it will go more quickly. When the bread is dried and thor-oughly cooled, process the slices in a food processor until you get fine crumbs.

Venison Strudel

WITH PLUM JAM, CHESTNUTS, AND BRUSSELS SPROUTS

MARIO LOHNINGER Venison is very popular in Austria. We eat it in the fall and winter, when people do a lot of hunting. This is an interesting way to serve it, with a crispy crust and a layer of Powidl, plum jam, over the loin. The jam plays off the sweetness of the meat, and the crust keeps the juices in and the venison soft and tender. The chestnuts and Brussels sprouts are a nice wintry accompaniment.

1. Bring a large pot of water to a boil and salt it until it tastes like seawater (about 2 teaspoons per quart). Blanch the chestnuts in the boiling water for 3 to 4 minutes. Drain. When the chestnuts are just cool enough to handle, pull off and discard their shells. This gets harder to do as the chestnuts cool, so work quickly while they are still warm. Rewarm them in the microwave if peeling becomes too difficult.

2. Sprinkle the sugar in an even layer in a heavy skillet. Cook the sugar over medium heat, without stirring, until it melts and turns into a dark amber caramel (swirl the pan if the caramel colors unevenly), about 7 minutes. Add the cream and chestnuts (stand back when you do this—the caramel may spatter). Simmer, partly covered, until the chestnuts are tender, 45 minutes to 1 hour. Season with salt and pepper. Cover and keep warm.

3. Cook the bacon in a large skillet over medium heat until it is lightly browned but not yet crisp, about 3 minutes. Use a slotted spoon to transfer the bacon to paper towels to drain. Pour off all but 1 tablespoon of the fat in the pan, and add the Brussels sprouts. Season with salt and pepper, add the bacon, and toss until the sprouts are cooked through, 10 to 15 minutes. Cover and keep warm, or reheat before serving

4. Season the venison loin with salt and pepper. Heat a sauté pan over high heat for 5 minutes, then add the canola oil. Place the venison in the pan and sear both sides of the loin until brown, 2 minutes. Then let the venison cool.

CHESTNUTS AND BRUSSELS SPROUTS

7 ounces FRESH CHESTNUTS, shells scored with an X

3 tablespoons SUGAR

1 cup HEAVY CREAM

Fine SEA SALT and freshly ground BLACK PEPPER

4 thick slices BACON, sliced crosswise into matchsticks

1 pound BRUSSELS SPROUTS, trimmed and roughly sliced

VENISON STRUDEL

1 pound VENISON LOIN (see Sources, page 337)

Fine SEA SALT and freshly ground BLACK PEPPER

2 teaspoons CANOLA OIL

2 tablespoons POWIDL (see page 67)

3 sheets PHYLLO DOUGH, thawed if frozen (see Note, page 62)

2 tablespoons UNSALTED BUTTER, melted and cooled

SERVES 4 TO 6 AS A MAIN COURSE

5. Preheat the oven to 400°F.

6. Meanwhile, spoon the Powidl over the venison. Lay out one piece of phyllo dough, brush it with butter, and place the venison at the bottom. Trim the edges of the dough so that 1 to 2 inches of excess remain on either side of the venison. Roll the meat up in the pastry, tucking in the edges. Repeat this process, rolling the strudel in the remaining 2 sheets of buttered phyllo, trimming each sheet before rolling. Brush the last edge with butter and seal the edges neatly. Lightly brush the outside of the strudel with butter, and place it on a baking sheet.

7. Bake the strudel for 10 minutes. Then reduce the oven temperature to 325°F and bake until the internal temperature of the meat is 135°F, 8 to 10 minutes. Let it rest for 5 minutes, then slice the strudel crosswise and serve with the chestnuts and Brussels sprouts.

Quark Spätzle
WITH CHEESE

QUARK SPÄTZLE

1 cup QUARK CHEESE (see page 14)

4 extra-large EGGS

3 large EGG YOLKS

2 cups ALL-PURPOSE FLOUR

1 teaspoon fine SEA SALT

1/4 teaspoon freshly grated NUTMEG

Freshly ground WHITE PEPPER

6 tablespoons UNSALTED BUTTER

1 cup chopped ONION

Fine SEA SALT and freshly ground
    BLACK PEPPER

2 GARLIC CLOVES, chopped

1/2 NUTMEG, freshly grated

SEA SALT and freshly ground
    WHITE PEPPER

1/2 pound ALPINE GRUYÈRE-STYLE
    CHEESE, such as Hoch Ybrig or
    Gruyère (see Note), grated

1 cup WHITE BEEF STOCK (see
    page 333) or low-sodium canned
    beef broth

3 SHALLOTS, thinly sliced, for
    garnish

2 tablespoons chopped FRESH
    CHIVES, for garnish

SERVES 6 AS A SIDE DISH

Spätzle are tiny dumplings that you make by passing a thin batter through a colander (or a spätzle maker) into a pot of boiling water. You can serve them simply boiled and drained, topped with melted butter and poppy seeds, or fried with onions and cheese as we do here. This is a rich mountain-style skiers' dish that will really keep you going.

1. Prepare the spätzle: Bring a large pot of water to a boil and salt it until it tastes like seawater (about 2 teaspoons per quart). Whisk the Quark, eggs, and yolks in a large bowl. Use a rubber spatula to stir in the flour until smooth. Season with the salt, nutmeg, and white pepper.

2. Using half of the spätzle dough and working quickly, push the dough through the holes of a colander (or spätzle maker) into the boiling water. Stir the spätzle and cook until the water returns to a simmer, about 1 minute. Then, using a skimmer or a large slotted spoon, transfer the spätzle to another colander. Run cold water over the spätzle to stop them from cooking further. Set that batch of spätzle aside. When the water returns to a boil, make the rest of the spätzle, repeating the procedure.

3. Heat a large cast-iron skillet over medium heat. Add 3 tablespoons of the butter and then the onions. Season with salt and pepper, and cook, stirring occasionally, until soft and light brown, about 15 minutes. Add the garlic and cook until tender, another 2 minutes. Raise the heat to high and add the spätzle. Fry, stirring frequently, until the spätzle begin to turn golden, about 10 minutes. Season with the nutmeg, salt, and pepper.

4. Add the cheese and fry, stirring, until it begins to brown, about 10 minutes. Add 1/2 cup of the beef stock and cook, stirring often, until it is absorbed. Add more stock until a thick, soupy consistency is achieved.

5. Meanwhile, melt the remaining 3 tablespoons butter in a small saucepan over medium-high heat. Add the shallots, season with salt and pepper, and fry until they are brown and slightly crisp.

6. Serve immediately, garnished with the fried shallots and chives.

Note: Hoch Ybrig is made in Zurich from cow's milk. It is a buttery, nutty, pungent cheese, similar in flavor to Gruyère. It is available at specialty cheese stores (see Sources, page 337).

IRISH CHEDDAR
mild
100 g 26.90

Passion Fruit Parfait

1/2 pound bittersweet CHOCOLATE, finely chopped

10 tablespoons plus 1 teaspoon SUGAR

2 LARGE EGG WHITES

3/4 cup PASSION FRUIT PUREE (see Sources, page 337)

2 cups HEAVY CREAM

PASSION FRUIT SAUCE

5 tablespoons SUGAR

4 ripe PASSION FRUIT, halved, pulp and seeds scooped out (see page 235)

Fresh ORANGE JUICE, optional

SERVES 8 AS DESSERT

Here a tangy passion fruit parfait is piped into chocolate cones for a rather dramatic dessert. The chocolate is an excellent partner with the passion fruit, adding a touch of richness. You can skip the cones if they seem like too much work. Instead, serve the parfaits in wine or parfait glasses, and top them with shavings of good-quality bittersweet chocolate.

MARIO LOHNINGER This is what you make in the middle of winter when you get bored with apples and pears. Bright-tasting passion fruit makes you think of warm, tropical places, which is a nice thing in cold weather.

1. To form the cones, cut four 8-inch squares of parchment paper, then cut the squares diagonally into 2 triangles. Hold 1 triangle with the tip facing down. Twisting inward, bring in one of the corners until it meets the bottom tip. Hold the two tips together with your opposite hand and wrap around until a cone begins to form. Bring the corners to meet each other and twist until you have created a pointy cone. Keep twisting the cone tighter, until you have a 2-inch diameter at the base. Tape the cone along the crease and trim the base flat (so it stands up straight). Repeat with the remaining triangles of parchment.

2. Fill a bowl with ice water. To temper the chocolate, bring 1 inch of water to a simmer in the bottom of a double boiler. With the water barely simmering, place the chocolate in the top of the double boiler (or use a saucepan with a metal bowl suspended over it) and let it melt, stirring as little as possible while ensuring that it is smooth. Place the bottom of the pot or bowl in the cold water and whisk the chocolate constantly until thick. Place the pot or bowl back over the simmering water and let it melt, without stirring, until glossy. Immediately pour the chocolate into a paper cone, turning the cone to coat the inside in a layer of chocolate, then pour the chocolate back into the bowl. Stand the cone upside down on a wire rack to dry and repeat with the other cones.

3. In a small saucepan, combine 1/2 cup (8 tablespoons) of the sugar with 6 tablespoons of water and cook over medium heat, stirring, until the sugar has dissolved. Turn the heat to low while you beat the egg whites.

4. Place the egg whites in a clean bowl of an electric mixer fitted with the whisk attachment and beat them until foamy. Add 2 tablespoons of the sugar and beat until the whites hold shiny, not quite firm peaks.

5. Raise the heat to high under the sugar syrup, place a candy thermometer in the pan, and let the syrup heat until it reaches 240°F. With the mixer on medium speed, drizzle the hot syrup in a steady stream down the side of the egg white bowl, taking care not to let the syrup hit the whisk. Whip until cool, 5 to 8 minutes.

6. In a bowl, whisk the remaining teaspoon of the sugar with the passion fruit puree and gently fold this mixture into the egg whites. Whip the cream and fold it in. Pipe or spoon the filling into the chocolate cones. Freeze until ready to serve, up to 1 day.

7. To prepare the sauce, in a small saucepan over medium heat, combine the sugar with $1/4$ cup of water and bring to a boil, stirring until the sugar dissolves. Simmer for 1 minute, then let cool.

8. In the bowl of a blender, combine the passion fruit pulp and seeds with the sugar syrup and liquefy. Strain the mixture through a fine-mesh sieve. Thin with orange juice if desired.

9. To serve, place the passion fruit sauce on serving plates and place a chocolate cone on top.

Walnut Praline Cake

1 cup plus 3 tablespoons SUGAR

1 cup WALNUT HALVES, toasted

2 tablespoons UNSALTED BUTTER

4 large EGGS, separated

1/3 cup plus 2 tablespoons CONFEC-
TIONERS' SUGAR

2 ounces MILK CHOCOLATE, melted
and cooled

Pinch of SALT

MAKES ONE 10-INCH CAKE,
8 SERVINGS

DAVID BOULEY This is a very delicious cake, but when I first suggested putting it in the cookbook, Mario didn't want to. I think Austrians take some things for granted, like this traditional dessert. Since I didn't grow up there, I can see how good those things really are!

We did change the recipe somewhat. We put more milk chocolate in it because I wanted it a little moister. We added more walnuts, too, and roasted them to get a deeper flavor. It's a wonderful cake, and it's very easy to make. It's mind-blowing served right out of the oven, so to really impress someone, serve it while it's still warm. It's much more aromatic and lighter that way, and the chocolate is still a little gooey.

1. Preheat the oven to 325°F. Butter a 10-inch round cake pan. Line a baking sheet with buttered parchment paper.

2. Prepare the praline: Sprinkle 1/4 cup of the sugar in an even layer in a heavy skillet. Cook over medium heat, without stirring, until it melts and turns into an amber caramel (swirl the pan if it colors unevenly), about 5 minutes. Remove the pan from the heat and add the walnuts and butter (stand back, the caramel may sputter), stirring with a wooden spoon. Continue to cook until any hard bits of the caramel melt. Spread the nuts on the prepared baking sheet to cool.

3. Transfer the nuts to a food processor and pulse until coarsely ground. Set the nuts aside.

4. Whisk the egg yolks and confectioners' sugar together in a bowl, and stir in the melted chocolate. Set it aside.

5. Place the egg whites in a clean bowl of an electric mixer fitted with the whisk attachment, and beat at medium speed until foamy. Sprinkle 1/2 cup of the remaining sugar and the salt over the egg whites, and beat on high speed until soft peaks form. Gradually sprinkle in the remaining 7 tablespoons sugar, and beat until stiff, glossy peaks form.

6. Whisk a little of the egg white mixture into the chocolate mixture. Then gently fold the remaining whites into the chocolate. Fold in the walnuts.

7. Scrape the batter into the prepared cake pan and bake until the cake is golden brown on top but still moist inside, about 45 minutes. Let it cool in the pan.

Chocolate Bread Pudding Soufflé

2 tablespoons UNSALTED BUTTER, melted

½ cup plus 2 tablespoons SUGAR

1 cup WALNUTS

8 tablespoons (1 stick) UNSALTED BUTTER, softened

4 ounces EXTRA-BITTER CHOCOLATE, melted

6 large EGGS, separated

½ cup BRIOCHE or WHITE BREAD CRUMBS, preferably homemade (see Note, page 107)

SOUR CHERRY COMPOTE

½ cup SUGAR

1 cup SOUR CHERRIES, pitted

CHOCOLATE SAUCE

¼ cup SUGAR

10 ounces EXTRA-BITTER CHOCOLATE, chopped

2 tablespoons UNSALTED BUTTER, cold

Lightly whipped CREAM, for serving

SERVES 4 AS DESSERT

This is Mario's version of *Mohr im Hemd*, a traditional Austrian dessert that combines nuts, eggs, chocolate, and bread crumbs. With a soft, almost liquid center, it's like a cross between a molten chocolate cake and a rich, nutty bread pudding. The sour cherry compote is delicious but optional.

1. Preheat the oven to 350°F. Brush the insides of four 8-ounce baking dishes (custard cups or ramekins) with the melted butter and coat them with the 2 tablespoons sugar.

2. Place the walnuts in a food processor with 2 tablespoons of the remaining sugar, and pulse until they resemble coarse meal. Set them aside.

3. Cream the softened butter in a bowl of an electric mixer fitted with the paddle attachment. Beat in the melted chocolate. Add the egg yolks one at a time, beating until each is incorporated.

4. In another clean bowl, whip the egg whites until foamy with the whisk attachment of an electric mixer. Then gradually add the remaining 6 tablespoons sugar and beat until soft peaks form.

5. Whisk a little of the egg whites into the chocolate mixture. Use a rubber spatula to gently fold in the rest of the whites—work slowly to avoid deflating them. Gently fold in the ground walnuts and the bread crumbs.

6. Fill the prepared dishes two-thirds full, and place them in a roasting pan. Pour very hot water into the pan, to come halfway up the sides of the baking dishes. Bake for 30 minutes.

7. To prepare the cherry compote, in a small saucepan, combine the sugar and ⅓ cup water and bring to a boil. Cook, stirring, until the sugar dissolves, about 2 minutes. Add the cherries and simmer over low heat until tender, about 10 minutes. Let cool.

8. Meanwhile, prepare the chocolate sauce: Place the sugar in a saucepan with 1⅓ cups water, and bring to a boil, stirring until the sugar is dissolved. Add the chocolate and remove the pan from the heat. Whisk the cold butter into the sauce. Cover to keep warm.

9. Serve the soufflés straight from the oven, with the warm chocolate sauce, cherry compote, and whipped cream.

Nuss Nudeln

HOMEMADE NOODLES WITH NUTS AND BROWNED BUTTER

2 small (about 1 pound) IDAHO
   POTATOES

Fine SEA SALT

²/₃ cup ALL-PURPOSE FLOUR

2 tablespoons SEMOLINA FLOUR

2 large EGG YOLKS

7 tablespoons UNSALTED BUTTER

¹/₂ cup very finely ground
   WALNUTS, hazelnuts, or almonds

¹/₃ cup CONFECTIONERS' SUGAR

SERVES 4 TO 6 AS DESSERT

MARIO LOHNINGER This is the same potato dough recipe as the Schupfnudeln (page 277), but it is served sweet. You can top them with melted butter, poppy seeds, nuts, and powdered sugar, or any combination. They can be served for dessert or as a lunch dish. We eat a lot of sweets for lunch in Austria. We might have a soup and then sweet noodles or dumplings. These noodles are the kind of thing that gives you energy for skiing or hiking. They are a little bit heavy, though—not what you want to eat right before going to bed.

1. Bring a large pot of water to a boil and salt it until it tastes like seawater (about 2 teaspoons per quart). Boil the potatoes in the water until tender, 25 minutes. Drain the potatoes and peel them as soon as they are cool enough to handle. Push them through a ricer or a coarse-mesh strainer.

2. Place 1¹/₄ loosely packed cups (about 8³/₄ ounces) of the riced potatoes in a large bowl. Stir in the flour, semolina, egg yolks, and ¹/₄ teaspoon salt, and knead to make a dough. Let it rest for 30 minutes. Cover with plastic.

3. Turn the dough out onto a board and form it into a long roll. Cut it into ¹/₂-inch-thick slices. Roll each slice into a 4-inch-long cylinder.

4. Bring a large pot of water to a boil and salt it until it tastes like seawater (about 2 teaspoons per quart). Add the noodles and boil until they float to the surface, 3 minutes. Drain, and lay them out on a clean dish towel.

5. Preheat the oven to 200°F.

6. Melt 2 tablespoons of the butter in a large sauté pan. Sauté half the noodles and half the nuts in the butter until the noodles begin to brown and the nuts are golden. Transfer to a bowl and keep warm in the oven. Wipe out the sauté pan, and sauté the remaining noodles and nuts in another 2 tablespoons of the butter. Add to the noodles in the oven.

7. Melt the remaining 3 tablespoons butter in the sauté pan over medium heat. Let the butter cook until the white milk solids fall to the bottom of the pan and turn nut-brown, about 5 minutes. Add the brown butter to the noodles, toss well, and sprinkle with the confectioners' sugar. Serve warm.

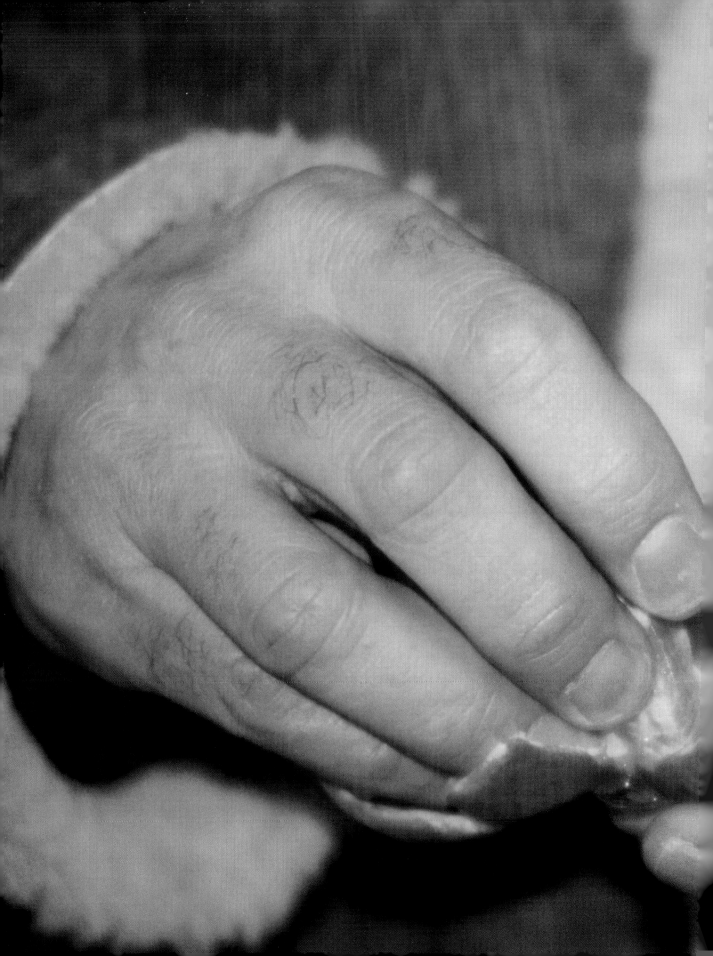

Spring

Salmon Torte

WITH HORSERADISH CREAM CHEESE MOUSSE AND SALMON CAVIAR

CREAM CHEESE FILLING

1/4 pound (1/2 cup) CREAM CHEESE, at room temperature

2 tablespoons PREPARED HORSERADISH

1 tablespoon plus 1 teaspoon fresh LEMON JUICE

2 teaspoons grated LEMON ZEST

CRÊPES

2 tablespoons UNSALTED BUTTER, melted

4 large EGGS, well beaten

Fine SEA SALT and freshly ground WHITE PEPPER

1 pound CURED or SMOKED SALMON, thinly sliced

1/4 cup chopped FRESH CHIVES

2 tablespoons CRÈME FRAÎCHE

2 tablespoons SALMON CAVIAR

SERVES 12 AS AN HORS D'OEUVRE

MARIO LOHNINGER Salmon torte is a perfect hors d'oeuvre. It's elegant and beautiful, with its layers of salmon, cream cheese mousse, and crêpes. It is very simple to make and has a lot of interesting flavors from the horseradish, salmon, and salmon roe. The key thing is not to let the crêpes (which are more like thin omelets, since they don't have any flour) take on any color when you cook them—they have a nicer look when they are pale and not browned. Then all you do is stack it all together and add the garnishes. I like to use salmon that I've cured myself (see page 328), but you can use smoked salmon too. This is also a good dish for brunch, and you can make it a day or two ahead.

1. Combine all the ingredients for the cream cheese filling in a small bowl, and mix well. Set it aside.

2. Place a nonstick sauté pan over medium heat. When the pan is hot, brush a thin film of the butter onto the bottom. Season the eggs with salt and pepper, and pour about 3 tablespoons into the pan (it should be a little thicker than a regular crêpe), swirling to cover the bottom of the pan. When the crêpe is just set, flip it over and cook the other side, about 1 1/2 minutes total. Transfer the crêpe to a plate. Continue with the remaining eggs, stacking the crêpes with waxed paper between the layers. You should have 4 crêpes.

3. Using a cake pan that is slightly smaller than your crêpes as a guide, trim the edges of each egg crêpe to form perfect circles.

4. Spread a thin layer of the cream cheese filling on 3 of the crêpes. Arrange slices of salmon in a single even layer on the first crêpe without leaving any spaces (trim the salmon slices if necessary). Stack the second crêpe on top of the first, and layer it with salmon in the same way. Repeat with the third crêpe and the remaining salmon, and then place the remaining plain crêpe on top.

5. Wrap the torte in plastic and freeze it for at least 1 hour, or as long as 2 days, before slicing it. When you take it from the freezer, press the chives all around the sides of the torte. Cut it into 12 wedges, and garnish each one with a drop of crème fraîche and a single egg of salmon roe. Let the slices thaw completely, 5 to 10 minutes, before serving.

Crab-Filled Avocado Dumplings

This is a creative way to present what is essentially a crab and avocado salad. The crabmeat is flavored with herbs and lime juice, then layered onto thin slices of avocado, which are molded into a dumpling-like sphere. You can serve these as an appetizer on small plates or as a passed hors d'oeuvre. Of the two optional garnishes, the onions add a zesty, piquant note while the chive sauce is creamy and suave—your choice.

NOTES FROM THE KITCHEN The only hard thing about this recipe is forming the dumplings, but don't be discouraged if the first few are a little messy—you'll get better at them. Even if they do come out less than perfect, no one will care because they're still going to taste great. You can serve the dumplings by themselves, or with cured salmon, smoked fish, or an arugula or mâche salad.

1. Prepare the crab filling: Toss the crabmeat with the lime juice and herbs in a small bowl, and season with salt and pepper. Set it aside.

2. In another bowl, whisk together all the ingredients for the chive cream, if using.

3. Halve the avocados lengthwise, remove the pits, and remove the peel. Rub the avocado flesh with some of the lime juice.

4. Cut a large piece of plastic wrap into six 6-inch squares. Drizzle a few drops of both olive oil and lime juice in the center of each square, and mix them together with your fingers. Sprinkle with salt and pepper.

5. Cut the avocados crosswise into very thin slices. Lay 4 to 5 overlapping slices in the center of each plastic square, making sure that the green tops overlap attractively on the underside (the side that will ultimately be showing). Place a scant tablespoon of crab filling on top of the avocado. Gather up the corners of the plastic wrap and twist them tightly with one hand while cupping the avocado in the other hand to form a ball. Keep twisting until the avocado has encased the crabmeat. (The dumplings can be made an hour in advance and kept refrigerated.)

6. Just before serving, unwrap the dumplings. Serve with the chive cream or the pickled spring onions, if desired.

CRAB FILLING
1 cup (1/2 pound) FRESH CRABMEAT, picked over

2 teaspoons fresh LIME JUICE

1 teaspoon chopped MIXED FRESH HERBS (such as tarragon, chervil, and chives)

Fine SEA SALT and freshly ground BLACK PEPPER

CHIVE CREAM (OPTIONAL)
1/2 cup SOUR CREAM

2 teaspoons fresh LIME JUICE, or to taste

2 tablespoons chopped FRESH CHIVES

Fine SEA SALT and freshly ground WHITE PEPPER, to taste

AVOCADO DUMPLINGS
3 ripe but not mushy AVOCADOS

JUICE of 2 LIMES

Extra-virgin OLIVE OIL

Fine SEA SALT and freshly ground BLACK PEPPER

PICKLED SPRING ONIONS, for serving (optional; see page 183)

SERVES 6 AS AN APPETIZER

Mâche Salad

WITH BACON AND QUAIL EGGS

WINE DRESSING

1 tablespoon PORT WINE

1 tablespoon MADEIRA

1 tablespoon BALSAMIC VINEGAR

½ teaspoon DRY VERMOUTH

⅛ teaspoon DIJON MUSTARD

2 tablespoons extra-virgin
    OLIVE OIL

1 tablespoon CANOLA OIL

1 teaspoon PUMPKIN SEED OIL
    (see page 247)

Fine SEA SALT and freshly ground
    BLACK PEPPER

MÂCHE SALAD

Three ½-inch-thick slices DARK
    WHEAT, pumpernickel, or rye
    BREAD

1 tablespoon UNSALTED BUTTER

Fine SEA SALT and freshly ground
    BLACK PEPPER

¼ pound sliced BACON, cut cross-
    wise into ½-inch-wide strips

6 QUAIL EGGS, at room
    temperature

¼ pound (2 quarts) MÂCHE or
    BABY LETTUCES or mixed baby
    greens (mesclun)

SERVES 6 AS AN APPETIZER OR
SALAD COURSE

This is a refined take on a favorite bistro country salad made with frisée, bacon, and poached eggs. This recipe calls for mâche (or baby greens) and tiny quail eggs. A hint of pumpkin seed oil in the dressing is a nod toward Austria, as are the dark-bread croutons.

MARIO LOHNINGER I learned this technique for cooking quail eggs when I was in Japan. You have to boil the eggs for exactly 2 minutes and 24 seconds to get a perfect, softly cooked yolk. If you leave them 6 seconds too long, they will overcook. I didn't believe those few seconds mattered when I first learned about it, but they do—they make the difference between a waxy yolk and a melting, liquid one. Be careful when you peel the eggs, too. There's a skin between the shell and the egg, and when you remove the shell you want to peel that skin off to get a smooth appearance. Then you can just cut them in half. They are beautiful.

1. Prepare the wine dressing: Combine the Port and Madeira in a small saucepan and bring to a simmer over medium heat. Cook until reduced by half, 2 minutes. Transfer to a bowl and add the vinegar, Vermouth, and mustard. Whisk to combine, and continue whisking while you slowly pour in the oils. Season with salt and pepper, and set aside.

2. Trim the crusts off the bread and cut the slices into croutons. Melt the butter in a skillet over medium-high heat and add the bread. Season with salt and pepper and toss. Fry until both sides are crisp, about 5 minutes. Transfer the croutons to a paper towel–lined plate.

3. Heat the bacon in a sauté pan and fry it gently until golden brown (not crisp), about 4 minutes. Drain the bacon on a paper towel–lined plate.

4. Bring 2 quarts water to a simmer. Fill a large bowl with water and ice. Add the quail eggs to the boiling water and cook, keeping the water at a simmer, for exactly 2 minutes, 24 seconds. Transfer the eggs to the ice water to stop the cooking. When they are cool, crack the shells very gently on a countertop and peel the eggs.

5. Put the mâche in a large salad bowl, and toss it with enough wine dressing to lightly coat the leaves. Taste, and add salt and pepper if needed. Then toss with the bacon and croutons. Divide the salad among six plates. Cut the quail eggs in half, place them on top of the salads, and serve.

Leaf Spinach
WITH POACHED EGG AND TRUFFLES

TRUFFLE VINAIGRETTE

1 tablespoon finely chopped FRESH
    BLACK TRUFFLE (see page 136)

1 teaspoon aged BALSAMIC VINEGAR

Fine SEA SALT and freshly ground
    BLACK PEPPER

1/4 cup extra-virgin OLIVE OIL

SPINACH PUREE

3 tablespoons UNSALTED BUTTER

3 SHALLOTS, diced

1 teaspoon fine SEA SALT

2 large GARLIC CLOVES, minced

1/2 cup HEAVY CREAM

1 sprig FRESH THYME

3/4 cup VEGETABLE STOCK (see
    page 332) or canned low-sodium
    vegetable broth

6 ounces (3 quarts) FRESH SPINACH
    LEAVES

Freshly ground WHITE PEPPER

Freshly grated NUTMEG

CAYENNE PEPPER

POACHED EGGS

Fine SEA SALT

1 tablespoon distilled WHITE VINEGAR

6 large EGGS, preferably farm-fresh

Freshly ground BLACK PEPPER

1/2 small FRESH BLACK TRUFFLE

SERVES 6 AS AN APPETIZER

This recipe is a warmer, heartier version of the Mâche Salad on page 132. Instead of a raw, refreshing salad, in this one spinach greens are simmered with shallots and herbs and thickened with cream. A poached egg is placed in the center of this soft green nest, and then the whole dish is decadently covered with black truffles. It's sophisticated comfort food at its best.

MARIO LOHNINGER This is a rich mountain dish that you can serve for lunch, brunch, or even as a light supper. Be sure to spike the water with vinegar when poaching the eggs, and they will come out perfectly.

1. Prepare the truffle vinaigrette: In a small bowl, whisk together the truffle, vinegar, and a pinch of salt and pepper. Whisking constantly, drizzle in the olive oil until well combined. Set it aside.

2. Prepare the spinach: Melt the butter in a wide saucepan or large sauté pan over medium-high heat. Let the butter cook until the white milk solids fall to the bottom of the pan and turn nut-brown, about 5 minutes. Add the shallots and 1/2 teaspoon of the salt and cook, stirring, until the shallots begin to soften, 5 minutes. Add the garlic and cook for 2 more minutes.

3. Add the cream and thyme to the pan, and bring the liquid to a boil. Simmer until reduced by about one third, 3 to 4 minutes. Pour in the vegetable stock and let the liquid return to a boil. Then add the spinach. Cook gently, stirring and tossing, until the spinach is tender, about 2 minutes.

4. Remove the thyme sprig. Using a slotted spoon, transfer the spinach to a blender or food processor, reserving 1/2 cup of the cooking liquid. Puree the spinach, and season it with the remaining 1/2 teaspoon salt, white pepper and nutmeg to taste, and a pinch of cayenne. If necessary, add some of the reserved cooking liquid so the puree is just loose enough to pour. Cover to keep warm, or reheat before serving.

5. To poach the eggs, bring a saucepan of water to a boil and salt it until it tastes like seawater (about 2 teaspoons per quart). Add the vinegar. Break 1 egg into a shallow dish. Swirl a spoon in the simmering water to create a slow whirlpool, and gently slide the egg into the water. Cook until the white is solidified but the yolk is still soft, about 4 minutes. Remove the egg from the water with a slotted spoon, blot it dry with paper towels, and season it with salt and pepper. Transfer the cooked egg to a covered dish to keep warm. Repeat, poaching each egg in the same manner.

6. If necessary, reheat the spinach puree. Pour it into a serving dish. Carefully spoon the eggs on top. Grate the truffle over the eggs, and then spoon the truffle vinaigrette over them. Serve immediately.

TRUFFLES Truffles are a highly prized fungus that forms underground on the roots of trees, primarily oak and hazelnut trees. While truffles have been cultivated in other parts of the world with some success, the earthy black truffles of Périgord and Loti in France, and the savory, prized white Alba truffles of Italy's Piedmont, are considered the highest quality. Truffles are generally hunted with the aid of a pig or dog trained to detect their unique scent. Mature truffles are gathered from fall to early spring. Look for firm, round, highly fragrant truffles in season at specialty food stores. They can be gently scrubbed clean with a brush. Store them along with eggs in an egg carton, or in a bag of rice, and they will infuse the food surrounding them with their intriguing flavor and aroma.

The summer truffle, not yet mature and less intense, is available at a much more affordable price during the summer. You can also buy canned and frozen truffles—choose high-quality flash-frozen ones when texture matters. Truffle oil, a flavorless oil infused with truffles, is a good way to perfume a dish with the dusky scent of truffles and lend a depth of flavor for a fraction of the cost. Quality matters, so be sure you have good, fresh truffle oil and store it tightly sealed in the refrigerator—when it stops smelling like truffles, it's too old. For mall-order sources for fresh truffles and truffle products, see Sources, page 337.

Grostl of Maine Lobster

WITH VEAL RAVIOLI, FRESH PEAS, AND LEMON SHALLOTS

LEMON SHALLOTS

9 SHALLOTS, halved lengthwise

1/2 cup fresh LEMON JUICE

1 tablespoon grated LEMON ZEST

1 tablespoon SUGAR

Fine SEA SALT and freshly cracked
  BLACK PEPPER

2 tablespoons UNSALTED BUTTER

1/4 cup DRY WHITE WINE

3 sprigs FRESH THYME, preferably
  lemon thyme

2 cups CHICKEN STOCK
  (see page 333)

RED WINE SAUCE

4 cups PORT WINE

4 cups DRY RED WINE

6 ounces (about 36) SHALLOTS,
  coarsely chopped

12 CORIANDER SEEDS

5 WHITE PEPPERCORNS

1/2 BAY LEAF, preferably fresh

DAVID BOULEY Grostl is a dish that you are likely to find up in the mountains of Austria. It's very hearty, made with whatever scraps and leftovers the cook has around—potatoes, ham, boiled beef, cheese. It's the kind of dish that's perfect when everyone is going out to ski or hike and needs the energy. But a heavy, traditional Grostl has no place in the city. So we designed another version, substituting lobster, foie gras, and veal shank for the traditional "leftovers." It is lighter than the original, but a lot more complex and interesting.

1. Prepare the lemon shallots: Lay the shallot halves flat on a board and partially slice them at 1/4-inch intervals, stopping short of the base so the slices remain connected, like a fan. Combine the lemon juice, zest, sugar, a pinch of salt, and a very generous shower of black pepper in a resealable plastic bag. Add the shallots, seal the bag, toss well, and refrigerate overnight.

2. Drain the marinated shallots, reserving the marinade. Melt the butter in a large pan over medium heat. Add the shallots and cook, stirring, until they are slightly limp, about 2 minutes. Add the reserved marinade, the wine, and the thyme sprigs, and bring to a simmer. Simmer until the liquid has reduced and is clinging to the shallots, about 15 minutes. Then add 1 cup of the chicken stock. Simmer until the liquid once again has reduced enough to cling to the shallots, about 20 minutes. Then add the remaining

NOTES FROM THE KITCHEN This is one of the most popular dishes at the Danube. You can see why: If you can't decide whether to order the veal ravioli or the lobster or the foie gras on the menu, you can order this and get it all. It's labor-intensive to make at home, but not difficult, and many of the components can be prepared at least a day ahead. To spread the cooking over three days, follow this order: Two days ahead, prepare the red wine sauce (Steps 3 and 4). One day ahead, prepare the pea sauce (Steps 5 and 6), make the veal ravioli (page 143), and marinate the shallots (Step 1). On the day you'll be serving the Grostl, cook the lobster in the morning. Then all you have to do in the evening is to finish the lemon shallots (Step 2) and cook the ravioli, prepare the pea garnish, reheat it all, and serve (Steps 9 through 13).

PEA SAUCE

1 tablespoon plus 1 teaspoon
UNSALTED BUTTER

2 SHALLOTS, thinly sliced

Fine SEA SALT and freshly ground
BLACK PEPPER

1/3 cup DRY WHITE WINE

1 GARLIC CLOVE, minced

1 BAY LEAF, preferably fresh

2 cups CHICKEN STOCK (see
page 333) or canned low-sodium
chicken broth

2 cups freshly SHELLED PEAS

10 FRESH CHIVES (optional)

3 sprigs FRESH PARSLEY

3 sprigs FRESH CHERVIL

1 sprig FRESH TARRAGON

Leaves from 1 sprig FRESH THYME

2 live LOBSTERS (1 1/4 to 1 1/2
pounds each)

Fine SEA SALT

VEAL RAVIOLI (recipe follows)

1 cup freshly shelled BABY PEAS or
regular peas

4 tablespoons UNSALTED BUTTER

Freshly ground BLACK PEPPER

SERVES 4 AS A FISH COURSE

1 cup stock and reduce until the shallots are soft and the liquid is thickened, 20 to 30 minutes. Set aside.

3. Prepare the red wine sauce: Combine the Port, red wine, and chopped shallots in a large saucepan, and bring to a boil. Simmer until the shallots have turned deep red, 30 minutes. Using a slotted spoon, transfer the shallots to a smaller pot. Cover them with 1 cup of the Port-wine mixture and cook over low heat until that liquid is reduced by half and the shallots are very soft and very dark red, about 20 minutes. Transfer the shallots to a blender or food processor, and puree until smooth.

4. Meanwhile, continue to simmer and reduce the remaining wine in the other pan. Toast the coriander seeds in a small dry skillet over medium heat until fragrant, about 3 minutes. Add them, along with the white peppercorns and bay leaf half, to the simmering wine. Reduce the wine until large bubbles begin to form on the surface and it is thick enough to thinly coat the back of a spoon, about 2 hours. Add 1 tablespoon of the shallot puree to the sauce and whisk to combine. Cool and refrigerate until serving time. (Any extra shallot puree makes a terrific topping for pasta, or it can be added to a stew, soup, or salad.) The red wine sauce can be made up to 2 days ahead. Strain the sauce before refrigerating.

5. Prepare the pea sauce: Heat the butter in a saucepan over medium heat until the white milk solids fall to the bottom of the pan and turn nut-brown, about 2 minutes. Add the sliced shallots and season with salt and pepper. Cook, stirring occasionally, until the shallots are soft and light brown, about 5 minutes. Add the wine, garlic, and bay leaf, and simmer until the wine has evaporated, about 5 minutes. Add the chicken stock and bring to a boil.

6. Fill a large bowl with water and ice, and have ready a smaller bowl that will fit in the ice water. Add the peas to the sauce, keeping it at a boil, and cook until they are slightly underdone, about 2 minutes. Remove the bay leaf. Transfer the mixture to a blender (or use an immersion blender), add the fresh herbs, season with salt and pepper, and process until smooth. Then push the puree though a fine-mesh sieve into the smaller bowl and place this in the ice water. Stir constantly until the sauce is cool (this will help retain the color). Transfer the sauce to a container, cover, and refrigerate immediately. The pea sauce can be made up to 1 day ahead.

7. Prepare the lobsters: Fill a bowl with water and ice. Bring a large pot of water to a boil, and salt it until it tastes like seawater (about 2 teaspoons per quart). To kill the lobsters, insert a thin, sharp knife between their eyes and down through their heads, or briefly hold their heads in the boiling water. Separate the lobster heads from their tails by twisting them off at the abdomen; twist off the claws. (If desired, freeze the heads and use them for a stock or sauce.) Drop the tails and claws into the boiling water and poach until slightly underdone, about 4 1/2 minutes for the tails and 5 minutes for the claws. (To test for doneness, break off the small pincer beneath the claw to expose the meat. The flesh should remain intact, feel somewhat firm to the touch, and be just starting to turn opaque.) Drain and immediately transfer to the ice water.

8. When the lobster is cool, use the back of a large knife or cleaver to smash the claw shells. Remove the claw meat intact. Use a strong set of kitchen shears to cut down the underside of the tail, and remove the tail meat. Rinse the meat and refrigerate it, covered, until ready to use. The lobster can be cooked up to 8 hours ahead.

9. While the pasta is cooking, prepare the pea garnish: Fill a bowl with water and ice. Bring a small pot of water to a boil and salt it until it tastes like seawater (about 2 teaspoons per quart). Add the peas and blanch for 1 minute. Drain, and immediately plunge them into the ice water. Drain well.

10. Melt 1 tablespoon of the butter in a large skillet over medium heat, and let it cook until the white milk solids fall to the bottom of the pan and turn nut-brown, about 2 minutes. Add the blanched peas and heat them through. Season with salt and pepper, and cover to keep warm.

MARIO LOHNINGER Traditionally Grostl is a country kind of dish, with sautéed onions, cubed braised meats, bacon, ham, potatoes, blood sausage . . . whatever leftovers are around. You cook it in an iron pan, scraping up the browned crust around the edges and mixing it in so it's crunchy, like a corned beef and potato hash. Sometimes it's served for lunch with a sunny-side-up fried egg on top. That's how I like to eat it when I go home to Austria, with a salad on the side. But you could make it with anything, and people do.

These days chefs are coming up with interesting and creative combinations for a more contemporary Grostl. They keep the idea of using three or four different components, but make it more refined. That's what we did here; we made it sophisticated but kept the spirit of the dish.

11. Bring a large pot of water to a boil and salt it until it tastes like seawater (about 2 teaspoons per quart). Cook the ravioli in the boiling water until tender, about 5 minutes. Then drain and add them to the pan with the peas.

12. Melt the remaining 3 tablespoons butter in a saucepan over medium-low heat. Add the lobster and warm it just until it is heated through, about 5 minutes. In a small saucepan, gently warm the red wine sauce over medium heat. In another small saucepan, warm the pea sauce over medium heat. (You can froth the pea sauce in a blender or with an immersion blender if you like.) In yet another small saucepan, warm the lemon shallots over medium heat.

13. To serve, place 2 ravioli and a spoonful of lemon shallots in the center of each plate. Top with hot lobster pieces, and scatter the green pea garnish around this. Drizzle the pea and red wine sauces over all.

Roasted Foie Gras

At the Danube, the Grostl is sometimes served with slices of roasted foie gras. If you make the foie gras, use the pan drippings to enrich the red wine sauce. Slice the roasted foie gras diagonally into 4 to 6 thick slices, and lay a slice beside the shallots on each plate. If you like, you can substitute foie gras for the veal ravioli.

2 slices from the larger lobe of grade-A FOIE GRAS (see page 206)
Fine SEA SALT and freshly ground BLACK PEPPER
WONDRA FLOUR, for dusting (see Notes, page 250)
CANOLA OIL

1. Preheat the oven to 400°F.

2. Season the foie gras with salt and pepper on both sides, and sprinkle a little flour on top. Heat a small ovenproof sauté pan over medium-high heat until it is very hot. Add a couple of drops of canola oil and tilt the pan to thinly coat the bottom. Place the foie gras in the pan, flour side down. Cook until it is deeply browned, about 2 minutes, then turn the foie gras over.

3. Place the pan in the oven and roast until there is just a little resistance in the center of the foie gras when gently poked, about 2 minutes.

Veal Ravioli

These ravioli are also delicious on their own, topped with a little brown butter and some herbs.

1 "osso bucco" cut VEAL SHANK (2^1/$_2$ pounds)

Fine SEA SALT and freshly ground BLACK PEPPER

^{1}/$_4$ cup CANOLA OIL

1^1/$_2$ teaspoons UNSALTED BUTTER

1 large CARROT, cut into rounds

1 CELERY STALK, chopped

1 small ONION, chopped

1 PLUM TOMATO, cubed

1 GARLIC CLOVE, smashed

^{1}/$_2$ cup DRY WHITE WINE

1 quart VEAL STOCK (see page 335)

3 BLACK PEPPERCORNS

1 sprig FRESH THYME

1 BAY LEAF, preferably fresh

3 tablespoons finely chopped FRESH PARSLEY

CORNMEAL, for dusting

1 recipe EGG PASTA DOUGH (see page 328), rolled out

1 EGG WHITE, beaten

MAKES ABOUT 60 RAVIOLI

1. Season the veal all over with salt and pepper. Heat a large, heavy oven-proof pot or Dutch oven over high heat. Add the canola oil and let it heat for 30 seconds. Then add the veal shank and sear on all sides, about 20 minutes. Transfer the shank to a plate. Discard the oil and wipe out the pot.
2. Place the pot over medium heat. Add the butter, carrot, and celery, and cook for 5 minutes, scraping the bottom and sides of the pot with a wooden spoon. Add the onion and cook, stirring occasionally, until it is soft and caramelized, about 20 minutes.

3. Meanwhile, preheat the oven to 400°F.

4. Add the tomato and garlic to the pot and cook until soft, about 10 minutes. Pour in the wine and bring to a simmer, stirring and scraping the bottom and sides of the pot. Simmer until the wine is reduced by half, about 12 minutes.

5. Return the veal shank to the pot, pour in the stock, and bring it to a simmer. Cover the pot, transfer it to the oven, and bake for 1 hour.

6. Meanwhile, make a sachet: Place the peppercorns, thyme, and bay leaf in a 6-inch square of cheesecloth, and tie it securely with kitchen string.

7. Add the sachet to the pot and cook, uncovered, basting the veal occasionally, until it is extremely tender, 2 to 3 hours. Remove the pot from the oven and let it cool.

8. Discard the sachet. Pull the meat off the veal bones. Strain the stock, reserving the solids. Push the meat and the vegetables through the fine holes of a meat grinder into a bowl. (Alternatively, pulse them together in a food processor until very finely chopped but not pureed.) Season the veal mixture with salt and pepper. Stir in the parsley and add a few table-spoons of the strained stock to form a moist, but not loose, ravioli filling. Cover the bowl with plastic wrap and refrigerate until you are ready to form the ravioli. The filling can be made up to 2 days in advance.

9. To form the ravioli, dust a baking sheet with cornmeal. Spread out one of the rolled pasta sheets horizontally, and brush the lower half of the dough with egg white. Spoon quarter-size dollops of veal filling at 4-inch intervals on the lower half of the dough. Fold the top half over and seal it around the filling, making sure there are no air bubbles. Cut the ravioli into circles or squares, using a pastry wheel, cookie cutter, or knife. Transfer the ravioli to the prepared baking sheet as they are done, keeping them covered with a clean dish towel as you work. Repeat, using all the pasta dough and filling, and placing the ravioli on more cornmeal-dusted baking sheets as needed. Cover the ravioli with plastic wrap and refrigerate until ready to use. The ravioli can be made up to 1 day ahead.

Rösti Potato Halibut

WITH RHUBARB SAUCE AND FENNEL CONFIT

Cooking fish in a potato crust is a classic French technique. Cooking fish in rösti potatoes is Austria's take on it. The result is the same: The grated potatoes fry into a crisp brown crust that contrasts with the soft fish it encloses. The subtle nuttiness of sesame and pumpkin seeds mixed into the potato gives this dish an extra dimension of flavor. As a garnish, David likes to subvert expectations by serving a bracingly tart fruit sauce of rhubarb and raspberry to counter the sweetness of the fennel confit. It also looks quite stunning, with shades of fuchsia, pale green, and gold on the plate.

1. Preheat the oven to 200°F.

2. Trim the fennel bulbs and halve them lengthwise. Remove the core from each half by making a V-shaped cut around it. Use a mandoline or sharp knife to thinly slice the fennel bulbs crosswise. Place the slices in a baking dish and cover with the canola and olive oils. Add the ginger, lemon halves, bay leaf, and kaffir lime leaf if using. Bake uncovered until the fennel is perfectly soft and flavored by the aromatics in the oil, 1 1/2 to 2 hours. Let the confit cool.

3. While the fennel is baking, prepare the rhubarb sauce: Sprinkle the sugar in an even layer in a heavy pan. Cook over medium heat, without stirring, until it melts and turns into a medium amber caramel (swirl the pan if the caramel darkens unevenly), about 5 minutes. Take the pan off the heat and quickly pour in the vinegar (stand back—the caramel will spatter). Stir and scrape the sides of the pan, loosening any crystals that have hardened, until the liquid is smooth.

FENNEL CONFIT

3 medium (about 2 1/4 pounds) FENNEL BULBS, fronds reserved

2 cups CANOLA OIL

1/2 cup OLIVE OIL

One 2-inch-long piece FRESH GINGER, halved

1/2 LEMON, halved

1 BAY LEAF, preferably fresh

1 large KAFFIR LIME LEAF (optional), see Notes

RHUBARB SAUCE

3 tablespoons SUGAR

2 tablespoons RASPBERRY VINEGAR

4 cups (about 1 1/2 pounds) sliced RHUBARB

3/4 cup RASPBERRIES

Fine SEA SALT and freshly ground BLACK PEPPER

1 tablespoon UNSALTED BUTTER, cold

NOTES FROM THE KITCHEN You can coat any fish fillet in a potato crust and get excellent results, but it works particularly well with halibut, which tends to dry out if it's cooked at too high a temperature. The potato crust insulates the halibut and keeps it from touching the hot pan directly.

Any extra fennel confit would be marvelous as part of a salad, or tossed with pasta, herbs, and plenty of grated pecorino cheese.

RÖSTI POTATO HALIBUT

2 IDAHO POTATOES (about 1 pound total), peeled, thinly sliced cross-wise, then sliced lengthwise into matchsticks

3 1/2 tablespoons UNSALTED BUTTER

2 teaspoons PUMPKIN SEEDS, toasted and chopped (see Notes)

2 teaspoons BLACK SESAME SEEDS

Fine SEA SALT and freshly ground BLACK PEPPER

Four 1 1/2-inch-thick pieces HALIBUT (about 4 ounces each)

1 1/2 tablespoons CANOLA OIL

1 GARLIC CLOVE, halved

1 sprig FRESH ROSEMARY

SERVES 4 AS A FISH COURSE

4. Add the rhubarb, raspberries, salt, and pepper to the pan. Cook over medium-low heat until the rhubarb has begun to soften, about 5 minutes. Then add enough water to come level with the rhubarb (you will probably need less than 1 cup). Cook gently until the rhubarb is entirely soft and its flavor is concentrated, about 20 minutes. Push the mixture through a fine-mesh sieve set over a clean saucepan, and discard the solids. Set the sauce aside, reserving the 1 tablespoon butter.

5. To prepare the rösti potatoes, bring a large pot of water to a boil and salt it until it tastes like seawater (about 2 teaspoons per quart). Boil the potatoes for 2 minutes, then drain. Spread the potatoes out on a wire rack so they dry as they cool.

6. Melt 1 1/2 tablespoons of the butter in a small pan or in a microwave. Transfer the cooled potatoes to a bowl and stir in the melted butter, chopped pumpkin seeds, sesame seeds, and salt and pepper to taste. Season both sides of the fish with salt and pepper. Divide the potato mixture among the fish pieces, pressing down to cover the top of each piece of fish with a neat 1/2-inch-thick layer of potatoes.

7. Warm a large skillet over medium-high heat. Add the oil and heat it until it begins to shimmer. Add the fish, potato side down. (Have faith; just let it fall.) Cook until the potatoes are browned, 6 to 8 minutes, giving the pan a gentle shake after about 3 minutes. Flip the fish over, and add the remaining 2 tablespoons butter, the garlic, and the rosemary to the pan. Spoon the foaming butter over the fish. Flip the fish and cook for another minute.

8. While the fish is cooking, finely mince 1 tablespoon of the reserved fennel fronds. Place the minced fronds in a small bowl and add 4 teaspoons of the oil from the fennel confit. Season with salt and pepper.

9. Remove the sliced fennel from the oil and place it in a small saucepan. (If desired, reserve the remaining fennel oil, strained, for another use, such as dressing salads or pasta.) Season the fennel with salt and pepper, and warm over low heat.

10. Warm the rhubarb sauce over medium heat, and swirl in the 1 tablespoon cold butter. Season with additional salt and pepper if desired.

11. To serve, pour a small pool of rhubarb sauce onto each plate. Garnish with fennel confit and dabs of fennel oil. Place a piece of fish, potato side up, in the center.

Notes: To toast pumpkin seeds, place them in a small heavy pan over medium-high heat. Toast, tossing constantly, until the seeds are brown and fragrant and beginning to pop, 2 to 3 minutes. Transfer to a plate to cool. Kaffir limes are a bitter, bumpy-skinned citrus fruit. Their wonderfully fragrant leaves are used frequently in Southeast Asian cooking and are available in Asian specialty stores.

Soft-Shell Crab

WITH FENNEL, TOMATO, AND POMELO

TOMATO VINAIGRETTE

2 pounds (about 4 large) RIPE TOMATOES, cored and quartered

3 GARLIC CLOVES, smashed

1 large sprig FRESH BASIL (about 12 leaves)

1 teaspoon SUGAR

1/2 teaspoon fine SEA SALT

1/4 teaspoon cracked BLACK PEPPER

3 teaspoons fresh LEMON JUICE

1 teaspoon CHAMPAGNE VINEGAR

1/4 cup CANOLA OIL

1 tablespoon extra-virgin OLIVE OIL

1 POMELO, or 1 large grapefruit

1 large FENNEL BULB (about 3/4 pound), trimmed, 1/4 cup chopped fronds reserved

Grated ZEST and fresh JUICE of 1 LIME

Fine SEA SALT and freshly ground BLACK PEPPER

2 tablespoons extra-virgin OLIVE OIL

2 tablespoons GRAPESEED, canola, or other flavorless OIL, plus additional for frying

1 cup plus 2 tablespoons ALL-PURPOSE FLOUR

DAVID BOULEY Pomelos, native to Malaysia and Indonesia, are yellow or green thick-skinned relatives of the grapefruit with a sweet flavor and slightly drier flesh. One of the things I love about this dish is the way the pomelo breaks apart and adds little sweet-tart bites that contrast beautifully with the sweetness of the tomato, fennel, and crab. The tempura batter gives the crab a nice crunch but keeps it light even though it's fried.

MARIO LOHNINGER Soft-shell crab is certainly not an Austrian thing, but it's very popular in the United States. I learned how to cook it when I worked for Wolfgang Puck in California, actually. They go crazy for soft-shells on the West Coast. When you do them right, they are crunchy on the outside and juicy inside. To keep them really juicy, you should clean them yourself at home instead of having the fishmonger do it. It just takes a minute, and that way you won't lose all the juices.

1. Prepare the tomato vinaigrette: Place the tomatoes in a saucepan with the garlic, basil, sugar, salt, and pepper. Cook very gently on the lowest heat until the tomatoes are soft and melting, about 1 hour. Push the tomatoes through a fine-mesh sieve set over a glass measuring cup. You should have at least 2 cups. Return the mixture to a clean saucepan and simmer over medium-low heat until it is reduced to the consistency of thick tomato juice (it should measure 1 1/2 cups), about 20 minutes. Add the lemon juice, vinegar, and salt and pepper to taste. Whisk in the oils. Set the dressing aside.

2. Prepare the salad: Use a sharp knife to cut the top and bottom off the pomelo. Stand it up on a cutting board and cut the peel and white pith away from the fruit, following the curve with your knife, so that the segments are exposed. Hold the peeled fruit over a bowl and cut out the segments, letting them fall into the bowl along with the juice. Use a slotted spoon to transfer the segments to a cutting board and slice them into thirds. Reserve 2 tablespoons of the juice. Set the pomelo segments aside.

1/2 cup CORNSTARCH or rice flour

2 teaspoons BAKING POWDER

3 cups SODA WATER (seltzer)

6 fresh SOFT-SHELL CRABS, cleaned (see below)

1/4 pound (2 quarts) BABY ARUGULA

SERVES 6 AS A FISH COURSE

3. Using a mandoline or a large sharp knife, shave the fennel into nearly transparent slices. Place the fennel in a bowl, add the lime zest, season with salt and pepper, and mix gently. In another bowl, whisk together the reserved 2 tablespoons pomelo juice and 1 tablespoon lime juice. Season with salt and pepper. Whisk in the olive and grapeseed oils. Lightly dress the fennel with this mixture, and toss to combine. Set the fennel salad aside.

4. To prepare the crabs, pour 1/2 inch of grapeseed oil into a heavy skillet or Dutch oven and heat it to 375°F. In a bowl, whisk together the flour, cornstarch, baking powder, and 1 teaspoon salt. Whisk in the soda water to make a thin batter.

5. Dip the crabs into the batter one by one, and fry them in batches in the hot oil until golden brown. Use a thermometer to ensure that the oil remains at 375°F. Transfer the fried crabs to a paper towel-lined plate, and season them with salt and pepper.

6. Transfer the pomelo segments to a saucepan and stir in 2 tablespoons of the tomato vinaigrette. Warm the mixture over medium heat.

7. In a bowl, dress the arugula with some of the tomato vinaigrette. Season with salt and pepper.

8. To serve, place some fennel salad on each plate and scatter pieces of pomelo over the fennel. Top with a crab, garnish with the arugula, and drizzle a bit more of the tomato vinaigrette around the plate.

HOW TO CLEAN SOFT-SHELL CRABS Although you can have your fishmonger clean them for you, you'll get a slightly more flavorful crab by doing it yourself, just before cooking. Place each crab on a cutting board and use a sharp knife to cut straight across the front of the crab, removing less than a 1/2-inch strip, which will include the eyes and mouth. Pull up on half of the top shell to expose the gills, and pull them away. Repeat on the other side. Turn the crab upside down and pull off the tail flap.

Warm Rabbit Salad

WITH FOIE GRAS, WHITE ASPARAGUS, AND TARRAGON-RIESLING SAUCE

Two of Austria's delicacies, white asparagus and Riesling wine, are paired here in a stunning salad with rabbit and foie gras. The tarragon-Riesling sauce is made with a blend of spices and herbs that highlight the spice notes of the wine, while the white asparagus is prepared in a typical method—in broth with a pinch of sugar. Foie gras makes this dish memorable.

NOTES FROM THE KITCHEN As a special treat, sometimes we will sear the rabbit kidneys and serve them with the salad. They have a great flavor. Or if you don't want to bother with the foie gras, simply sauté the rabbit liver and serve that with the salad instead.

1. Prepare the asparagus: Fill a large bowl with water and ice. Bring a large saucepan of water to a boil. Divide the asparagus into two bundles and tie them, not too tightly, with kitchen string. Add enough sugar and salt to the boiling water so that you can just taste it (about 1 teaspoon salt and 1 tablespoon sugar per quart of water). Slide the asparagus bundles into the boiling water and simmer, covered, until tender, about 10 minutes. Transfer the bundles to the ice water, remove the string, and let cool. Drain when cool and pat dry. Reserve 1 cup of the cooking water.

2. Combine the chicken stock, reserved 1 cup asparagus cooking water, shallot, and the 1 teaspoon sugar in a medium saucepan over medium heat. Season with salt and pepper. Cook until the sugar has dissolved. Then whisk in the vinegar and olive oil. Arrange the asparagus spears in a single layer on a dish or a deep platter, and pour the marinade over them. Let marinate at room temperature for at least 2 hours, or as long as 8 hours.

3. Make the tarragon-Riesling sauce: Place the stock, wine, mustard, coriander seeds, and herbs in a blender, and blend on high speed. With the blender running, add the olive oil in a thin stream. Season with the salt and pepper. Fill a large bowl with water and ice, and place a smaller metal bowl inside it. Push the sauce through a fine-mesh sieve into the metal bowl and stir until cold. The sauce can be prepared 4 hours ahead.

4. When you are ready to cook the rabbit, preheat the oven to 400°F.

MARINATED ASPARAGUS

12 spears WHITE ASPARAGUS, peeled, tough ends snapped off

1 teaspoon SUGAR, plus additional for cooking the asparagus

Fine SEA SALT

1 cup CHICKEN STOCK (see page 333) or canned low-sodium chicken broth

1 large SHALLOT, finely chopped

Freshly ground BLACK PEPPER

1/3 cup CHAMPAGNE VINEGAR

2 tablespoons extra-virgin OLIVE OIL

TARRAGON-RIESLING SAUCE

5 tablespoons CHICKEN STOCK (see page 333) or canned low-sodium chicken broth

5 tablespoons RIESLING or other dry but fragrant white wine, such as a Gewürztraminer

1 teaspoon DIJON MUSTARD

1 teaspoon CORIANDER SEEDS

1/2 cup loosely packed FRESH TARRAGON

1 cup loosely packed FRESH CHERVIL

1 1/2 cups loosely packed FRESH FLAT-LEAF PARSLEY

5 tablespoons extra-virgin OLIVE OIL

1/4 teaspoon SEA SALT, or to taste

Freshly ground BLACK PEPPER

ishes

tews, salads, & slaws, but if you're brave
'll best enjoyed when eaten raw. Too
se old favorites are a relati of the

1.00 a bunch

2 tablespoons UNSALTED BUTTER

1 sprig FRESH ROSEMARY

1 sprig FRESH THYME

1 SHALLOT, chopped

4 RABBIT LOINS (about 4 ounces each)

SEA SALT and freshly ground BLACK PEPPER

1 tablespoon CANOLA OIL

2 pieces FRESH FOIE GRAS (each about 1 inch thick)

3/4 cup WONDRA FLOUR (see Notes, page 250)

2 cups (1 ounce) MIXED BABY GREENS (mesclun)

2 RED RADISHES, thinly sliced

2 tablespoons extra-virgin OLIVE OIL

1 tablespoon BALSAMIC VINEGAR

Fine SEA SALT and freshly ground BLACK PEPPER

4 small slices prepared FOIE GRAS TERRINE (optional; see Sources, page 337)

SERVES 4 AS AN APPETIZER OR LIGHT MAIN COURSE

5. Melt the butter in a sauté pan over medium heat and let it cook until the milk solids fall to the bottom and turn nut-brown, about 5 minutes. Add the rosemary, thyme, and shallot, stir, and reduce the heat to low. Season the rabbit loins with salt and pepper, and add them to the pan. Cook the rabbit slowly and evenly, turning it often, until it is slightly pink in the center, 4 to 6 minutes depending on the size of the loin. Take care not to overcook it, or the meat will become dry. Transfer the rabbit to a cutting board and set it aside.

6. Heat the canola oil over high heat in a large ovenproof sauté pan. Season the foie gras with salt and pepper, and dredge it in the flour, shaking off any excess. Place the floured foie gras in the pan and cook until the underside is dark brown, about 1 minute. Flip the pieces over and place the pan in the oven. Bake until the foie gras is soft around the edges and offers the slightest resistance in the center, about 2 minutes. Transfer it to a plate and let it rest while you assemble the salad.

7. Gently warm the tarragon-Riesling sauce. Toss the mesclun and radishes with the olive oil, vinegar, and salt and pepper to taste. Place 3 asparagus spears on each plate, and top with the greens. Slice each rabbit loin lengthwise into 4 pieces, and nestle them in the salad. Slice each piece of foie gras in half, and place a piece alongside the salad. Dipping a knife in hot water, cut 4 slices from the terrine, about the same size as the foie gras, and place them on the other side of the salad. Drizzle the warm tarragon-Riesling sauce over the rabbit and around the salad. Serve.

MARIO LOHNINGER Rabbit is a very traditional food in Austria, especially in the springtime, when asparagus is in season. I ate it when I was a child, but my parents never told me what it was because I had my own rabbits. I had two, and my parents always gave me a hard time because I didn't clean up after them often enough. I got them from my grandparents, who had about a hundred bunnies. I never knew we ate them, though. Every once in a while I would go to eat at my grandmother's place, and she would serve us what she called fried chicken. One day she said, "How did you like it? You ate a rabbit." And I started to cry. I was only five or six.

Rabbits are cute the way they wrinkle their little noses, but at a restaurant, rabbit is an item you have to watch out for, because it overcooks. You can ruin it quickly. So watch it closely and make sure it doesn't overcook and toughen.

Wine-Braised Beef Cheeks

WITH CHANTERELLE GOULASH

BEEF CHEEKS

3 tablespoons CANOLA OIL

7 BEEF CHEEKS (about 3 1/2 pounds total), trimmed and halved

3 tablespoons UNSALTED BUTTER

2 CARROTS, quartered

2 CELERY STALKS, quartered

1 large ONION, quartered

2 GARLIC CLOVES, smashed

Fine SEA SALT and freshly ground BLACK PEPPER

2 teaspoons TOMATO PASTE

5 cups HEARTY RED WINE, preferably Zweigelt

2 cups PORT WINE

6 cups VEAL STOCK (see page 335)

10 BLACK PEPPERCORNS

5 to 6 PARSLEY STEMS

2 sprigs FRESH THYME

1 sprig FRESH ROSEMARY

1 BAY LEAF, preferably fresh

Americans don't think of cooking beef cheeks, but they can be the best part of the cow. They are shot through with veins of gelatin, which, when slowly braised, dissolve and thicken the meat juices, making them incredibly rich and succulent. The meat itself becomes melt-in-the-mouth tender, barely holding together on the plate, then breaking apart at the first touch of a fork. You might have to special-order beef cheeks from your butcher, but they are worth tracking down.

Here the beef cheeks are gently simmered with red wine and Port and served with a chanterelle goulash, orange and spice–glazed carrots, and sweet baby turnips.

1. Heat a large heavy stockpot over high heat. Add the canola oil and let it heat for 30 seconds. Then add the beef cheeks and sear them lightly on all sides, about 15 minutes. Transfer the beef cheeks to a platter, and discard the oil.

2. Reduce the heat to medium and add the butter, then the carrots, celery, onion, garlic, and salt and pepper to taste. Cook until the vegetables are soft and brown, about 30 minutes. Add the tomato paste and cook, stirring, for 30 seconds. Pour in 1 cup of the red wine and 1 cup of the Port, and simmer until the vegetables are syrupy and almost dry, about 15 minutes. Add another cup of the wine and the remaining Port, and simmer until slightly reduced, about 20 minutes. Return the beef cheeks to the pot and add the veal stock. Bring the stock to a simmer, uncovered, and cook gently for 2 hours.

NOTES FROM THE KITCHEN If you can find a dark, rich Zweigelt wine from Austria, use it here. Otherwise choose a hearty wine from the Rhône in France or an American Zinfandel. This dish can be served with either the carrots or turnips alone, but when time allows, it's prettiest with both. When you can't get chanterelles, substitute other mushrooms, such as oyster, shiitake, or cremini. Serve this dish with the Chive Dumplings on page 200 or with mashed potatoes.

CARROTS IN CARROT SAUCE

1 1/2 tablespoons UNSALTED
    BUTTER

1 SHALLOT, thinly sliced

1/2 pound CARROTS, cut into
    1/4-inch-thick rounds

10 CORIANDER SEEDS

10 BLACK PEPPERCORNS

3 ALLSPICE BERRIES

1 WHOLE STAR ANISE

1 sprig FRESH THYME

1 BAY LEAF, preferably fresh

1 cup VEGETABLE STOCK
    (see page 332)

1 cup CHICKEN STOCK (see
    page 333), plus additional to taste

Fine SEA SALT

CAYENNE PEPPER

Fresh JUICE of 3 ORANGES, plus
    additional to taste

Freshly ground WHITE PEPPER

3/4 pound BABY CARROTS

TURNIPS

1 pound BABY TURNIPS, trimmed

1 VANILLA BEAN, split lengthwise,
    seeds scraped out with a knife

1 tablespoon SUGAR

1 cup (2 sticks) UNSALTED BUTTER,
    cut into cubes

Fine SEA SALT

3. Place the peppercorns, parsley stems, thyme, rosemary, and bay leaf in a 6-inch square of cheesecloth. Tie it securely with kitchen string, add it to the pot, and continue to simmer for 1 hour.

4. Now begin to check the cheeks with a fork, transferring them to a clean platter when they are tender. Set them aside. Pour the braising liquid through a coarse-mesh strainer set over a clean pot, pushing down on the solids to extract all the liquid. Set it aside.

5. Pour the remaining 3 cups red wine into a saucepan and bring it to a simmer over medium heat. Simmer until the wine is reduced to 1/4 cup, about 1 hour. Reheat the braising liquid and skim off the foam. Add the reduced wine, 1 tablespoon at a time, until the sauce has a balanced acidity (you may not need all of it). Set it aside.

6. To prepare the carrot sauce, melt the butter in a large saucepan over low heat. Add the shallot and cook, stirring occasionally, until soft and translucent, about 10 minutes—do not allow it to brown. Add the carrots and continue to cook, without browning, until they are beginning to soften, about 15 minutes.

7. Place the coriander, peppercorns, allspice berries, star anise, thyme, and bay leaf in a 6-inch square of cheesecloth. Tie it securely with kitchen string and add it to the carrots. Stir in the vegetable and chicken stocks, and salt and cayenne pepper to taste. Loosely cover the pot and cook gently, at a bare simmer, until the carrots are very tender, about 1 hour.

8. Meanwhile, bring the orange juice to a simmer in a small saucepan and let it reduce to 1/4 cup, about 40 minutes.

9. When the carrots are tender, place them in a blender with the cooking liquid. Add the reduced orange juice to taste and blend, adding fresh orange juice and/or chicken stock if needed, until the sauce is smooth and thin enough to pour. Season with salt and white pepper.

10. Fill a bowl with water and ice. Bring a pot of water to a boil and salt it until it tastes like seawater (about 2 teaspoons per quart). Add the baby carrots and boil until crisp-tender, 5 to 7 minutes. Drain, and plunge them into the ice water to cool. Drain well and toss with the carrot sauce. Set aside.

11. Prepare the turnips: Fill a bowl with water and ice. Bring a pot of water to a boil and salt it until it tastes like seawater (about 2 teaspoons per quart). Add the turnips and boil until tender, 12 to 15 minutes. Drain, and plunge them into the ice water. When the turnips are cool, peel them and halve any that are large.

12. Warm 2 tablespoons water in a saucepan over medium heat. Add the scraped vanilla bean seeds and the sugar. When the mixture is hot, add the butter, piece by piece, whisking constantly to keep the sauce smooth. Season with salt. Add the cooked turnips and cover to keep warm.

13. Prepare the chanterelle goulash: Melt the butter in a saucepan over medium heat. When it foams, add the shallots and cook, stirring occasionally, until tender, about 7 minutes. Do not allow the shallots to brown. Add the chanterelles, season with salt and pepper, and toss until soft, about 8 minutes. Add 1 cup of the reserved wine sauce and cover to keep warm.

14. Gently warm the carrots in their sauce, thinning the sauce with additional chicken stock or orange juice if necessary to keep it very loose, and cover to keep warm. Warm the beef cheeks in the wine sauce.

15. To prepare the scallions, fill a bowl with water and ice. Bring a pot of water to a boil and salt it until it tastes like seawater (about 2 teaspoons per quart). Add the scallions and boil for 30 seconds, then drain and transfer to the ice water. Drain well, pressing down on the scallions with paper towels. In a small saucepan, warm the scallions with 3 tablespoons of the chive paste, and season with salt and pepper. Use the remaining chive paste for another purpose.

16. To serve, divide the chanterelle goulash among the plates and garnish with the parsley leaves. Top each portion with 2 beef cheeks. Garnish with the carrots and turnips. Place ¼ teaspoon of the scallions on top of each beef cheek, and drizzle the circumference of the plate with whipped cream.

CHANTERELLE GOULASH

2 tablespoons UNSALTED BUTTER

2 SHALLOTS, sliced

1/2 pound CHANTERELLE MUSHROOMS, trimmed

Fine SEA SALT and freshly ground BLACK PEPPER

SCALLIONS

Fine SEA SALT

Freshly ground BLACK PEPPER

2 cups sliced SCALLIONS (about 2 bunches), white and light green parts only

6 tablespoons CHIVE PASTE (see page 200, Step 1)

10 FRESH PARSLEY LEAVES, thinly sliced

1/2 cup HEAVY CREAM, whipped

SERVES 6 AS A MAIN COURSE

Rhubarb Buttermilk Parfait

Tart and creamy, this red and white parfait is the essence of springtime. It can be made a day or two ahead, so it's very convenient for a dinner party. Serve it with crisp cookies such as the Vanilla Butter Crescents on page 318.

1. Preheat the oven to 300°F.

2. Place all the ingredients for the rhubarb-raspberry sorbet in a 9- by 12-inch baking pan and cover with foil. Bake until the rhubarb and raspberries are falling apart and syrupy, about 1 hour. Let the mixture cool slightly, then transfer it to a blender or food processor and puree. Pass the mixture through a fine-mesh sieve and discard the solids. Let the puree cool thoroughly. Chill the puree until it is very cold, at least 4 hours.

3. Freeze the rhubarb mixture in an ice cream machine according to the manufacturer's instructions. You can store the sorbet in the freezer for up to 3 days.

4. Prepare the buttermilk parfait: Line an 8-cup loaf pan or terrine mold with plastic wrap. Combine the buttermilk, sugar, and lime juice in a bowl and mix well to dissolve the sugar.

5. Place the leaf gelatin in a small bowl and cover it with cold water. Let it soften for 5 minutes. Then drain the gelatin and pat it dry with a paper towel.

6. Put 2 tablespoons of the buttermilk mixture in a small saucepan and bring it to a bare simmer. Remove the pan from the heat and mix in the gelatin, stirring until it dissolves. Pass the buttermilk-gelatin mixture through a fine-mesh sieve into the rest of the buttermilk mixture. Mix well.

RHUBARB-RASPBERRY SORBET

6 cups (2 pounds) sliced RHUBARB

1/2 pint RASPBERRIES

2/3 cup SUGAR

1 VANILLA BEAN, split lengthwise, seeds scraped out with a knife

BUTTERMILK PARFAIT

1 1/4 cups BUTTERMILK, cold

1/2 cup SUGAR

2 tablespoons fresh LIME JUICE

1 sheet (about 3 grams) LEAF GELATIN (see Sources, page 337)

1 cup HEAVY CREAM

GARNISH

1 pint ripe STRAWBERRIES, sliced

3 tablespoons CONFECTIONERS' SUGAR

SERVES 8 AS DESSERT

7. Whip the cream until it holds soft peaks. Fold the cream into the butter-milk mixture. Pour the mixture into the prepared loaf pan and smooth the top. Freeze the parfait until it is set, at least 4 hours or as long as overnight.

8. Remove the rhubarb-strawberry sorbet from the freezer, and let it soften for about 15 minutes. Then spread the sorbet over the buttermilk parfait and smooth the top. Cover with plastic wrap and freeze for at least 3 hours, or as long as overnight.

9. For the garnish, combine the strawberries and confectioners' sugar in a bowl, and let macerate for 30 minutes at room temperature. Then puree a third of the berries in a food processor or blender, and mix the puree into the remaining sliced berries.

10. Unmold the parfait, peel off the plastic wrap, and slice it into 1-inch-thick pieces. Serve the slices garnished with the strawberries.

Brandteigkrapfen

SWAN-SHAPED CREAM PUFFS

PASTRY CREAM FILLING

2 VANILLA BEANS, split lengthwise, seeds scraped out with a knife

1 3/4 cups WHOLE MILK

1 1/4 cups SUGAR

2 large EGG YOLKS

1/3 cup CORNSTARCH

5 large EGG WHITES

CHOUX PASTE

9 tablespoons (1 stick plus 1 tablespoon) UNSALTED BUTTER

Pinch of fine SEA SALT

1 cup ALL-PURPOSE FLOUR

3 to 4 large EGGS

SERVES 6 AS DESSERT

Swan-shaped cream puffs are not the kind of dessert one would attempt on a whim, but they do make for a very special treat. The only trick is to be sure to cook the batter long enough once the flour has been added. It should thicken into a near-intractable paste and stick to the spoon. Then immediately transfer the mixture to an electric mixer to beat in the eggs. After that, forming the swan shapes is easy. These puffs are filled with vanilla custard, but ice cream and sorbet are also fine options. Have the camera ready before you serve them.

1. Prepare the pastry cream filling: Combine the vanilla seeds and 3/4 cup of the milk in a saucepan and warm over medium heat, but do not let it boil. In a bowl, whisk the remaining 1 cup milk with 1 cup of the sugar, the egg yolks, and the cornstarch.

2. Add a few tablespoons of the hot vanilla milk to the egg yolk mixture, and whisk to combine. Whisking constantly, pour all the egg yolk mixture into the hot milk. Cook over medium-low heat, stirring, until the mixture thickens enough to coat the back of a spoon well, about 8 to 10 minutes. Transfer the custard to a shallow bowl, press plastic wrap over the surface, and let it cool.

3. In a clean bowl of an electric mixer fitted with the whisk attachment, beat the egg whites on medium speed until foamy. Add the remaining 1/4 cup sugar and beat at high speed to form stiff, but not dry, peaks. Whisk one fourth of the whites into the custard to lighten it. Then gently fold in the remaining whites, cover, and refrigerate for at least 30 minutes or as long as overnight.

4. Preheat the oven to 425°F, and line two baking sheets with parchment paper.

5. Prepare the choux paste: Combine 1 $\frac{1}{4}$ cups water with the butter and salt in a saucepan, and bring to a boil. Add the flour all at once, and stirring constantly and vigorously with a wooden spoon, cook over medium-low heat until the dough comes together in a ball around the spoon, about 5 minutes. Transfer the dough to the bowl of an electric mixer fitted with the paddle attachment, and beat until slightly cooled, about 1 minute. Add 3 eggs one by one, beating to incorporate. The mixture should be smooth and thick enough to briefly hold a mark when poked. If it is too stiff, add the fourth egg.

6. Transfer the mixture to a pastry bag (or use a resealable plastic bag with one corner cut off), and pipe twelve 2-inch rounds of dough, spaced 1 inch apart, on one of the prepared baking sheets. Pipe out 12 thin swan's-neck shapes (a thin line with curlicues at each end) on the other baking sheet. Put the sheets in the oven and prop the oven door open with the end of a wooden spoon. Bake the swans' necks for 15 minutes and the larger rounds for 20 minutes. Transfer the pans to wire racks to cool.

7. Slice each round in half horizontally, and then cut each top piece in half. Spoon or pipe 1 tablespoon of the pastry cream filling into the bottom of each round. Place a swan's neck upright in the pastry cream, and flank it with the pastry halves, arranging them to look like wings.

Marmalade Palatschinken

CRÊPES WITH HOMEMADE JAM

RASPBERRY JAM

2 cups FRESH RASPBERRIES

1 cup SUGAR

APRICOT JAM

1 pound FRESH APRICOTS, pits
removed, cut into 1/2-inch cubes

1 cup SUGAR

1 tablespoon fresh LEMON JUICE

CRÊPES

1 1/2 cups ALL-PURPOSE FLOUR

2 tablespoons SUGAR

Pinch of fine SEA SALT

1 large EGG YOLK

2 large EGGS

1 1/3 cups WHOLE MILK

1 1/3 cups HEAVY CREAM

1 teaspoon grated LEMON ZEST

1 VANILLA BEAN, split lengthwise,
seeds scraped out with a knife

2 tablespoons UNSALTED BUTTER,
melted

CONFECTIONERS' SUGAR, for
serving

SERVES 8 TO 10 AS DESSERT

This appears to be a very plain dessert—just thick crêpes rolled up with jam. But if you use the best quality jam, preferably homemade, and serve the crêpes fresh from the pan when they are still hot and tender, it's a revelation. A dollop of whipped cream or crème fraîche, or perhaps a scoop of vanilla ice cream, is not strictly necessary but wouldn't be out of place.

1. Prepare the raspberry jam: Combine the ingredients in a small saucepan and bring to a simmer over medium heat, stirring until the sugar is dissolved. Let simmer until loosely set, 15 to 30 minutes. The jam is ready if a few drops of the syrup firm up and gel when dripped onto a cold plate. Skim off any foam and refrigerate until completely set, about 3 hours. The jam will keep for at least 1 week in the refrigerator.

2. Prepare the apricot jam in the same manner. It will keep for 1 week in the refrigerator.

3. Prepare the crêpes: Combine the flour with the sugar and salt in a large bowl. In a separate bowl, whisk together the egg yolk, eggs, milk, cream, lemon zest, and vanilla seeds. Add the egg mixture to the flour mixture and whisk until smooth. Let rest for 30 minutes in the refrigerator. Whisk again before using.

4. Heat a seasoned crêpe pan (or a nonstick sauté pan) over medium heat. When the pan is hot, brush a thin film of melted butter over the bottom. Add enough batter to cover the pan to a depth of 1/8 inch, about 3 to 4 tablespoons (it shouldn't be too thin). When the crêpe is browned on the bottom, flip it over and cook the other side, 1 1/2 to 2 minutes total. Transfer the crêpe to a plate and keep it warm in a 200°F oven. Repeat until all the batter has been used.

5. Fill each crêpe with 2 tablespoons jam (some with raspberry, some with apricot), roll it up, and serve warm, sprinkled with confectioners' sugar.

Salzburger Nockerln
SWEET SOUFFLÉS WITH RASPBERRIES AND CREAM

NOTES FROM THE KITCHEN The Nockerln can also be served family-style, in one large dish: Put the raspberries and cream in the dish, top with the batter, and bake for 8 to 10 minutes. You can substitute lingonberry jam for the raspberries if you want, or use other berries such as strawberries or blackberries.

1. Preheat the oven to 400°F.
2. Place ³/4 cup of the raspberries in a bowl and toss with the 2 tablespoons sugar. Let macerate for 15 minutes.
3. Using a fork or a potato masher, mash the raspberries to a puree. Push the puree through a fine-mesh strainer set over a bowl. Add the remaining ¹/4 cup raspberries and toss to coat them in the raspberry puree.
4. Divide the cream among 6 shallow ovenproof dishes, such as crème brûlée dishes or ramekins. Divide the raspberry mixture among the dishes.
5. Using an electric mixer fitted with the whisk attachment, beat the egg whites and salt until the whites are very foamy. Gradually add the remaining ¹/4 cup sugar, beating just until stiff peaks form.
6. In a separate bowl, beat the egg yolks, rum, vanilla seeds, and citrus zests together. Fold one third of the egg whites into the yolk mixture to lighten it. Then fold the lightened yolks into the rest of the whites. Sift the flour over the eggs and gently fold to combine.
7. Drop large dollops of the egg mixture onto the raspberries in the dishes, mounding it high. Bake until the Nockerln are set and the peaks are browned, 4 to 6 minutes. Serve immediately, with vanilla ice cream if desired.

1 cup FRESH RASPBERRIES

¹/4 cup plus 2 tablespoons SUGAR

6 tablespoons HEAVY CREAM

5 large EGG WHITES

Pinch of fine SEA SALT

2 large EGG YOLKS

2 teaspoons DARK RUM

¹/2 VANILLA BEAN, split lengthwise, seeds scraped out with a knife

¹/4 teaspoon grated LEMON ZEST

¹/4 teaspoon grated ORANGE ZEST

1 tablespoon plus 1 teaspoon ALL-PURPOSE FLOUR

VANILLA ICE CREAM, for serving (optional)

SERVES 6 AS DESSERT

MARIO LOHNINGER Salzburger Nockerln is from my hometown—I grew up in Salzburg. But oddly, I have never made this recipe in the traditional way. The original method calls for sautéing quenelles of the soufflé batter in clarified butter in a cast-iron pan, then mounding it into three peaks in a large dish (the peaks are supposed to represent the three mountains that ring Salzburg). These days most chefs just bake the nockerln in the oven like a soufflé. That's what I always did. Still, it's embarrassing to be from Salzburg and never to have made the dish the way it was created. Once I was in Japan giving a demonstration and the students asked me to make the nockerln the old-fashioned way. I didn't do it—I didn't want to be embarrassed in front of hundreds of people. I will try it one of these days . . . but it's hard when this version is so easy and so delicious.

Summer

Chicken Schnitzel

24 CHICKEN WINGS, wing tips
   removed
Fine SEA SALT and freshly ground
   BLACK PEPPER
1 ½ cups ALL-PURPOSE FLOUR
3 EGGS, beaten
1 ½ cups BREAD CRUMBS,
   preferably homemade (see Note,
   page 107)
CANOLA OIL, for frying
24 FRESH PARSLEY LEAVES
1 LEMON

SERVES 10 TO 12 AS AN
HORS D'OEUVRE

The South does not have the last word on fried chicken. It's a very popular dish in Vienna, too, where it's called *Backhendl*. There was a long
period of time—up until the latter half of the nineteenth century, in fact—
when chicken was a delicacy that only the rich could afford (unlike pork
and beef, which were less expensive). Serving Backhendl was a sign of
prosperity, and there is still much ceremony surrounding the preparation
of the dish. The type of chicken is paramount: It should be plump and
tender and not too old. The pieces are seasoned and coated exactly like
Wiener Schnitzel—dipped sequentially in flour, eggs, and bread crumbs—
and fried until perfectly golden brown and very crisp. But unlike pork
and veal schnitzel, which are served year-round, Backhendl is a summer
dish, served preferably outdoors in a lovely garden, with lemon wedges,
fried parsley, a salad, and a cool bottle of local white wine.

MARIO LOHNINGER We use only the wings in this chicken schnitzel
because it makes a good hors d'oeuvre for passing. The wings stay very
juicy and are cute to serve, like little fried lollipops. It's a very popular
dish—not complicated, but tasty.

1. Using a sharp knife, separate the lower joint of each chicken wing from
the upper joint, and remove the skin (discard the upper joint). Push the
flesh down toward the ball joint and detach the larger bone, making a
plump ball of meat at one end and a bare bone at the other. Season them
with salt and pepper.
2. Place the flour in a bowl, the eggs in another bowl, and the bread
crumbs in a third. Season the flour and the eggs with salt and pepper.

3. Dredge the chicken wings in the flour and shake off the excess. Dip the wings in the egg and shake off any excess. Then cover the wings completely with the bread crumbs. Reshape the wings into perfect "lollipops" before setting them on a plate.

4. Pour oil to a depth of 1 inch in a deep frying pan (or fill a deep-fryer), and heat it to 350°F. Fry the chicken in batches (do not crowd the pan) until dark brown, 2 1/2 to 3 minutes. Drain on a paper towel–lined plate, and season with salt and pepper. Fry the parsley in the hot oil until crisp, 5 to 10 seconds, and remove it with a slotted spoon.

5. Use a sharp knife to cut the top and bottom off the lemon. Stand it up on a cutting board, and cut the peel and white pith away from the fruit, following the curve with your knife, so that the segments are exposed. Hold the peeled fruit over a bowl and cut out the segments, letting them fall into the bowl. Use a slotted spoon to transfer the segments to a cutting board, and slice them at 1/4-inch intervals to make tiny wedges. Garnish each chicken wing with a piece of lemon and a leaf of fried parsley.

Tuna with Pickled Spring Onions

AND SESAME-MUSTARD SEED DRESSING

Combining raw sashimi-quality tuna, sesame, soy sauce, and ginger, this dish is more Asian in style than Austrian, and in fact it was inspired by David's many trips to Japan. However, there is a crossover when it comes to the mustard. Instead of the usual wasabi bite, the kick here comes from freshly ground yellow mustard seeds—a very Austrian ingredient. Be sure to use whole mustard seeds and grind them yourself. The preground stuff is bland and pasty compared to freshly ground.

NOTES FROM THE KITCHEN The mustard-sesame dressing in this dish is wonderful—thick and rich like an aïoli but with a punch from the ginger. Everyone who works at the Danube really loves it, and at the end of the night members of the staff migrate to the kitchen and make a snack of raw tuna cubes smothered in leftover dressing. It's also great on sandwiches, or thinned with a little oil and used as a salad dressing for hardy greens like arugula or watercress.

1. Prepare the pickled onions: Cut the green stalks from the onion bulbs and reserve them for another use. Halve the onions lengthwise and remove the yellow-green cores. With a sharp knife or a mandoline, cut the onions lengthwise into paper-thin slices. Place the lime juice in a bowl and whisk in the honey. Whisk in the coriander, mustard seeds, canola and olive oils, salt, and pepper to taste. Marinate the onions in this mixture for at least 4 hours before using. The pickle will last up to 4 days, covered, in the refrigerator.

2. Prepare the soy-lime dressing: Combine the soy sauce, lime juice, vinegar, honey, and ginger juice in a bowl, and whisk in the sesame oil. Season with salt and pepper. Add the chopped cilantro and refrigerate, covered, for at least 2 hours or as long as overnight. Pass the dressing through a fine-mesh strainer before using.

PICKLED ONIONS

4 SPRING ONIONS, each 2 to 3 inches in diameter (see Notes)

1/2 cup fresh LIME JUICE

2 1/2 tablespoons HONEY

3/4 teaspoon GROUND CORIANDER

3/4 teaspoon YELLOW MUSTARD SEEDS

1 1/2 teaspoons CANOLA OIL

1 1/2 teaspoons extra-virgin OLIVE OIL

1/2 teaspoon fine SEA SALT

Freshly ground BLACK PEPPER

SOY-LIME DRESSING

1 tablespoon SOY SAUCE

1 tablespoon fresh LIME JUICE

1 tablespoon RICE WINE VINEGAR

1 1/2 teaspoons HONEY

1/4 teaspoon GINGER JUICE (see Note, page 90)

1 tablespoon SESAME OIL

Fine SEA SALT and freshly ground BLACK PEPPER

1 sprig FRESH CILANTRO, roughly chopped, including the stem

3. Prepare the sesame-mustard dressing: Combine the canola and sesame oils in one bowl, and combine the rice wine vinegar and soy sauce in another. Place the egg yolk, honey, ground mustard seeds, garlic, and ginger juice in a blender, and blend to combine; then add a few drops of the vinegar-soy mixture. With the motor running, drizzle in some of the oil mixture until the dressing is combined and thickened. Thin it by pouring in a thin stream of the vinegar-soy mixture; then thicken again by drizzling in more of the oil. Continue alternating the additions until all the ingredients are used. Season with salt and pepper, and set aside.

4. Prepare the herb vinaigrette: Place the herbs, oil, and vinegar in a blender and blend to combine. Season with salt and pepper, and set aside.

5. Slice half the tuna into 16 equal slices, and cut the other half into 1-inch cubes.

6. To serve, toss the lettuce with enough strained soy-lime dressing to lightly coat the leaves. Season the tuna slices with sesame-mustard dressing. Drop the tuna cubes into the sesame-mustard dressing and gently toss to coat. In the center of each plate, spread out about 1 tablespoon pickled onions, being careful to drain off excessive amounts of the pickle juice. Fan out the onions attractively to make a nice bed for the tuna. Drape 2 slices of tuna over the onions, and place 2 tuna cubes near the edge. Garnish with the lettuce. Drizzle with herb vinaigrette and serve immediately, while the tuna is cold.

Notes: Grind yellow mustard seeds in an electric spice mill, or use a mortar and pestle. Purchased mustard powder is a much tamer spice, making it well worth the effort to grind your own.

Spring onions are not necessarily a product of the spring season or a particular type of onion; rather they are immature onion bulbs, usually from white onions, sold fresh, with their greens still attached (they are sometimes called green onions). Spring onions tend to be milder than full-sized onions. Scallions—onions that have been harvested before their white base has swelled into a round bulb—are milder and smaller than spring onions.

SESAME-MUSTARD SEED DRESSING

1/2 cup plus 2 tablespoons CANOLA OIL

2 teaspoons SESAME OIL

2 tablespoons plus 2 1/4 teaspoons RICE WINE VINEGAR

1 tablespoon SOY SAUCE

1 EGG YOLK

2 teaspoons HONEY

1 tablespoon plus 1 teaspoon finely ground YELLOW MUSTARD SEEDS (see Notes)

1/4 teaspoon chopped GARLIC

2 1/2 teaspoons GINGER JUICE (see Note, page 90)

Fine SEA SALT and freshly ground BLACK PEPPER

HERB VINAIGRETTE

2 tablespoons chopped FRESH CHIVES

1 tablespoon chopped FRESH PARSLEY

1 teaspoon chopped FRESH TARRAGON

3 tablespoons extra-virgin OLIVE OIL

2 teaspoons CHAMPAGNE VINEGAR

Fine SEA SALT and freshly ground BLACK PEPPER

1 pound very fresh TUNA LOIN

1/4 pound (2 quarts) MIXED BABY GREENS (mesclun)

SERVES 8 AS AN APPETIZER

Salmon Ravioli
WITH AVOCADO MOUSSE

TOMATO-BASIL GELÉE

1 1/2 grams (about 1/2 sheet) LEAF GELATIN (see Sources, page 337)

1/2 cup TOMATO WATER (see page 329)

4 teaspoons CHAMPAGNE

1/4 cup BASIL OIL (see page 330)

Fine SEA SALT and freshly ground BLACK PEPPER

MUSTARD-DILL CREAM

2 1/2 tablespoons DIJON MUSTARD

2 tablespoons chopped FRESH DILL

1 tablespoon plus 2 teaspoons SUGAR

1 tablespoon fresh LEMON JUICE

1 teaspoon extra-virgin OLIVE OIL

2/3 cup HEAVY CREAM

Fine SEA SALT and freshly ground BLACK PEPPER

AVOCADO MOUSSE

2 ripe AVOCADOS

Fresh JUICE of 2 LIMES

CAYENNE PEPPER

Fine SEA SALT and freshly ground BLACK PEPPER

2 tablespoons diced SHALLOT

2 tablespoons diced RED BELL PEPPER

SALMON

3/4 pound CURED SALMON, thinly sliced (see page 328, or use purchased cured or smoked salmon)

SERVES 12 TO 14 AS AN APPETIZER

MARIO LOHNINGER We serve this as an *amuse bouche* at the restaurant. *Amuses bouches* are hard to figure out, especially for lunch, when you have to be able to serve them quickly. You need something that is quick to put on the plate, and something mainstream that everyone will like. This works well. It's fun and special enough, but can also be prepared an hour or two in advance.

1. Prepare the gelée: Place the gelatin in a dish of cold water, and let it soak until pliable, about 5 minutes. Transfer to a paper towel and pat dry.

2. Combine the tomato water and the Champagne in a saucepan, and warm the mixture over medium-low heat. Add the softened gelatin and heat gently, whisking constantly, until the gelatin has dissolved (do not let the mixture boil). Strain into a bowl and refrigerate until gelled, about 2 hours.

3. Whisk the basil oil into the gelée, 1 tablespoon at a time, until the gelée is broken up, green, and lightly flavored with basil. Season it with salt and pepper, and set it aside.

4. Prepare the mustard-dill cream: Combine the mustard, dill, sugar, and lemon juice in a bowl, and whisk until the sugar has dissolved. Whisking constantly, drizzle in the olive oil. Whisk until smoothly combined.

5. Using an electric mixer or a whisk, whip the cream to form soft peaks. Set aside 1/4 cup of the whipped cream, and fold the rest into the mustard mixture. Season with salt and pepper, and set it aside.

6. Scoop the avocado flesh out of its skin and push it through a fine-mesh strainer into a bowl. Season with the lime juice and with cayenne pepper, salt, and black pepper to taste. Add the shallot and red bell pepper. Gently fold the reserved 1/4 cup whipped cream into the avocado mixture.

7. To assemble, lay out the slices of salmon and use a 4- or 5-inch cookie cutter to cut them into rounds (or place a dish of this diameter on the salmon and use the tip of a sharp knife to trace around the edge of the dish). Place a dollop (about 1 1/2 teaspoonfuls) of avocado mousse in the center of each salmon round. Fold each round into a half-moon. Spoon 2 tablespoons of the gelée onto the center of each plate and spread it out thinly. Place a ravioli on top. Use two small spoons to form the mustard-dill cream into an oval quenelle, and place one on top of each ravioli.

Mackerel "Herring Style"
WITH CUCUMBER-AND-BIBB-LETTUCE VINAIGRETTE

MACKEREL TARTARE

6 ounces skinless MACKEREL FILLETS

1 very small GARLIC CLOVE

Fine SEA SALT

3 tablespoons CRÈME FRAÎCHE

1 teaspoon chopped FRESH DILL

1/2 teaspoon PREPARED
     HORSERADISH

1/4 teaspoon CHAMPAGNE VINEGAR

Pinch of ground toasted CARAWAY
     SEEDS (see Note, page 100)

1/4 cup finely diced CUCUMBER

1/4 cup finely diced COOKED BEET

1/4 cup finely diced APPLE

Freshly ground BLACK PEPPER

VINAIGRETTE

1 head BIBB LETTUCE

3/4 cup seeded, diced CUCUMBER

1/2 cup packed PARSLEY LEAVES

Pinch of ASCORBIC ACID (optional;
     see Note, page 18)

1 tablespoon fresh LEMON JUICE

1 tablespoon CHAMPAGNE VINEGAR

Fine SEA SALT and freshly ground
     BLACK PEPPER

3 tablespoons CANOLA OIL

2 tablespoons extra-virgin OLIVE OIL

3 1/2 ounces (about 3 1/2 cups) MIXED
     BABY GREENS (mesclun)

SALMON ROE, for garnish

SERVES 4 AS AN APPETIZER

DAVID BOULEY Mario and I wanted to put fresh herring on the menu, but we couldn't find a consistent source for the best product from the North Sea. So we came up with this dish using mackerel, an underused fish in this country. When you marinate the raw mackerel, it becomes very mellow in flavor. It's a clean-tasting fish, not a bit "fishy" or strong. We marinate the mackerel in Bibb lettuce and cucumber juices, then mix it with beet and apple for sweetness and a little crunch. It's both light and refreshing.

1. Cut the thin ends off the mackerel fillets and set them aside. Cut the thick parts of the fillets crosswise into 8 thin, wide slices. Lay the slices flat on a plate, wrap tightly with plastic wrap, and refrigerate.

2. Roughly dice the thin ends of the fillets. Using a mortar and pestle, smash the garlic and a pinch of salt into a paste.

3. In a bowl, whisk together the crème fraîche, dill, horseradish, vinegar, caraway, and garlic paste. Gently stir in the diced mackerel, cucumber, beet, and apple. Season with salt and pepper. (Do not mix too much or the salad will turn pink from the beet.)

4. Prepare the vinaigrette: In an electric juicer, juice the lettuce, cucumber, and parsley (alternatively, puree the vegetables in a food processor or blender, adding a little water if necessary). Add a pinch of ascorbic acid, if desired, to keep the juice bright green. You should have 3/4 cup juice. Whisk in the lemon juice, vinegar, and salt and pepper to taste. Whisking constantly, drizzle in the oils and whisk until combined. Set aside 1/4 cup of this vinaigrette for the salad greens.

5. Pour the remaining vinaigrette into a shallow, wide bowl. Marinate the mackerel slices in the vinaigrette at room temperature for at least 10 and no more than 20 minutes. Season the slices with salt and pepper.

6. To serve, toss the greens with 3 tablespoons of the reserved vinaigrette. Make two small oval mounds of the diced mackerel tartare in the center of each plate. Top each mound with a mackerel slice. Spoon the remaining vinaigrette on top of and around the mackerel. Garnish with the baby greens and salmon roe.

Coriander-and-Pepper-Crusted Monkfish

WITH GARGANELLI AND TOMATO BROTH

FENNEL CONFIT

3 medium FENNEL BULBS (about
2 1/4 pounds total)

2 cups CANOLA OIL

1/2 cup OLIVE OIL

One 2-inch-long piece FRESH
GINGER, halved

1/2 LEMON, halved

1 large KAFFIR LIME LEAF
(optional; see Notes, page 148)

1 small BAY LEAF, preferably fresh

7 ounces SEA BEANS, rinsed
(optional; see Note)

TOMATO BROTH

2 tablespoons extra-virgin OLIVE OIL

1 cup sliced ONION

2 SHALLOTS, sliced

Fine SEA SALT and freshly ground
BLACK PEPPER

3 large TOMATOES (about 1 1/2 pounds
total), cored and roughly chopped

3 GARLIC CLOVES, chopped

1/2 cup DRY WHITE WINE

3 tablespoons DRY VERMOUTH

2 cups CHICKEN STOCK (see
page 333) or canned low-sodium
chicken broth

1 cup TOMATO WATER (see page 329)

3 FRESH BASIL STEMS

1 teaspoon CORIANDER SEEDS

1 BAY LEAF, preferably fresh

Fresh JUICE of 1/2 LEMON

MARIO LOHNINGER This is a light summertime dish made with a tomato consommé and fennel confit, and finished with a little pesto. The monkfish has a coating of coriander and peppercorns. It's a little crunchy and has a spicy bite that works well with the sweetness of the tomatoes. You can use purchased pasta if you don't want to make the garganelli, but make sure it's a nice, thick, fresh pasta that will soak up the flavors.

1. Preheat the oven to 200°F.

2. Trim the fennel bulbs and halve them lengthwise. Remove the core from each half by making a V-shaped cut around it. Use a mandoline or a sharp knife to thinly slice the fennel crosswise. Place the slices in a baking dish, and cover with the canola and olive oils. Add the ginger, lemon halves, kaffir lime leaf, if using, and bay leaf. Bake, uncovered, until the fennel is perfectly soft and flavored by the aromatics in the oil, 1 1/2 to 2 hours. Let cool.

3. If using the sea beans, bring a pot of water to a boil and salt it until it tastes like seawater (about 2 teaspoons per quart). Fill a bowl with water and ice. Blanch the sea beans in the boiling water until crisp-tender, 1 to 2 minutes. Drain and immediately transfer to the bowl of ice water. Allow to cool, and then drain. Set them aside.

4. Prepare the tomato broth: Heat a large pot over medium heat and add the olive oil. Add the onion and shallots, season with salt and pepper, and cook until tender and translucent, about 7 minutes. Add the tomatoes and garlic, and cook without browning, stirring occasionally, until the garlic is tender, 2 minutes. Pour in the white wine and vermouth, bring the liquid to a simmer, and cook until reduced by half, about 10 minutes. Add the chicken stock, tomato water, basil stems, coriander seeds, and bay leaf. Cook gently until the flavor is concentrated, about 45 minutes. Strain through a fine-mesh sieve, pushing on the solids to extract all the liquid. Correct the seasoning with salt, pepper, and the lemon juice. Set the broth aside.

1 recipe EGG PASTA DOUGH (see page 328), or 1 pound purchased fresh pasta

PESTO

2 cups packed FRESH BASIL LEAVES (from 1 large bunch)

2 small GARLIC CLOVES

2 teaspoons PINE NUTS

1/2 cup extra-virgin OLIVE OIL

1/4 cup grated PARMIGIANO-REGGIANO CHEESE

Fine SEA SALT and freshly ground BLACK PEPPER

MONKFISH

2 tablespoons CORIANDER SEEDS

2 teaspoons BLACK PEPPERCORNS

2 teaspoons WHITE PEPPERCORNS

4 MONKFISH FILLETS (3 to 4 ounces each)

Fine SEA SALT

2 tablespoons CANOLA OIL

2 tablespoons UNSALTED BUTTER

1/2 cup chopped FRESH CHIVES

SERVES 4 AS A FISH COURSE

5. To make the garganelli, cut the rolled pasta dough into 2-inch squares. Set each square on a wooden gnocchi roller, and place a chopstick across the tip of one corner of the dough. Roll up from one corner to its opposite corner, so you get a little ribbed cylinder. (Alternatively, you may roll up the dough on a chopstick without using a gnocchi roller.)

6. Prepare the pesto: Combine the basil, garlic, and pine nuts in a food processor or blender, and process to a rough puree. With the motor running, drizzle in the olive oil. Add the cheese, and salt and pepper to taste, and process to combine.

7. Drain the fennel (if desired, reserve the oil for another use, such as dressing salads or pasta), and place it in a large bowl. Toss in the sea beans, if using, and stir in enough pesto to lightly coat the vegetables. Cover to keep warm.

8. Toast the coriander seeds in a dry pan until golden brown and fragrant, 2 minutes. Crush them roughly in a coffee grinder, and then transfer them to a wide, shallow bowl. Combine the black and white peppercorns, and toast them in a pan until fragrant, 2 to 3 minutes. Use the coffee grinder to very coarsely grind the pepper. Stir the pepper into the coriander, and set aside.

9. Bring a large pot of water to a boil and salt it until it tastes like seawater (about 2 teaspoons per quart). Cook the garganelli until it is al dente, then drain well. Add the garganelli to the fennel mixture. Cover to keep warm.

10. Warm the tomato broth over low heat.

11. Preheat the oven to 425°F.

12. Season the monkfish with salt. Heat two large ovenproof sauté pans over high heat. Roll the monkfish in the cracked spices, and shake off the excess. Add 1 tablespoon canola oil to each pan, and when it is hot, add the monkfish. Sear the fillets, about 2 minutes, then turn them over. Put the pans in the oven and roast until the fish feels solid to the touch, approximately 3 minutes. Transfer the pans back to the stove over medium-high heat. Add 1 tablespoon butter to each pan, and baste the fish until the butter begins to brown. Remove the fish from the pans and roll each fillet in the chopped chives. Let rest for 1 minute before slicing into medallions.

13. To serve, place some fennel confit in the center of a shallow soup plate. Lay pieces of pasta around the circumference. Place 1 sliced fillet on the plate, and spoon the tomato broth around all.

Note: Sea beans, also known as samphire, salicornia, or glasswort, are thin, branchy green plants with a saline crispness. They grow on the coasts of both the Atlantic and Pacific Oceans (as well as in Europe). Sea beans are sold fresh from summer through fall, and are also available pickled and jarred in gourmet food stores.

Maine Lobster

WITH WILD MUSHROOMS, SPINACH TORTELLINI, AND SAFFRON-CURRY BROTH

SPINACH-MUSHROOM TORTELLINI

2 1/2 ounces HEN-OF-THE-WOODS MUSHROOMS

3 ounces (about 6 medium) SHIITAKE MUSHROOMS

2 ounces (8 or 9) CHANTERELLE MUSHROOMS

3 1/2 ounces WHITE MUSHROOMS

2 tablespoons UNSALTED BUTTER

1 SHALLOT, minced

Fine SEA SALT and freshly ground BLACK PEPPER

2 tablespoons HEAVY CREAM

1/2 teaspoon fresh LEMON JUICE, or more to taste

1 GARLIC CLOVE, smashed to a paste

2 ounces (1 packed cup) SPINACH LEAVES

1 teaspoon finely chopped FRESH TARRAGON

CORNMEAL, for dusting the pan

1 recipe EGG PASTA DOUGH (see page 328), or 1 pound purchased fresh lasagna noodles

1 EGG WHITE, beaten

4 live LOBSTERS, about 1 1/4 pounds each

There is a lot going on in this dish, and not much of it is Austrian, save for the mushrooms and spinach in the tortellini. But Austrians love curry sauces and often borrow those flavors from the East. Here the lobster is set off with an earthy, spicy curry sauce tinged with ginger, lemongrass, kaffir lime, and saffron, and sweetened with fresh mango and pineapple. The tortellini make it a spectacular dish, but they aren't strictly necessary; basmati rice would also make a fine accompaniment.

NOTES FROM THE KITCHEN If you can't find hen-of-the-woods or chanterelle mushrooms, substitute oyster, cremini, or extra shiitake.

1. Prepare the tortellini filling: Place all the mushrooms in a food processor and pulse until they are the size of small pebbles (do not reduce them to a paste). In a sauté pan over medium heat, cook 1 tablespoon of the butter until the white milk solids fall to the bottom of the pan and turn nut-brown. Add the shallot, season with salt and pepper, and cook, stirring often, until the shallot is softened and translucent, 2 to 3 minutes. Add the mushrooms and season again with salt and pepper. Cook until the mushrooms release their juices, then begin to look dry, 7 to 10 minutes. Add the cream and cook until slightly thickened, about 3 minutes. Season with the lemon juice to taste, and set aside to cool.

2. Heat a clean sauté pan over medium heat. Add the remaining 1 tablespoon butter and when it foams, add the garlic. Let cook for a minute, then add the spinach. Season with salt and pepper, and toss until wilted, 1 minute. Transfer the spinach to a cutting board. When it is cool, chop the spinach very fine, almost to a paste. Combine the mushrooms with the spinach, and add the tarragon. Season with salt and pepper if necessary.

SAFFRON-CURRY SAUCE

2 tablespoons CANOLA OIL, plus extra for the lobster heads

1 cup chopped ONION

1/3 cup chopped CARROT

1/4 cup chopped FENNEL

1/4 cup chopped CELERY

1/4 cup chopped PARSNIP

2 WHITE MUSHROOMS, sliced

2 PLUM TOMATOES, sliced

1/2 cup chopped FRESH PINEAPPLE

1/2 cup diced FRESH MANGO

1/2 stalk LEMONGRASS, smashed with the side of a knife and cut into 2-inch lengths

One 1-inch-long piece FRESH GINGER

2 small GARLIC CLOVES, chopped

1 WHOLE STAR ANISE

1 teaspoon SAFFRON THREADS

1/2 cup DRY VERMOUTH

1 tablespoon plus 2 teaspoons CURRY POWDER

1 3/4 cups CHICKEN STOCK (see page 333) or canned low-sodium chicken broth

1/2 cup DRY WHITE WINE

3 KAFFIR LIME LEAVES (see Notes, page 148)

7 tablespoons UNSALTED BUTTER

1 tablespoon FRESH CILANTRO LEAVES, sliced into thin strips

Fresh LEMON JUICE, to taste

1/2 MANGO, diced

3. Assemble the tortellini: Scatter cornmeal over a large baking sheet. Lay out the rolled pasta dough and cut it into 2-inch squares. Place a small dollop of spinach-mushroom filling (the size of a quarter) in the center of each square. Brush beaten egg white around the filling and fold the squares diagonally into triangles, pressing with your fingers to seal the edges and making sure there are no air bubbles. Pull up the corners of the long side of the triangle, and pinch them together to form tortellini. Place them on the prepared baking sheet. As you work, cover the finished tortellini with a towel so they don't dry out. Set the sheet of tortellini aside.

4. Next, cook the lobsters: Fill a bowl with water and ice. Bring a large pot of water to a boil and salt it until it tastes like seawater (about 2 teaspoons per quart). To kill the lobsters, insert a thin, sharp knife between their eyes and down through their heads, or briefly hold their heads in the boiling water. Separate the lobster heads from their tails by twisting them off at the abdomen; twist off the claws. Set the heads and bodies aside for the curry sauce. Drop the tails and claws into the boiling water, and poach until slightly underdone, about 4 1/2 minutes for the tails and 5 minutes for the claws. (To test for doneness, break off the small pincer beneath the claw to expose the meat. The flesh should remain intact, feel somewhat firm to the touch, and just be starting to turn opaque.) Drain, and immediately transfer to the ice water.

5. When the lobster is cool, use the back of a large knife or cleaver to smash the claw shells. Remove the claw meat intact. Use a strong set of kitchen shears to cut down the underside of the tail, and remove the tail meat. Rinse the meat and refrigerate it, covered, until ready to use.

6. Preheat the oven to 425°F.

7. Prepare the saffron-curry sauce: Brush the reserved lobster heads and bodies with oil, and place them on a baking sheet. Roast until the shells brown around the edges, about 20 minutes. Set them aside.

8. Heat the 2 tablespoons oil in a large saucepan over medium heat. Add the onion, carrot, fennel, celery, parsnip, and mushrooms, and cook gently until the vegetables are soft but not brown, 10 minutes. Add the plum tomatoes, pineapple, mango, lemongrass, ginger, garlic, and star anise. Cook, stirring occasionally, until the tomatoes, pineapple, and mango have broken down, about 20 minutes.

9. Meanwhile, crush the saffron and steep it in a small dish with the Vermouth, 5 minutes.

10. Add the curry powder to the vegetables and cook, stirring, for 30 seconds. Then pour in the chicken stock, $3/4$ cup water, the wine, and the saffron mixture. Heat the liquid gently, scraping the sides and bottom of the pan with a wooden spoon. Add the roasted lobster shells and kaffir lime leaves, and simmer the sauce until its flavor is concentrated, about 2 hours. Pour the sauce through a fine-mesh sieve into another saucepan, and set it aside.

11. Gently melt 4 tablespoons of the butter in a saucepan over medium-low heat. Add the cold lobster and allow it to heat through, about 5 minutes.

12. Gently warm the curry sauce over low heat. Add the remaining 3 tablespoons butter, the cilantro, and lemon juice to taste. In another saucepan, warm the diced mango with a few tablespoons of the curry sauce.

13. Bring a large pot of water to a boil and salt it until it tastes like seawater (about 2 teaspoons per quart). Cook the tortellini in the boiling water, 5 minutes. Drain and keep warm.

14. Prepare the mushrooms: Heat a sauté pan over medium heat, add the butter, and cook until the white milk solids fall to the bottom of the pan and turn nut-brown, 5 minutes. Add the mushrooms and season with salt and pepper. Cook, stirring, until the mushrooms begin to soften, about 5 minutes. Then add the chicken stock, bay leaf, and thyme. Simmer until the mushrooms are tender, about 7 minutes; then add the spinach and cook, stirring, until wilted, 2 minutes. Add the tortellini to the pan and gently reheat the pasta.

15. Arrange some tortellini and mushrooms in the center of each plate. Top with pieces of lobster. Scatter some diced mango on top of each piece of lobster. Spoon a little of the saffron-curry sauce around the plate, and serve.

WILD MUSHROOMS

2 tablespoons UNSALTED BUTTER

$1/4$ pound HONSHIMEJI or SHIITAKE MUSHROOMS

Fine SEA SALT and freshly ground BLACK PEPPER

$1/4$ cup CHICKEN STOCK or broth (see page 333)

1 BAY LEAF, preferably fresh

1 FRESH THYME SPRIG

3 ounces ($1^1/2$ cups packed) baby SPINACH LEAVES

SERVES 4 TO 6 AS A MAIN COURSE

Mushroom Goulash
WITH CHIVE DUMPLINGS

CHIVE DUMPLINGS

2 cups roughly chopped FRESH
    CHIVES (1-inch lengths)

2 cups FRESH PARSLEY LEAVES

1/2 cup SOUR CREAM

1/2 cup CRÈME FRAÎCHE

Fine SEA SALT and freshly ground
    BLACK PEPPER

3 large EGGS

3 large EGG YOLKS

2 3/4 cups ALL-PURPOSE FLOUR

Freshly grated NUTMEG

Freshly ground WHITE PEPPER

MUSHROOM GOULASH

4 tablespoons UNSALTED BUTTER

2 SHALLOTS, cut into very small
    cubes

1 GARLIC CLOVE, minced

1/4 pound CHANTERELLE or pied de
    mouton MUSHROOMS, trimmed

1/4 pound BLACK TRUMPET
    MUSHROOMS, trimmed

MARIO LOHNINGER In summer we collect a lot of mushrooms in the woods around my parents' house near Salzburg. Serving a mushroom goulash highlights all the different varieties you can find, especially the chanterelles and porcini. We serve it for lunch, as a side dish, or sometimes as an appetizer. You can make it a vegetarian dish, but I love the flavor of the chicken stock.

1. Prepare the chive paste: Place the chives, parsley, sour cream, crème fraîche, and salt and pepper to taste in a blender and blend until smooth.

2. To prepare the dumplings, place 1 cup plus 2 tablespoons of the chive paste in a bowl, and whisk in the eggs and egg yolks (reserve the rest of the chive paste). Use a rubber spatula to fold in the flour, nutmeg, a generous amount of salt, and white pepper. (This dough should taste highly seasoned, as cooking will mellow it.)

3. Bring a large pot of water to a boil and salt it until it tastes like seawater (about 2 teaspoons per quart). Working in three batches, quickly push the dough through a colander or spätzle maker set over the boiling water. Stir the dumplings with a fork and poach them until the water returns to a boil. Then immediately scoop them out with the strainer and place them in another colander. Run cold water over the dumplings to stop them from cooking further. Set them aside.

4. Prepare the mushroom goulash: Melt the butter in a large sauté pan over medium heat. Add the shallots and garlic, and cook without browning, stirring occasionally, until soft and translucent, 2 to 3 minutes. Add all the mushrooms and cook, stirring, until they release their juices, 6 to 7 minutes. Strain the mushroom mixture in a sieve set over a bowl. Add the paprika to the pan, heat briefly, then add the strained mushroom juices. Whisk in the crème fraîche, and return the mushrooms to the pan. Heat gently to incorporate the flavors without letting the liquid reach a simmer. Season to taste with salt and pepper, and keep warm.

1/4 pound YELLOWFOOT CHANTERELLE, golden chanterelle, or chanterelle MUSHROOMS, trimmed

1/2 teaspoon SWEET HUNGARIAN PAPRIKA

2 tablespoons CRÈME FRAÎCHE

Fine SEA SALT and freshly ground BLACK PEPPER

4 tablespoons UNSALTED BUTTER

Fine SEA SALT and freshly ground BLACK PEPPER

6 tablespoons CHICKEN STOCK (see page 333)

1 1/2 tablespoons chopped MIXED FRESH HERBS (such as a mix of tarragon, parsley, chervil, basil, and marjoram)

SERVES 4 TO 6 AS A SIDE DISH, APPETIZER, OR LIGHT MAIN COURSE

5. Melt 2 tablespoons of the butter in a wide pan over medium heat, and cook until the white milk solids fall to the bottom of the pan and turn nut-brown, about 5 minutes. Add half the dumplings and season with salt and pepper. Cook, stirring, until brown around the edges, about 7 minutes. Then stir in 1 1/2 tablespoons of the remaining chive paste and 3 tablespoons of the chicken stock, and cook for 1 minute. Transfer the ingredients to a bowl. Wipe out the pan and repeat with the remaining 2 tablespoons butter, the rest of the dumplings, another 1 1/2 tablespoons chive paste, and the remaining 3 tablespoons chicken stock. Toss all the dumplings in the bowl, and sprinkle with the mixed herbs.

6. To serve, place some of the dumplings in the center of each plate, and spoon the mushroom goulash on top.

Whole Roasted Foie Gras

WITH CHERRIES

1 whole grade-A FOIE GRAS (about
    1½ pounds; see page 206)

Fine SEA SALT and freshly ground
    BLACK PEPPER

WONDRA FLOUR, for dusting (see
    Notes, page 250)

1 teaspoon CANOLA OIL

1 large SHALLOT, quartered

2 GARLIC CLOVES, smashed

2 sprigs FRESH THYME

1 sprig FRESH SAGE

2 BAY LEAVES, preferably fresh

8 FRESH BING CHERRIES, pitted

CHERRY SAUCE

3 tablespoons SUGAR

¾ cup PORT WINE

1½ pounds FRESH BING CHERRIES,
    pitted

2 tablespoons aged BALSAMIC
    VINEGAR

SERVES 10 TO 12 AS AN
APPETIZER

NOTES FROM THE KITCHEN Cherries, cooked with Port for sweetness and balsamic vinegar for acidity, are a perfect accompaniment in the summer season. But other fruits work well during other times of the year, such as poached quince in fall, oranges in winter, or rhubarb in spring. You can also serve the cherry sauce with seared foie gras slices if you prefer, or even with a foie gras terrine.

1. Preheat the oven to 375°F.

2. Clean the foie gras with a wet cloth. Set the foie gras with the smoothest side up, and score the top at 1-inch intervals in a checkerboard pattern. Season with salt and pepper, and dust lightly with Wondra all over. Heat a heavy ovenproof, flameproof skillet or casserole over high heat until it is very hot. Add the canola oil and then the foie gras, and sear it quickly on all sides, 2 to 3 minutes. Remove the skillet from the heat and transfer the foie gras to a plate.

3. Scatter the shallot, garlic, and herbs in the bottom of the casserole, and place the foie gras on top. Roast in the oven for about 5 minutes. Then baste it with the hot fat accumulating in the pan, and reduce the oven temperature to 350°F. Add the 8 pitted cherries and continue to roast until the foie gras is cooked to medium-well, 5 to 10 minutes. It should feel pretty soft but have a bit of resistance in the center. Let it rest for 5 minutes, until the internal temperature is 128°F.

4. Meanwhile, prepare the cherry sauce: Sprinkle the sugar evenly over the bottom of a heavy saucepan set over medium-high heat. Cook without stirring until the sugar melts and turns into an amber-brown caramel, 5 to

MARIO LOHNINGER It's always fun to roast a foie gras whole. People expect seared slices, and serving the whole thing is an exciting presentation at the table. Roasting gives the foie gras a more velvety texture than searing it, though you do lose a little of the flavor you would get from the caramelized crust. It's more delicate, which is a nice change. It's also convenient for serving ten or twelve people at a time, and is quite impressive at a dinner party.

7 minutes. Swirl the pan if the caramel browns unevenly. Pour the Port into the pan (stand back—it will spatter and boil up), and stir to dissolve the caramel. Raise the heat and simmer until the port is reduced and syrupy, about 7 minutes. Add the cherries and reduce the heat. Cook gently, covered, until the cherries are tender and the juice is quite thick, about 5 minutes. Remove from the heat and stir in 1 tablespoon of the foie gras fat from the roasting pan. Then stir in the balsamic vinegar.

5. Slice the foie gras and serve it with the cherry sauce.

FOIE GRAS *Foie gras* means "fat liver," and this luxuriously rich and tender meat is indeed the liver of a duck (or sometimes a goose) that has been force-fattened using a traditional process dating back three thousand years to ancient Egypt. Much of the world's best foie gras comes from southwestern France, but the southern regions of Hungary's Great Plains also boast a significant foie gras production, mainly from geese. Hungarian goose livers are enjoyed throughout Eastern Europe and are imported elsewhere. Increasingly, reputable producers are raising fowl for foie gras in this country, including some high-quality duck farms on Long Island and in New York's Hudson Valley.

Foie gras is sold raw (usually vacuum-packed) for cooking and can be roasted, seared, poached, or made into a terrine or pâté. You can also buy prepared foie gras terrine and pâté, though for the best quality, make sure there are no other meats or livers added. Truffles are always a fine addition, however.

A whole lobe of raw foie gras should be pale—practically white—and large. Look for grade-A liver, which has fewer veins. Let the foie gras come to room temperature, then split the lobes apart with your hands and gently pull out the veins, trying to avoid breaking the lobes. You can order foie gras from a good butcher, or by mail order (see Sources, page 337). Whenever you cook foie gras, save the fat left in the pan to use as a cooking oil. It will give other foods a rich flavor; potatoes fried in foie gras fat are especially wonderful.

Salt-Crusted Lamb

WITH GREEN TOMATO JAM

MARIO LOHNINGER This is a traditional dish from Salzburg, my home-town. Salzburg used to be famous for its salt; that's how it got its name. Salt was more powerful than gold—at one point it was a currency—and it made Salzburg a very rich town. So cooking things in salt is a common technique there.

You can put a salt crust on any meat. It's good with beef and venison, as well as lamb. First you surround the meat with herbs, pine needles, grape leaves, or hay, then you cover it in a salt crust. The salt makes the herb flavors sink into the meat and cooks it gently so it comes out per-fect and tender. The thing is to make a very stiff dough, as stiff as you can work with. Anything too wet will oversalt the meat.

You can serve this lamb with anything, but the green tomato jam is especially good—a nice relish to make at the end of summer, when the last tomatoes are left on the vine.

1. Prepare the tomato jam: Place the coriander seeds in a small skillet and toast them over medium-high heat until fragrant, about 2 minutes. Transfer them to a mortar or electric spice mill and grind coarsely. Set them aside.

2. Place 1/2 cup water in the bottom of a heavy saucepan. Add the corn syrup to this pool, and mound the sugar over it. Warm the mixture over low heat, stirring constantly, until all the sugar has dissolved, 3 to 5 min-utes. Raise the heat to high and simmer, stirring and scraping around the sides of the pan, until the sugar begins to darken, 6 to 8 minutes. Cook, stirring, until the sugar is amber colored and caramelized, 7 minutes. Then add the onions and olive oil (stand back—the caramel will sputter). Reduce the heat to medium and cook, stirring, until the onions begin to soften, 3 to 5 minutes. Add the sherry vinegar and stir and scrape the sides of the pan, loosening any crystals that have hardened, stirring until the liquid is smooth. Add the green tomatoes, ground coriander seeds, lemon slices, and bay leaves. Season with the salt, and add pepper to taste. Raise the heat and bring the mixture to a simmer. Cook gently until the tomatoes begin to break down but have not completely lost their shape, 15 to 20 minutes.

GREEN TOMATO JAM

1/2 teaspoon CORIANDER SEEDS

1 teaspoon LIGHT CORN SYRUP

3/4 cup SUGAR

2 small ONIONS, sliced

3 tablespoons extra-virgin OLIVE OIL

2 tablespoons SHERRY VINEGAR

2 pounds (about 5 large) GREEN TOMATOES, roughly chopped

1/2 LEMON, peeled, white pith removed, sliced crosswise

4 BAY LEAVES, preferably fresh

2 teaspoons fine SEA SALT, or to taste

Freshly ground BLACK PEPPER

SALT-CRUSTED LAMB

3 2/3 cups KOSHER SALT

1 1/2 cups ALL-PURPOSE FLOUR

6 large EGG WHITES

1 tablespoon CANOLA OIL

2 racks of BABY LAMB, frenched, about 4 pounds

Freshly ground BLACK PEPPER

2 cups loosely packed MIXED FRESH HERBS (any combination of basil, mint, thyme, rosemary, marjoram, sage—as great a variety as possible)

SERVES 4 AS A MAIN COURSE

3. Preheat the oven to 350°F.

4. Prepare the salt crust: In a small bowl, stir the kosher salt and flour together. In a separate bowl, whisk the egg whites until frothy; then whisk in the salt mixture. Work the mixture with your hands, adding water as necessary (about 2 tablespoons), until it resembles a crumbly dough.

5. Heat the canola oil in a large sauté pan over medium-high heat until it is very hot. Season the lamb with pepper, add it to the pan, and sear until brown, about 2 minutes on each side.

6. Spread a thin layer of the dough in a 9-by-13-inch metal pan. Sprinkle half of the fresh herbs over this, then arrange the racks of lamb on top. Cover with the rest of the fresh herbs, followed by the remaining dough, patting it around the lamb to form a crust (the crust should cover the meat completely, leaving only the rib bones exposed). Using an instant-read thermometer, make a hole in the crust over the center of one of the racks (so you can check the temperature of the meat as it cooks without break-ing the crust).

7. Bake for 15 minutes, or until an internal temperature of 130°F has been reached. Break the lamb out of the salt crust by pulling upward on the rib bones. Let the meat rest for a few minutes before slicing it. Serve the meat with the green tomato jam.

Braised Veal Shank

WITH PORCINI RISOTTO

VEAL

1 VEAL SHANK (about 4 ½ pounds)

4 GARLIC CLOVES, cut into matchsticks

2 sprigs FRESH MARJORAM

4 tablespoons UNSALTED BUTTER, softened

Fine SEA SALT and freshly ground BLACK PEPPER

1 large ONION, sliced ½ inch thick

10 PEARL ONIONS, blanched and peeled (see Note, page 58)

1 CARROT, thickly sliced

1 small CELERY ROOT, trimmed, quartered, and thickly sliced

1 PARSNIP, thickly sliced

¾ cup DRY WHITE WINE

1 large TOMATO

10 FRESH CHIVES, finely sliced

1 tablespoon chopped FRESH PARSLEY LEAVES

When fresh porcini mushrooms are available, you'll want to use them in everything. They have an earthy, pungent flavor that smells just like the forest at the end of August, when the leaves are starting to fall from the trees. Here they add meatiness and their pleasant slippery texture to risotto, which soaks up all that good rich flavor. While it's an ideal accompaniment to the braised veal shank, the risotto is also exceptional on its own, or as a side dish for roasted chicken or grilled steak.

DAVID BOULEY In the summer you can hike up to a little restaurant on a peak in the Austrian mountains, and they will usually serve you a hearty dish like this one. It's the kind of thing you do with a group, with everyone enjoying a drink of beer or wine on the terrace, taking in the view, and discussing the morning hike.

The trick to braising is to cook the meat slowly so the fibers soften and become tender, soaking up the collagen in the meat.

1. Preheat the oven to 500°F.

2. Using a thin, sharp paring knife, poke shallow holes in the veal shank at regular intervals. Push a piece of garlic or a single marjoram leaf deep into each hole, using all the garlic and marjoram. Rub 1 tablespoon of the soft butter over the veal roast, and season it well with salt and pepper.

3. Lay the onion rounds in a single layer on the bottom of a wide casserole, and then set the veal shank on top. Spread the pearl onions, carrot, celery root, and parsnip around the veal shank. Pour the white wine over the vegetables, and place the casserole in the oven. Roast, uncovered, for 30 minutes.

4. Check the pan and add some water if the wine has evaporated. Roast, basting with the pan juices every 45 minutes, until the meat is very tender, about 2 hours longer.

PORCINI MUSHROOM RISOTTO

4 to 5 cups CHICKEN STOCK (see page 333) or canned low-sodium chicken broth

4 GARLIC CLOVES

3 tablespoons UNSALTED BUTTER

1 cup chopped ONION

Fine SEA SALT and freshly ground BLACK PEPPER

1 1/4 cups ARBORIO RICE

1/2 cup DRY WHITE WINE

2 tablespoons extra-virgin OLIVE OIL

10 PORCINI MUSHROOMS, trimmed and diced

2 tablespoons MASCARPONE CHEESE

2 tablespoons finely chopped MIXED FRESH HERBS (such as tarragon, chervil, parsley, and chives)

1/4 cup grated PARMIGIANO-REGGIANO CHEESE

SERVES 4 TO 6 AS A MAIN COURSE

5. Meanwhile, peel the tomato: Fill a bowl with water and ice. Bring a saucepan of water to a boil. Use the tip of a knife to score the skin of the tomato with a small X, and blanch the tomato in the boiling water for 30 seconds. Transfer the tomato to the ice water to cool; then use a knife to peel off its skin. Core and halve the tomato, scoop out and discard the seeds, and dice the flesh.

6. Remove the veal shank from the pan and scoop out the vegetables and discard. Cover the meat to keep warm. Skim the fat from the pan juices, and strain the skimmed juices through a fine-mesh sieve.

7. Place the remaining 3 tablespoons butter in a pan over medium heat. Cook until the white milk solids fall to the bottom of the pan and turn nut-brown, about 5 minutes. Whisk in the strained veal juices, diced tomato, chives, and parsley. Set the sauce aside.

8. Prepare the risotto: Bring the chicken stock to a gentle simmer, and keep it over low heat. Mince 2 cloves of the garlic. Set a large saucepan over medium heat, add 2 tablespoons of the butter, and when it foams, add the onion. Season with salt and pepper, and cook gently, stirring occasionally, until the onions are soft and lightly golden, about 7 minutes. Add the minced garlic and cook, stirring, for another minute. Add the rice and cook, stirring, for 3 minutes. Pour in the white wine. When the wine has evaporated, add 1/2 cup of the hot chicken stock. Cook, stirring, until the stock has been absorbed. Repeat, adding the stock 1/2 cup at a time as soon as the previous addition has been absorbed.

9. Meanwhile, smash the remaining 2 garlic cloves with the side of a knife. Heat the olive oil in a pan over high heat and add the garlic. Add the porcini, season with salt and pepper, and cook, stirring, until the mushrooms are tender, about 5 minutes. Stir in the remaining 1 tablespoon butter.

10. When the rice is beginning to soften but the grains are still hard at the center, add the mushrooms. Pour some hot chicken stock into the mushroom pan, scrape the bits and juices up from the pan, and pour this into the rice. Continue stirring the risotto and adding stock until the rice is creamy and al dente, about 25 minutes total. Immediately before serving, stir in the mascarpone, herbs, and Parmigiano-Reggiano cheese.

11. Reheat the tomato-veal sauce over medium heat. Baste the shank with the sauce, and serve the veal with the risotto.

RISOTTO There are places in Austria where the food speaks of centuries of interchange with countries in the Middle East and with closer neighbors, particularly Italy, Germany, Hungary, the Czech Republic, and Switzerland. So it's no surprise that a canon of Italian (often referred to as "Venetian") recipes exists in Austrian cuisine. Though most people think of risotto only as Italian, it is quite commonly made in Austria as well. Pumpkin, asparagus, saffron, and wild mushroom risotto are favorites, seen on many modern-day Austrian menus.

Kaiserschmarrn

SWEET PANCAKES WITH RUM-SOAKED RAISINS

Kaiserschmarrn means "emperor's fluff," or "emperor's nonsense," and was named in honor of Kaiser Franz Joseph I. Neither fluffy nor nonsensical, this thick, sweet pancake is nonetheless delicious, filled with rum-soaked raisins and flavored with vanilla. It makes a very substantial dessert on its own, and is best served lightened up a bit with a fruit compote or sliced fresh plums, peaches, or nectarines.

1. Place the raisins in a small bowl and cover them with 1 1/2 tablespoons of the rum. Let sit for at least 4 hours, or preferably overnight.

2. Preheat the oven to 350°F.

3. In a bowl, whisk the egg yolks with the 2 tablespoons sugar until smooth and creamy. Add the sour cream, crème fraîche, vanilla seeds, and the remaining 2 tablespoons rum, and whisk until smooth. Using a rubber spatula, fold in the flour.

4. In a clean bowl of an electric mixer fitted with the whisk attachment, whip the egg whites until foamy. Add the salt and the remaining 1/2 cup sugar, and whip until stiff peaks form. Fold the egg whites into the batter.

5. Melt the butter in a 10-inch high-sided sauté pan (preferably a seasoned cast-iron pan), and when the butter foams, pour in the batter. Drain the raisins and sprinkle them over the top. Transfer the pan to the oven and bake until a knife inserted in the center comes out clean, 25 to 30 minutes.

6. Use two spoons to tear the Kaiserschmarrn into 6 equal pieces. Sprinkle with confectioners' sugar, and serve warm.

2 tablespoons GOLDEN RAISINS

3 1/2 tablespoons STROH RUM (see Note, page 298) or dark rum

5 large EGG YOLKS

1/2 cup plus 2 tablespoons SUGAR

1/2 cup SOUR CREAM

1/3 cup CRÈME FRAÎCHE

1 VANILLA BEAN, split in half lengthwise, seeds scraped out with a knife

3/4 cup sifted ALL-PURPOSE flour

8 large EGG WHITES

1/2 teaspoon SALT

1 tablespoon UNSALTED BUTTER

CONFECTIONERS' SUGAR, for serving

SERVES 6 AS DESSERT

Viennese Iced Coffee

WITH HIPPENSPIRALE

10 tablespoons (1 stick plus 2 tablespoons) UNSALTED BUTTER,
melted

1 cup CONFECTIONERS' SUGAR

3/4 cup ALL-PURPOSE FLOUR

2 large EGG WHITES

1/2 cup HEAVY CREAM

1 tablespoon SUGAR

1 pint VANILLA ICE CREAM

4 shots ESPRESSO (about 1 cup),
chilled

BITTERSWEET CHOCOLATE CURLS
(shaved with a vegetable peeler),
for garnish

ICED COFFEE SERVES 4 AS
DESSERT; MAKES 50 SPIRAL-
SHAPED *TUILES*

If whipped cream–capped hot coffees and mochas are de rigueur in Vienna's coffeehouses in the winter, fall, and spring, iced coffee is what one orders in the summertime. This one, with both whipped cream and ice cream, is substantial enough to serve as dessert. Pair it with Hippenspirale or other crisp cookies.

NOTES FROM THE KITCHEN *Tuiles* are traditionally made by curving the just-baked thin wafers over a wineglass or rolling pin so they resemble roof tiles when cooled. At the Danube, we cut these *tuiles* into long 8- by 1/2-inch rectangles, then wrap them around the handle of a wooden spoon to form strawlike spirals. To do this, you'll need to make a stencil: Use a craft knife to cut a long thin rectangle out of the middle of a piece of stiff cardboard or plastic. Place the stencil on a baking sheet, and spread the batter over the cutout so that the cookie is a perfect rectangle when you lift the cardboard. Reuse the same stencil for each cookie; then bake the cookies as directed. While they are still hot, spiral them around the handle of a wooden spoon. Made either way, they are the perfect crunchy, fragile accompaniment to Viennese iced coffee.

1. Gently mix the butter, confectioners' sugar, flour, and egg whites to-gether in a bowl. Cover with plastic wrap and let sit for 2 hours at room temperature.
2. Preheat the oven to 350°F.
3. Line several baking sheets with parchment paper or nonstick liners. Dip a spoon or spatula in water, and spread about 1/2 tablespoon of the batter into a very thin round on the baking sheet to form each *tuile*. Bake only about 6 *tuiles* at a time, since you need to mold them when they are still hot. Bake until they are light golden brown, about 7 minutes.

4. Transfer the baking sheet to a rack, immediately lift up a corner of a *tuile* with a knife, and drape the cookie over a rolling pin or the side of a wine bottle to mold it into a curve. As soon as the shape holds, transfer the cookie to a platter. Repeat until all the *tuiles* are made.

5. For the iced coffee, whip the cream with the sugar in a mixing bowl until it holds soft peaks.

6. Using two teaspoons to form small oval scoops of ice cream, place 3 scoops into each of four martini glasses, wineglasses, or tall parfait glasses. Pour a shot of cold espresso into each glass. Top with a dollop of whipped cream, and garnish with chocolate curls. Serve with the *tuiles*.

Signature
Dishes

All of these cocktail recipes were created by Albert Trummer (see page 226), the Danube's original bartender—or, as Albert likes to say, "bar chef." He is quite right to favor this term; with his ingenious use of homemade fruit purees, infused syrups, and fresh herbs, he is indeed a "chef" in his own right. When he started at the Danube in 1998, Albert, from Graz, Austria, had already spent ten years training with some of Europe's most celebrated bartenders. This experience, coupled with his brilliant creativity, made him ideal to put together a signature cocktail list for the Danube. These are some of his favorites.

The Danube Cocktail
ELDERFLOWER CHAMPAGNE

2 ounces D'Arbo elderflower syrup (see Sources, page 337)
4 ounces Schlumberger Cuvée Klimt Austrian sparkling wine (or other dry sparkling wine)

Pour the elderflower syrup, according to taste, into a cocktail shaker. Add 1 cup cracked or crushed ice and the sparkling wine, stir gently, and strain into a champagne flute.

Rose Fashion

1 sugar cube
1 dash Angostura bitters
1 drop rose water
3 ounce Woodford Reserve (or other premium bourbon)
Twist of thin-cut lemon peel

1. Place the sugar cube in the bottom of a double old-fashioned glass or other heavy-bottomed tumbler. Add the Angostura bitters, the rose water, and a teaspoonful of water. Crush and stir the sugar with a muddler or the handle of a sturdy wooden spoon until the sugar has dissolved.
2. Add the bourbon and 2 or 3 large ice cubes, and stir 20 times. Twist the lemon peel over the top and serve.

Bouley's Truffle Martini

3 ounces Richard Hennessy cognac
1½ teaspoons Grand Marnier, preferably Centenaire
1½ teaspoons fresh lime juice
7 thin slices white or black truffles

1. In a cocktail shaker, combine the cognac, Grand Marnier, lime juice, and 2 of the truffle slices. Add 1 cup cracked or crushed ice, shake vigorously for 10 seconds, then strain into a chilled cocktail glass.
2. Serve on a plate with the remaining truffle slices fanned out around the base of the glass.

Blueberry Martini

½ ounce freshly squeezed lime juice
½ ounce simple syrup (see Note, page 229)
8 blueberries, plus additional for garnish
2 ounces Montecristo Rum (or other aged, medium-bodied rum)
Mint sprigs, for garnish (optional)

1. Pour the lime juice and the simple syrup into a cocktail shaker, add the blueberries, and crush them with a muddler or the handle of a sturdy wooden spoon.
2. Add the rum and 1 cup cracked or crushed ice, shake vigorously for 10 seconds, and strain into a chilled cocktail glass. Garnish, if desired, with a few blueberries impaled on a small sprig of mint.

Raspberry Dream

8 fresh raspberries

1 ounce fresh lime juice

$1/2$ ounce simple syrup (see Note)

2 ounces añejo tequila, such as Chinaco or Herradura

1 teaspoon Grand Marnier

1. In a food processor or blender, puree the raspberries with the lime juice and simple syrup.

2. Pour the mixture into a cocktail shaker and add the tequila and Grand Marnier. Add 1 cup cracked or crushed ice, shake vigorously for 10 seconds, and strain into a champagne flute.

Big Apple

2 green apples, cored and roughly chopped

$1/2$ ounce fresh lime juice

$1/2$ ounce simple syrup (see Note)

2 ounces Grey Goose or other premium vodka

1 ounce Cointreau

1. Place the apples in a blender or food processor and puree, adding a little water if necessary. Measure out $1^1/2$ ounces (use the rest for another purpose).

2. Return the $1^1/2$ ounces apple puree to the blender or food processor and add the lime juice and simple syrup. Blend, then pass through the mixture through a fine-mesh strainer.

3. Put the mixture in a cocktail shaker along with the vodka and the Cointreau, add 1 cup cracked or crushed ice, and shake vigorously for 10 seconds. Strain into a chilled cocktail glass and serve.

Note: To make simple syrup, half fill a clean bottle with superfine ("bar") sugar, top off with water, and shake vigorously until the sugar dissolves. Let it settle and shake again briefly to dissolve any residual grains.

Klimt's Cherry Cocktail

7 fresh, pitted cherries

1 ounce Grey Goose or other premium vodka

1 ounce fresh lime juice

$1/2$ ounce simple syrup (see Note)

2 ounces Schlumberger Cuvée Klimt Austrian sparkling wine (or other dry sparkling wine)

1. In a cocktail shaker, crush the cherries with a muddler or the handle of a sturdy wooden spoon.

2. Add the vodka, lime juice, and simple syrup. Pour in 1 cup cracked or crushed ice, shake vigorously for 10 seconds, then strain into a large, chilled cocktail glass and top with the sparkling wine.

Passion

4 passion fruit

1 ounce fresh lime juice

$1/4$ ounce añejo tequila, such as Chinaco or Herradura

$1/4$ ounce Cointreau

2 teaspoons simple syrup, or to taste (see Note)

2 ounces Moët & Chandon champagne (or other brut champagne)

1. Halve the passion fruit, scoop out the seeds and juicy pulp, and put it into a food processor or blender. Add the lime juice, tequila, Cointreau, and simple syrup. Blend well.

2. Pass the mixture through a fine-mesh strainer (for a fruitier flavor, this step can be omitted, retaining the seeds). Pour into a tall glass three-quarters full of cracked or crushed ice and top off with the champagne.

Oysters

WITH BEET SORBET AND SOUR CREAM

BEET SORBET

3 cups BEET JUICE (see Note)

1/2 cup plus 2 tablespoons
    BALSAMIC VINEGAR

Fresh JUICE of 1/2 LEMON,
    or to taste

Fine SEA SALT and freshly ground
    BLACK PEPPER

SOUR CREAM SAUCE

1/2 cup SOUR CREAM

5 teaspoons OYSTER LIQUOR
    (see page 231)

2 tablespoons TOMATO WATER
    (optional; see page 329)

1/2 teaspoon freshly squeezed
    LEMON JUICE

Fine SEA SALT and freshly ground
    BLACK PEPPER

12 BLUEPOINT OYSTERS, shucked,
    liquor reserved (see page 231)

SERVES 6 AS AN APPETIZER

In this favorite Danube *amuse bouche*, cool oysters are layered like a parfait with vibrant magenta beet sorbet and a cap of sour cream froth. Served in a martini glass, it's an oyster cocktail unlike any other.

DAVID BOULEY The beet sorbet is the most important part of this dish. It's what brings the oyster together with the sour cream foam, making a liaison between the two. It softens the saltwater from the oyster with its sweetness and mitigates the richness of the airy foam. It all comes together in the mouth. The thing that's important here is balance. Too much sorbet and sour cream and you won't taste the oyster. But a little bit of each is transcendent.

Of course you need good beets, ones with a deep flavor. Once you have that, the idea is to elevate them to the highest level. But elevating doesn't mean exploiting. You can make a silly chip out of a beet, which won't add anything to a dish, or you can maintain its integrity. The sorbet accomplishes that.

1. Prepare the beet sorbet: Combine the beet juice and vinegar in a saucepan, and season with the lemon juice, salt, and pepper. Bring to a simmer and cook over low heat until reduced to 1 1/2 cups, 20 to 30 minutes. Let cool, then refrigerate for at least 4 hours. Freeze the sorbet in an ice cream maker according to the manufacturer's instructions.

2. Just before serving, prepare the sour cream sauce: Combine the sour cream, oyster liquor, tomato water, if desired, and lemon juice in a blender. Season to taste with salt and pepper, and blend until very foamy.

3. To serve, place a scoop of beet sorbet in the bottom of each of six martini glasses. Place 2 oysters in each glass, and fill to the top with sour cream foam.

Note: If you don't have a juicer, you can buy fresh beet juice at a local juice bar or bottled at some larger health food stores.

SHUCKING OYSTERS Scrub the oyster shells with a brush under running water, preferably about 1 hour before shucking, and refrigerate them flat (in two layers if necessary). To shuck them, insert an oyster knife into the joint of the shell and twist the knife to loosen the shell. Holding the oyster upright, slide the knife along the top of the shell to detach the meat. Discard the upper shell and cut through the muscle that holds the oyster to the bottom shell. Strain the liquid through a sieve lined with several layers of cheesecloth. Pat the oyster with a clean towel to remove any grit from the flesh. Either pour the strained oyster liquor back over the oyster or save it for use in a recipe.

Marinated Sea Scallops
WITH PASSION FRUIT AND BLACK TRUFFLE

This intricate dish is a balancing act of flavors. At its heart are raw pearly-sweet scallops, which should be as fresh as possible. They are sharpened by a tart but bright passion fruit vinaigrette, countered with celery to add a crisp crunch and freshness, and given a softer bite and sweetness by some Granny Smith apple. Earthy truffle oil and sliced truffles contribute their own potent scent, just enough to meld the somewhat disparate-seeming ingredients without overpowering any of them.

NOTES FROM THE KITCHEN This has to be prepared just before serving, and the timing is everything. If the scallops are allowed to sit in the passion fruit dressing too long, they will toughen and "cook" like a ceviche. Keeping everything separate until the last minute will give you silky, soft scallops, which is what you want here.

This recipe works best with scallops purchased in the shell, which have a more delicate flavor. Either shell them at home (see page 251) or have the fishmonger do it for you.

1. Prepare the passion fruit vinaigrette: Halve the fruits and scoop out the pulp. Reserve the pulp of 1 fruit for garnish. Place the rest of the pulp in a blender or food processor and add the coconut milk, 1 tablespoon of the lemon juice, the lime juice, and salt and pepper to taste; pulse several times to combine. With the motor running, gradually pour in the canola oil and blend until the dressing is emulsified. Strain through a fine-mesh sieve and discard the solids. Set the vinaigrette aside.

2. In a bowl, whisk together the crème fraîche, 1¹/₂ teaspoons of the lemon juice, the shallot, and salt and pepper to taste. Set the sauce aside.

9 ripe PASSION FRUIT (see page 235)

3 tablespoons COCONUT MILK

2¹/₂ tablespoons fresh LEMON JUICE

1 tablespoon fresh LIME JUICE

Fine SEA SALT and freshly ground BLACK PEPPER

1¹/₄ cups CANOLA OIL

¹/₂ cup CRÈME FRAÎCHE

2 tablespoons minced SHALLOT

4 CELERY STALKS

1 teaspoon extra-virgin OLIVE OIL, plus additional for drizzling

¹/₂ teaspoon BLACK TRUFFLE OIL (see Sources, page 337)

6 large SEA SCALLOPS (see page 251)

FLEUR DE SEL, for garnish (see Note, page 53)

¹/₄ pound (about 2 quarts) MIXED SALAD GREENS, including mâche, yellow frisée, and celery leaves

1 GRANNY SMITH APPLE

1 small FRESH BLACK TRUFFLE (optional)

SERVES 6 AS AN APPETIZER

3. Bring a pot of water to a boil and salt it until it tastes like seawater (about 2 teaspoons per quart). Fill a bowl with water and ice. Peel the celery, pulling out the strings. Slice the celery very thin with a mandoline or a sharp knife. Blanch the celery in the boiling water for 30 seconds, then drain and immediately transfer to the ice water to cool. Drain well and transfer to a paper towel-lined plate. Blot the celery dry with more paper towels. Then transfer it to a bowl and toss with the 1 teaspoon olive oil, the truffle oil, and salt and pepper to taste.

4. A few minutes before serving time, slice the scallops crosswise into 5 or 6 thin rounds each. Season them with the remaining 1 tablespoon lemon juice, fleur de sel, pepper, and a drizzle of olive oil.

5. Place the greens in a bowl and drizzle them with some of the passion fruit vinaigrette. Julienne the apple by cutting it into very thin slices, then cutting the slices into very thin strips (you don't need to peel it). If using the truffle, shave it into thin, even slices with a truffle shaver or a mandoline.

6. Spread 1 tablespoon of the marinated celery on each of six plates. Divide the scallop slices among the plates. Drizzle some of the passion fruit vinaigrette on and around the scallops, and do the same with the crème fraîche sauce. Divide the greens among the plates and garnish each plate with a few slices of truffle, if desired, some apple, and a scattering of the reserved passion fruit pulp.

PASSION FRUIT
There is no replacement for the acidic tang of fresh, ripe passion fruit in this recipe, and they are not that hard to find. Gourmet stores usually have them, and even some large supermarkets carry them. Look for heavy, full-feeling fruit and let them ripen at room temperature for a few days until their skin has become crinkly.

Tyrolean Wine Soup
WITH FRESH TROUT AND SMOKED TROUT CRÊPES

CRÊPES

½ cup plus ½ tablespoon HEAVY CREAM

1 EGG, beaten

Fine SEA SALT and freshly ground WHITE PEPPER

2 tablespoons UNSALTED BUTTER, melted

TROUT FILLING

2 tablespoons CRÈME FRAÎCHE

2 tablespoons SOUR CREAM

Fresh LEMON JUICE, to taste

CAYENNE PEPPER, to taste

Fine SEA SALT and freshly ground BLACK PEPPER

3 ounces SMOKED TROUT, skin and bones removed, flaked

Tyrolean wine soup is a delicate first course from the South Tyrol. It is based on a good, full-bodied, preferably homemade consommé that is flavored with regional wine and then beaten with egg yolks for a foamy, sabayon-like texture. Traditionally the soup would be served simply, perhaps with toasted brioche croutons and a sprinkling of freshly grated nutmeg. This version is more involved, with the addition of fresh trout fillet and plump smoked trout crêpes floating in each bowl.

MARIO LOHNINGER Fish mousses and spreads are popular in Austria, especially in Salzburg. You can make them from any fish, but freshly smoked trout and salmon are the most common. They are usually served on bread or toast as a starter or a snack, or even as a light lunch. For this recipe you could float a crouton with the smoked trout mousse on top of the soup instead of making the crêpes, but wrapping it up in the crêpes is more refined.

1. Preheat the broiler. Line a baking sheet with parchment or waxed paper. In a bowl, whisk the cream into the beaten egg and season with salt and white pepper. Heat a seasoned ovenproof 9- or 10-inch crêpe pan or non-stick sauté pan over medium heat, and brush the bottom with a light coat of melted butter. Pour in enough batter to just cover the bottom, 2 to 3 tablespoons, swirling the batter as soon as it hits the pan. Allow to cook for a minute or two, until the bottom of the crêpe is browned, then place the pan under the broiler to cook the top, 1 minute. When the top is cooked through, turn the pan upside down over the prepared baking sheet and tap it, dropping the crêpe. Continue in the same manner, stacking the crêpes on the baking sheet with parchment or waxed paper layered between them. You will need 4 crêpes in good shape (you can freeze the rest, wrapped in plastic, leaving the parchment between the layers). Let cool completely before handling.

1 tablespoon UNSALTED BUTTER

1 tablespoon extra-virgin OLIVE OIL

½ cup diced BRIOCHE or white bread

1 boneless BROOK TROUT, head and tail removed, fillets separated and cut into 8 equal pieces

Fine SEA SALT and freshly ground WHITE PEPPER

2 EGG YOLKS

1 cup HEAVY CREAM

3 cups OXTAIL CONSOMMÉ (page 74) or best-quality purchased beef broth

1 cup RIESLING or dry white wine

Freshly grated NUTMEG

MICRO GREENS (such as cress and/or mustard greens), for garnish (optional)

SERVES 8 AS AN APPETIZER

2. Reduce the oven temperature to 275°F. To prepare the trout filling, mix the crème fraîche, sour cream, lemon juice, cayenne, and salt and pepper to taste in a bowl. Then fold in the trout.

3. Spoon a heaping tablespoon of trout filling onto the bottom third of each crêpe. Roll it up, trim the edges, and cut each roll into 4 pieces. Place the crêpe rolls on a baking sheet and set in the oven to warm.

4. Heat the butter and olive oil in a small skillet over medium-high heat. Add the bread and fry, stirring, until golden, about 5 minutes. Drain on paper towels and reserve for the garnish.

5. Fill a pot with an inch of water, set a steamer basket over the water, and bring to a boil. Season the fresh trout pieces with salt and white pepper. Place them in the steamer, cover, and cook until just done, 1 to 2 minutes. Remove the steamer, transfer the fish to a board, and use a small knife to carefully peel off the skin. Keep the water at a simmer.

6. In a bowl, whisk the egg yolks to break them up. Then add the cream and whisk for 30 seconds. Heat the consommé until it is very hot, and pour it into a metal mixing bowl that will fit partway into the pot of simmering water (you can also use a double boiler for this). Set the bowl over the simmering water. Add the Riesling and then gradually whisk in the cream mixture, making sure the eggs don't curdle. Keep whisking until the soup is frothy and thickened, about 3 minutes. Season with salt, white pepper, and nutmeg.

7. To serve, place a piece of trout fillet and 2 crêpe rolls in the center of each of eight wide bowls. Spoon the soup on and around them, making sure to include as much froth as possible. If necessary, whisk the soup to make more froth. Garnish with the bread cubes, and a scattering of micro greens, if desired.

Beet Salad

WITH CARAWAY SEEDS AND WALNUT OIL

1 pound BABY RED BEETS, trimmed but not peeled

1 tablespoon CANOLA OIL

2 sprigs FRESH THYME

1 BAY LEAF, preferably fresh

Fine SEA SALT and freshly ground BLACK PEPPER

1 teaspoon CARAWAY SEEDS

1/4 cup plus 2 teaspoons CHAMPAGNE VINEGAR

1 tablespoon plus 2 teaspoons SUGAR, or to taste

6 tablespoons WALNUT OIL

MICRO CRESS, MÂCHE, or WATERCRESS LEAVES, for garnish

CHOPPED WALNUTS, for garnish

SERVES 4 TO 6 AS AN APPETIZER OR SIDE DISH

NOTES FROM THE KITCHEN The caraway here is a nice contrast to the beet's sweetness, as is the walnut oil, which has a slightly bitter note. This is a versatile salad that will go with practically anything as a side dish: meat, fish, pasta, or potatoes. For a substantial first course, you can add cheese: a goat cheese, fresh or aged, a nice granular aged Cheddar or Parmigiano-Reggiano, or even a blue cheese.

1. Preheat the oven to 425°F.

2. In an ovenproof dish, toss the beets with the canola oil, thyme, bay leaf, and salt and pepper to taste. Cover the dish with aluminum foil and roast until the beets are tender and cooked through, 45 minutes to 1 hour.

3. Meanwhile, make the dressing: Place 1 cup water in a saucepan, add the caraway seeds, and bring to a boil. Take the pan off the heat and stir in the vinegar and sugar. Whisk in the walnut oil, and season with salt and pepper.

4. When the beets are cool enough to handle, slip off their skins and place them in a bowl. Pour the dressing over them and let marinate for at least 1 hour. Serve garnished with the cress and walnuts.

DAVID BOULEY Many people associate beets with something they had when they were kids that was pickled or served out of a can. And many people don't understand that a good beet straight from the garden doesn't taste anything like that. A fresh beet, still with its greens attached, is tender and sweet, almost more like a fruit than a vegetable. It's not woody and tough, or dry like a potato. It's beautiful.

Beets are one of my favorite things—I've loved them since I was about eight or nine when I first realized what vegetables were supposed to taste like. I was on a farm helping out during the harvest. After gathering the produce, there was a big cookout, and all the root vegetables were wrapped in aluminum foil and roasted in an open fire. The beets got intensely sweet, and I thought they were the best vegetables I'd ever had.

This recipe shows off how simple and delicious a garden-fresh beet can be, so it's important to use baby beets that have been harvested within a few days of cooking.

Schlutzkrapfen

AUSTRIAN CHEESE RAVIOLI WITH HARVEST CORN AND SMOKED MUSHROOMS

Schlutzkrapfen are Austria's answer to Italian ravioli. A favorite in Carinthia, they're traditionally made with an egg pasta dough that is formed into puffy pillows, stuffed with a variety of fillings—including cheese, grated cooked potatoes, and/or spinach—and served with mint or other herbs. In this version, they hold a mixture of five cheeses: ricotta salata for its crumbly texture, mascarpone for milkiness, Quark for creaminess, and goat cheese and Parmigiano-Reggiano for spice and bite. The recipe calls for broiling the ricotta salata and smoking the mushrooms to add a deep, charred nuance; if you prefer a lighter-flavored dish, you can skip those steps.

NOTES FROM THE KITCHEN When the Danube first opened, every order of ravioli was made to order. The waiters would walk into the kitchen and over to the stairwell, where they'd bellow down to the ravioli maker in the prep kitchen below, "Two Cheese!" for two orders of cheese ravioli. Five minutes later, ten perfect ravioli would appear. The cook would plop them into the ready pot, and before they even knew it, they'd be on the plate and sauced, dark green drops of pumpkin seed oil rolling off their plump bellies. You can make them ahead, but freshness is part of the reason these are so good.

Be careful when smoking the mushrooms. Like anything you cook in a smoker, you don't want them to smell like an ashtray—and they will if you leave them in too long.

1. Preheat the broiler. Rub the ricotta salata with canola oil and place it under the broiler. Let it cook until the cheese blackens on top, 5 to 10 minutes, depending upon how close the cheese is to the heat source. Let the cheese cool. Then grate it, and place it in a bowl with the goat cheese, Quark, Parmigiano-Reggiano, mascarpone, and egg. Mix well. Use a wide rubber spatula to push the filling through a coarse-mesh strainer into a bowl. Season with salt and pepper.

2. Melt the butter in a small skillet over medium heat, and add the shallots and garlic. Cook gently, stirring occasionally, until translucent, about 3

CHEESE RAVIOLI

1/2 pound RICOTTA SALATA or mild feta cheese

CANOLA OIL

1/2 cup (about 1/4 pound) FRESH GOAT CHEESE

1/4 cup QUARK CHEESE (see page 14), thick yogurt, or crème fraîche

1/4 cup grated PARMIGIANO-REGGIANO CHEESE

1/4 cup MASCARPONE CHEESE

1/2 EGG (see Note)

Fine SEA SALT and freshly ground BLACK PEPPER

1 tablespoon UNSALTED BUTTER

2 tablespoons minced SHALLOT

1 small GARLIC CLOVE, minced

1 ounce (about 2 cups) BABY SPINACH LEAVES

Freshly grated NUTMEG

CORNMEAL, for dusting the pan

1 recipe EGG PASTA DOUGH (see page 328)

1 EGG WHITE, beaten

CORN SAUCE

6 ears FRESH CORN, shucked

Fine SEA SALT

2 tablespoons UNSALTED BUTTER

3 SHALLOTS, thinly sliced

1 small GARLIC CLOVE, chopped

1 1/2 cups CHICKEN STOCK (see page 333) or canned low-sodium chicken broth

2 tablespoons CRÈME FRAÎCHE

Freshly ground BLACK PEPPER

MUSHROOMS

WOOD CHIPS, soaked, for smoking
(see Note, page 23)

1 large HEN-OF-THE-WOODS
MUSHROOM (about 1/2 pound), or
1/2 pound other wild mushrooms
such as oyster, chanterelle,
or black trumpet, trimmed

1 GARLIC CLOVE, thinly sliced

1 sprig FRESH THYME

3 tablespoons UNSALTED BUTTER

1/3 cup CHICKEN STOCK (see
page 333) or canned low-sodium
chicken broth

1/4 pound (about 2 quarts) BABY
SPINACH LEAVES

Fine SEA SALT and freshly ground
BLACK PEPPER

1/4 cup hulled PUMPKIN SEEDS

1 teaspoon CANOLA OIL

PUMPKIN SEED OIL, for garnish
(see following page)

SERVES 8 AS AN APPETIZER

minutes (do not let the shallots begin to brown). Add the spinach leaves
and cook, stirring, until they are wilted and cooked through, about 3 minutes. Season with nutmeg, salt, and pepper. Spread the mixture out on a
cutting board to cool, then chop it very fine. Stir 1 tablespoon of this mixture into the cheese filling. Discard the rest of the spinach mixture.

3. To form the ravioli, dust a baking sheet with cornmeal. Spread out the
rolled pasta dough horizontally, and brush the egg white on the lower half of
the dough. Spoon quarter-size dollops of cheese at 4-inch intervals on the
lower half of the dough. Fold the top over and seal it around the filling, making sure there are no air bubbles. Cut the ravioli into circles or squares, using
a pastry wheel, cookie cutter, or knife. As they are formed, transfer the ravioli to the prepared baking sheet. Keep them covered with a clean dish towel
as you work; then cover the pan with plastic wrap until ready to use.

4. Prepare the corn sauce: Hold each ear of corn upright in a large, deep
bowl and slide a thin knife along the cob to cut off the kernels. Set the kernels aside. Break the cobs in half and place them in a stockpot. Cover with
water, season with a large pinch of salt, and simmer until the corn flavor is
concentrated and the stock is slightly reduced, about 1 hour. Strain and
reserve the liquid.

5. Melt the butter in a saucepan over medium heat and add the shallots.
Cook gently, stirring occasionally, until soft and translucent, about 5 minutes. Add the garlic and cook until soft, about 2 minutes. Add the corn kernels and cook for 3 minutes longer. Pour in the chicken stock and simmer
until the corn is completely soft, 20 to 30 minutes.

6. Let the mixture cool for 10 minutes, then transfer the contents of the
pan to a blender and blend until smooth. Use a wide rubber spatula to
push the puree through a fine-mesh sieve into a saucepan, and discard

DAVID BOULEY When I was in Austria, I noticed that people would dry mountain cheeses in the heat next to their
oven or near the fireplace. Sometimes the cheese just dries out a bit, getting stronger and firmer as the water
evaporates. Other times it's left until it blackens, giving it a smoky taste. The concentrated flavor and low moisture
content make it good for filling the Schlutzkrapfen. We add smoked mushrooms to heighten the smokiness, and
then pumpkin seeds for crunch and a nutty flavor. The corn sauce provides a soft, sweet contrast to the intensity
of the dish.

the solids. Heat the puree and thin it with $1/2$ to 1 cup of the corncob stock—the sauce should still coat the back of a spoon. Season with salt and pepper. Add the crème fraîche and cover to keep warm.

7. If you are smoking the mushroom on an outdoor grill, light the grill and when it's hot, place the soaked wood chips in the smoker tray (or in a disposable aluminum pan set over the coals). If smoking in a wok, line the wok with aluminum foil and place it over high heat for several minutes; add the wood chips and drizzle them with 2 tablespoons water, tossing the chips until they are dry and burned at the edges. Lightly oil a rack and place it over the wood chips.

8. Place the mushroom, garlic, and thyme in the center of a large piece of aluminum foil and twist the ends together to seal. Lay the package on the rack over the wood chips, and cover. Let smoke, opening the grill every few minutes to release some of the smoke and to monitor the cooking process. Reduce the heat (or spread the coals) if the chips begin to smoke profusely—the smoke should just curl gently around the cover. Cook until the mushroom begins to soften and brown on the edges, about 15 minutes. Transfer the packet to a plate to cool.

9. Heat a wide sauté pan over medium-high heat. Add the butter and cook until the white milk solids fall to the bottom of the pan and turn nut-brown, about 5 minutes. Immediately add the chicken stock and the mushroom, and simmer until the liquid is slightly thickened, 7 to 10 minutes. Add the spinach leaves and cook, stirring, until just wilted, about 2 minutes. Season with salt and pepper, and cover to keep warm.

10. Meanwhile, place the pumpkin seeds in a dry skillet over medium-high heat and toast, shaking as they begin to pop. When most have popped, about 5 minutes, sprinkle them with the canola oil and salt and transfer to a plate to cool.

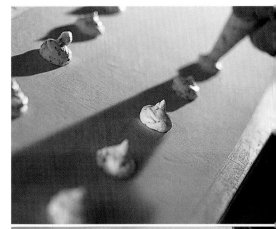

MARIO LOHNINGER The combination of the smoked mushrooms and the corn makes this dish very Austrian in style. Corn comes from the Americas, but it's very popular in Austria. All the southern areas grow corn, and it's eaten both fresh (on the cob and in soups and sauces) and dried and ground, like the Italian polenta. The smoked mushrooms are also typical—we Austrians like to smoke things, and mushrooms adopt the smoky flavors well. Usually this dish is made in a more rustic farmhouse style, with one or two big ravioli per person, but I like them smaller and more delicate.

11. Bring a large pot of water to a boil and salt it until it tastes like seawater (about 2 teaspoons per quart). Cook the ravioli in the boiling water until they are cooked through, 2 to 3 minutes. Drain.

12. Heat the corn sauce. If you want a frothy texture, use an immersion blender or regular blender to foam the sauce, blending for about 1 minute.

13. To serve, use a slotted spoon to divide about two thirds of the mushroom-spinach sauce among four plates. Toss the ravioli in the sauce remaining in the pan. Arrange the ravioli on the plates. Spoon the corn sauce on and around the ravioli. Drizzle with pumpkin seed oil and sprinkle with the roasted pumpkin seeds.

Note: To get half an egg, crack an egg in a small cup and beat well with a fork. Pour out half and use the remainder in the recipe.

STYRIAN PUMPKIN SEED OIL

Styrian pumpkin seed oil comes from the squat yellow-green pumpkins grown in Styria, the southeastern region of Austria. Styrian pumpkins have fibrous orange flesh and dark green, husk-less seeds. Their deep green oil has an earthy, nutty flavor with a hint of grassy sweetness. It's best used raw, as a garnish or salad dressing, or even as a dip for bread or vegetables. David particularly loves to drizzle the oil over delicate fish, topping it with a sprinkling of toasted pumpkin seeds for a simple yet memorable dish. Since pumpkin seed oil is sold in this country mainly for its health benefits (high in vitamins A, C, and E as well as potassium and essential fatty acids, it is used to treat a variety of health problems, especially those related to the bladder and prostate), it can usually be found at natural food stores (for mail-order information, see Sources, page 337). Like most nut and seed oils, pumpkin seed oil is highly perishable and should be refrigerated to extend its shelf life.

Sea Scallops, Crabmeat, and Baby Squid

WITH PARADEISER, CORIANDER, AND LEMON THYME SAUCE

The scallops here are prepared in an unusual manner. Before being seared they are deeply scored on one side in a crosshatch pattern. When they hit the pan, the crosshatch sections splay and caramelize, transforming into crunchy brown tentacle-like pieces that contrast with the soft pillowy interior. They also look beautiful, like chrysanthemums or golden sea anemones.

The seared scallops are served with sweet crabmeat and baby squid in a tomato broth that Mario likes to call "*Paradeiser*." Paradeiser is the Austrian word for tomato, taken from an old name for the fruit: the "paradise apple," or *paradeiserapfel*. In this dish, tomato water forms the base of a very light but perfumed sauce. It's probably fair to say that when David first made tomato water at Bouley restaurant over a decade ago, it was a revolutionary way to extract the intense flavor of ripe summer tomatoes. Here it's enhanced with the very Austrian flavor of coriander seed, along with lemon thyme and lemongrass.

DAVID BOULEY I got the idea for this technique from a Japanese cookbook about ten years ago. There was a picture of an eel fillet with a crosshatch pattern, and I wondered why they would do that. I realized that the scoring allows the marinade to sink in and encourages caramelization. So I tried it on a scallop. If you sear a scallop flat, you get only so much surface area to brown. By cutting it, a lot more of the sugars can come into contact with the heat of the pan. It's sweeter and makes a textural contrast with the rest of the scallop, which can be dense.

PARADEISER SAUCE

1 1/2 tablespoons CANOLA OIL

1 small ONION, thinly sliced

1/4 cup CORIANDER SEEDS

2 small GARLIC CLOVES, thinly sliced

1 tablespoon UNSALTED BUTTER

1 tablespoon OLIVE OIL

2 plum TOMATOES, chopped

1 teaspoon TOMATO PASTE

1 cup TOMATO WATER (see page 329)

5-inch-long piece of LEMONGRASS

One 15-ounce can San Marzano PLUM TOMATOES (see Notes), undrained

1/2 BAY LEAF, preferably fresh

1 sprig LEMON THYME or regular thyme, plus additional thyme leaves for garnish

1/4 teaspoon grated ORANGE ZEST

SEA SALT and freshly ground WHITE PEPPER

1. Prepare the Paradeiser sauce: Heat the canola oil in a large saucepan over medium heat. Add the onion and cook until wilted, about 5 minutes. Reduce the heat to low and cook, stirring frequently, until the onions are soft and golden, about 30 minutes.

2. Meanwhile, heat a small sauté pan over medium heat. Add the coriander seeds and toast, shaking the pan, until fragrant, about 2 minutes. Transfer the spices to an electric spice mill or a mortar and pestle, and grind.

SEAFOOD

1 cup FRESH CRABMEAT, picked
   over, at room temperature

2 tablespoons UNSALTED BUTTER,
   melted

2 tablespoons fresh LEMON JUICE

2 teaspoons chopped MIXED FRESH
   HERBS (parsley, tarragon,
   chervil, chives)

Fine SEA SALT

4 large SEA SCALLOPS
   (see following page)

2 SMALL SQUID, cleaned

2 tablespoons CANOLA OIL

Freshly ground WHITE PEPPER

WONDRA FLOUR, for dusting
   (see Notes)

SERVES 4 AS A FISH COURSE

3. When the onions are caramelized, add the garlic and cook until soft, about 3 minutes. Add the butter, olive oil, ground coriander, plum tomatoes, and tomato paste. Cook over medium-high heat for 1 minute, stirring constantly. Add the tomato water and bring to a simmer, scraping any brown bits from the bottom of the pan with a wooden spoon. Bruise the lemongrass with the back of a knife or a rolling pin, cut it into 1-inch pieces, and add them to the saucepan along with the canned tomatoes and their juices and the bay leaf. Reduce the heat to medium and simmer for 20 minutes. Add the lemon thyme and orange zest, and simmer another 5 minutes. Pass the mixture though a food mill or coarse-mesh strainer, then push the puree through a fine-mesh sieve. Season the sauce with salt and white pepper, and cover to keep it warm until ready to use.

4. Toss the crabmeat in a bowl with the melted butter, lemon juice, mixed herbs, and $3/4$ teaspoon salt. Score the tops of the scallops, making a checkerboard pattern $1/2$ inch deep. Detach the tentacles from the squid and cut the bodies in half lengthwise. Rinse and remove any remaining membrane. Cut the tentacles in half.

5. Heat two sauté pans over medium-high heat. Add 1 tablespoon of the canola oil to each pan. Season the scallops and squid with salt and white pepper, and dust the scallops with Wondra on both sides.

6. When the oil is hot, add the scallops to one pan, crosshatched side down, and press them gently with a spatula to flare the cut edges. Cook until browned, about $1 1/2$ minutes on each side. Add the squid pieces to the other pan and cook, turning once, until the bodies start to curl and the tentacles are cooked through, about $1 1/2$ minutes total.

7. To serve, ladle $1/4$ cup of the Paradeiser sauce into each heated soup bowl, and place a mound of crabmeat in the center. Top the crabmeat with a large scallop, and lay the squid pieces alongside. Garnish with the thyme leaves.

Notes: The San Marzano tomato is a long, thin, pointed tomato that contains less water and fewer seeds, and has a more intense color and flavor, than the more common Roma tomato. These meaty tomatoes make rich, highly flavored sauces. Look for canned imported San Marzanos at Italian specialty stores and gourmet food stores, and check to be sure that the can actually contains San Marzano tomatoes (as opposed to Roma tomatoes grown in San Marzano).

Wondra is a granulated flour that is designed to absorb readily into liquids. It is used to thicken gravy and sauces, and it also creates a uniquely crisp crust on meats and seafood. Look for Wondra flour in supermarkets.

SCALLOPS Live sea scallops are sometimes available in specialty markets, and they are worth the price. The shells should close up when you squeeze down on them, and they should smell fresh, not fishy. To shuck a live scallop, slide the blade of a sharp knife along the top shell to detach the scallop without cutting into it. Use the knife to detach the scallop from the bottom shell; then pull away the membrane and viscera that surround the scallop. When working with a scallop just cut from the shell, don't be surprised if it's still moving when you slice it, its flesh rolling back and forth like waves. It's not that the scallop is alive; it's simply reacting to the oxygen in the air.

If you don't have access to live sea scallops in the shell, "dry" (frozen) scallops are preferable to "wet" scallops. Since scallop boats stay at sea for days at a time, fast-frozen sea scallops tend to taste fresher than fresh scallops that have been soaked in brine and preservatives to keep them from spoiling. "Wet" scallops appear plumper, but they immediately lose their liquid to the pan as soon as they are heated, which slows their cooking and prevents them from developing a golden-brown, caramelized outer crust.

Almond-Crusted Halibut

WITH ASPARAGUS, PORCINI, AND KOHLRABI PUREE

KOHLRABI PUREE

2 tablespoons UNSALTED BUTTER

2 pounds (about 3 large) KOHLRABI, peeled, quartered, and thinly sliced

Fine SEA SALT and freshly ground BLACK PEPPER

ASPARAGUS SAUCE

2 pounds (2 bunches) ASPARAGUS, trimmed

3 tablespoons UNSALTED BUTTER

2 SHALLOTS, sliced

Fine SEA SALT and freshly ground BLACK PEPPER

2 GARLIC CLOVES, chopped

1/4 cup DRY WHITE WINE

3 cups VEGETABLE STOCK (see page 332) or canned low-sodium vegetable broth

2 sprigs FRESH THYME

1 BAY LEAF, preferably fresh

This dish combines the very contemporary French technique of using vegetable juices and broths as the foundation for a sauce with the distinctly Austrian flavors of asparagus and kohlrabi. It's a complex, meaty, earthy dish, thanks to the porcini, with a fresh grassy flavor from the asparagus and a nice nutty crunch from the almonds.

Halibut must be cooked more slowly than other fish—its strands of flesh have a tendency to be tough and springy. Slower, lower cooking allows them to relax.

NOTES FROM THE KITCHEN For a simpler dish, omit the kohlrabi puree and the porcini and serve the halibut with the asparagus sauce. You can also substitute other mushrooms for the fresh porcini, including cremini, portobello, shiitake, oyster, and chanterelle.

1. Prepare the kohlrabi puree: Melt the butter in a saucepan over medium heat until it foams. Add the kohlrabi and season with salt and pepper. Cook, stirring, until the kohlrabi softens and begins to turn translucent, about 10 minutes. Add 2 cups water, cover, and cook gently until completely soft, about 1 hour.

2. Fill a large bowl with water and ice. Transfer the kohlrabi mixture to a blender or food processor, and puree until smooth. Push the puree through a fine-mesh sieve into a second bowl, then place the bowl in the bowl of ice water and stir until the kohlrabi is thoroughly cooled. Refrigerate, covered, until ready to use.

3. Prepare the asparagus sauce: Snap off the top 4 inches of 12 stalks, and set them aside. Chop the rest of the asparagus into 1/2-inch pieces.

4. Melt 2 tablespoons of the butter in a saucepan over medium heat until it foams. Add the shallots and cook, stirring, until they are soft and translucent, about 5 minutes (do not let them begin to brown). Season with salt and pepper to taste. Add the garlic and continue to cook, stirring, for another minute. Add the chopped asparagus and continue to cook gently until it begins to soften, about 5 minutes. Season generously with salt and pepper.

PORCINI

1 tablespoon extra-virgin OLIVE OIL

½ pound PORCINI MUSHROOMS, trimmed and thickly sliced

2 GARLIC CLOVES, smashed

1 sprig FRESH THYME

Fine SEA SALT and freshly ground BLACK PEPPER

1 tablespoon UNSALTED BUTTER

HALIBUT

4 HALIBUT FILLETS (3 to 5 ounces each)

Fine SEA SALT and freshly ground BLACK PEPPER

½ cup finely chopped BLANCHED ALMONDS

2 teaspoons CANOLA OIL

1 tablespoon UNSALTED BUTTER

SERVES 4 AS A FISH COURSE

5. Pour the white wine into the pan and raise the heat to medium-high. Simmer until the liquid is reduced by half, about 3 minutes. Add the vegetable stock, thyme, and bay leaf, and simmer until the asparagus is cooked through, about 12 minutes longer.

6. Fill a shallow bowl with water and ice. Transfer the asparagus mixture to a blender or food processor, and puree until smooth. Push the puree through a fine-mesh sieve into a second bowl, then place it in the bowl of ice water and stir until the puree is thoroughly cooled. It will have the consistency of heavy cream. Refrigerate, covered, until ready to use.

7. Fill a bowl with water and ice. Bring a small pot of water to a boil, and salt it until it tastes like seawater (about 2 teaspoons per quart). Add the reserved asparagus tips. Cook until crisp-tender, 3 to 5 minutes. Drain, and transfer immediately to the ice water to cool. Drain again. Warm the remaining 1 tablespoon butter in a small saucepan over medium heat. Add the asparagus tips and 2 tablespoons of the asparagus puree, and cook until warmed through. Season with salt and pepper to taste.

8. Prepare the porcini: Heat a saucepan over high heat, then add the olive oil. Add the porcini, smashed garlic, and thyme, and season with salt and pepper. Toss and cook until the mushrooms are browned all over, about 5 minutes. Add the butter and toss to coat the mushrooms. Cover to keep warm.

9. Preheat the oven to 350°F.

10. Season both sides of the halibut fillets with salt and pepper. Place the almonds in a shallow dish and very firmly press one side of each fillet into the chopped nuts so that they adhere. Heat a large ovenproof sauté pan over medium-high heat. Add the canola oil, and when it begins to shimmer, add the fillets, almond side down. Cook until the almonds are browned, then turn the fillets over and transfer the pan to the oven. Bake until the fish is almost cooked through but feels slightly resistant to the touch, 6 to 7 minutes. Return the pan to the stove over medium heat. Add the butter and baste the fish with the foaming, browning butter for 1 minute.

11. Rewarm the kohlrabi puree and the asparagus sauce. To serve, spoon a round of kohlrabi puree onto each of four plates. Top each with a halibut fillet, almond side up. Garnish each plate with 3 asparagus tips and some sautéed porcini, and spoon the asparagus sauce around the fish.

John Dory in a Parsley Cloud
WITH CAVIAR SAUCE

1 whole JOHN DORY (about 2 pounds)
  or other firm white-fleshed fish,
  such as red snapper

FISH BROTH

1 tablespoon CANOLA OIL

Fine SEA SALT and freshly ground
  BLACK PEPPER

$1/2$ cup DRY WHITE WINE

$2^1/2$ cups sliced LEEKS (about 2
  large), white and light green parts
  separated

2 CELERY STALKS

1 small ONION, halved

2 GARLIC CLOVES, smashed

1 tablespoon WHITE PEPPERCORNS

1 BAY LEAF, preferably fresh

LEEKS AND SCALLOP MOUSSE

2 cups packed FRESH PARSLEY
  LEAVES

Fine SEA SALT and freshly ground
  BLACK PEPPER

$1/2$ pound DIVER SEA SCALLOPS
  (see page 251)

$1^3/4$ cups HEAVY CREAM

1 tablespoon UNSALTED BUTTER

In this dish, firm John Dory fillets are covered in a pale green parsley-scallop mousse and served with a tangy sauce studded with salty beads of caviar. The mousse seals the fish into a little packet, keeping it very moist during the steaming, and puffs into something light and ethereal. Every bite will melt in your mouth.

NOTES FROM THE KITCHEN This recipe makes extra fish stock, which can be refrigerated for up to 3 days or frozen for 2 months.

1. Fillet the John Dory (or have your fishmonger do it for you), reserving the bones. Wrap the fillets in plastic and place them in the refrigerator until you are ready to use them.

2. Prepare the fish broth: Heat a large stockpot over high heat, and add the canola oil. When it is hot, add the fish bones. Season with salt and pepper, and cook for 10 minutes. Pour in the white wine, bring it to a simmer, and cook for 10 minutes. Add the whites of the leeks (save the green), the celery, onion, garlic, white peppercorns, bay leaf, and 6 cups water. Simmer for 25 minutes. Strain, discarding the solids, and reserve.

3. Meanwhile, begin preparing the leeks and parsley: Fill a bowl with water and ice. Bring a pot of water to a boil and salt it until it tastes like seawater (about 2 teaspoons per quart). Blanch the leek greens in the boiling water until just tender, about 3 minutes. Use a strainer to scoop up the leeks and transfer them to the ice water to cool (keep the pot of water at a boil). Drain well and set aside.

MARIO LOHNINGER Since the fish is covered in mousse, it can be hard to see when it's done. I like to use a very thin knife or a thin metal skewer to test it. I want to be able to easily pierce the fish without resistance. If you cannot smoothly stick the knife through, you know the fish is not done. When it's done, you can't leave it over the heat anymore—you've got to pull it off immediately and be ready to serve it. But you can coat the fish in the parsley mousse ahead of time and then let it sit in the fridge for 4 or 5 hours (more than that and it will lose color and flavor). The sauce can be prepared several hours in advance, too. Reheat it very gently. Then the final cooking goes very quickly. This is a great dish for a dinner party.

CHAMPAGNE-CAVIAR SAUCE

2 tablespoons minced SHALLOT

1/4 cup HEAVY CREAM

1/4 cup CHAMPAGNE or dry white wine

Fine SEA SALT and freshly ground BLACK PEPPER

4 tablespoons UNSALTED BUTTER, cold, cut into pieces

3 tablespoons CAVIAR (see following page)

2 teaspoons fresh LEMON JUICE, or to taste

CANOLA OIL, for brushing

MICRO GREENS or parsley, for garnish (optional)

SERVES 4 AS A FISH COURSE

4. Boil the parsley leaves in the water until very soft but still green, about 5 minutes. Drain, transfer to the ice water to cool, then drain again, squeezing the leaves dry in a clean dish towel.

5. Place the blanched parsley in a blender, add 1/4 cup ice water, and blend on high speed, adding more ice water sparingly (up to another 1/4 cup) to achieve a smooth, thick puree. Season with salt and pepper. Strain through a fine-mesh sieve into a bowl, discarding the solids, and cover and refrigerate.

6. To prepare the scallop mousse, place the scallops in a food processor and blend until mostly smooth. With the processor running, slowly pour in 1 cup of the cream. Season with a large pinch of salt and pepper, and process, stopping often to scrape down the sides, until a smooth cream forms. Use a wide rubber spatula to push the mixture through a fine-mesh sieve into a bowl. Add 1/2 cup of the parsley puree, season with more salt and pepper if necessary, and mix well. Cover and refrigerate.

7. To finish the leeks, melt the butter in a small saucepan over medium heat. When it foams, add the remaining 3/4 cup cream and the blanched leeks, and simmer gently until the cream reduces enough to coat the leeks, about 7 minutes. Stir in 1 tablespoon of the parsley puree and season with salt and pepper. Cover to keep warm.

8. Prepare the Champagne-caviar sauce: Place 1 cup of the fish broth in a saucepan, add the shallot, and bring to a simmer over medium heat. Simmer until the mixture is reduced to 3 tablespoons, about 15 minutes. Then add the cream and cook until it is reduced by one third, about 7 minutes. Add the Champagne and bring to a simmer. Season with salt and pepper. Whisk in the cold butter piece by piece until the sauce thickens enough to lightly coat a spoon; then add the caviar. Stir in the lemon juice, and cover to keep warm.

9. Spoon the scallop mousse into a piping bag fitted with a flat ribbon tip (or use a resealable plastic bag with a 1-inch slit cut in one corner). Fill a pot with a few inches of water, set a steamer basket or bamboo steamer over the water (or place an upturned ramekin in the water and place a heatproof plate on top of it), and bring to a boil.

10. Season the John Dory fillets with salt and pepper, and cut them in half. Cut eight rectangles of parchment paper about 3 inches larger than the pieces of fish, and lightly brush one side of the papers with canola oil. Lay each piece of fish on the oiled side of a piece of parchment paper.

11. Pipe the mousse in wide ribbons over each fish fillet, making sure to cover the sides. When all of the fish has been covered, place a second piece of parchment, oiled side down, over the mousse and turn the packets over. Lift off the parchment paper and pipe more ribbons of mousse onto each piece.

12. Transfer the pieces of fish, on the parchment paper, to the steamer. Cover, and steam until the mousse is firm and the fish is cooked, 5 to 7 minutes. Cut each piece of fish in half crosswise. To serve, spoon a bed of warm leeks onto the center of each plate. Top with the pieces of fish, and spoon the caviar sauce around the leeks. Garnish with the micro greens or parsley.

CAVIAR

The better the quality of the caviar you use here, the better the dish will be. Sevruga or osetra is preferable, although you can use any type of sturgeon roe available. Osetra is favored for its slightly fruity, mellow flavor and firm texture. Sevruga eggs are more intense and bright-tasting, although the beads are smaller and a little soft. The highly prized beluga caviar is larger and crisper than either osetra or sevruga, but is probably best eaten alone if you are lucky enough to have any. You can also use high-quality American lumpfish caviar. Choose fresh, unpasteurized roe, sold refrigerated, which has more flavor and less added salt than jarred varieties. (For mail-order information, see Sources, page 337.)

Maine Lobster

WITH RED BEET FETTUCCINE AND BLACK TRUMPET MUSHROOMS

With a palette of magenta, orange, and burgundy, this dish is as breathtaking to look at as it is delightful to eat. The pasta is made with beet juice, which gives it a compelling sweetness and accounts for the intense red color. Black trumpet mushrooms add a dark bit of drama and a pungent flavor, which offsets the sweet saline character of the lobster. It's a demanding recipe but worth it.

NOTES FROM THE KITCHEN If you are pressed for time, you can skip the beet pasta and serve this with purchased fresh fettuccine.

1. Prepare the pasta: Bring the beet juice to a boil in a saucepan and simmer until it is reduced to $1/3$ cup, 30 to 40 minutes. Let it cool.

2. Combine the beet juice, egg yolks, and both flours in the bowl of a mixer fitted with a dough hook. Mix until a smooth dough forms. Knead the dough by hand for 5 minutes. Cover and let rest for 30 minutes before using.

3. With a pasta machine, roll out the pasta. Feed the rolled dough through the cutter attachment, sprinkle lightly with flour, and coil the fettuccine into six portion-size nests. Cover with plastic wrap until ready to use. The pasta can be made 1 day ahead and refrigerated, if desired.

4. Prepare the red wine sauce: Combine the Port and wine in a large saucepan, and add the shallots. Bring to a simmer over medium heat and cook until the shallots have turned red, 30 minutes. Strain the shallots, reserving all the wine. Place the shallots in a small pan and cover them with 1 cup of the wine mixture. Simmer until the liquid is reduced and the shallots are very soft and very dark red, about 20 minutes. Transfer the shallot-wine mixture to a blender and blend on high speed until you have a smooth puree. Reserve.

PASTA

2 cups BEET JUICE (see Note, page 230)

4 large EGG YOLKS

$1/3$ cup SEMOLINA FLOUR (see Note)

1 cup ALL-PURPOSE FLOUR, plus additional for rolling

RED WINE SAUCE

6 cups PORT WINE

6 cups DRY RED WINE

$1\,1/2$ cups sliced SHALLOTS

12 CORIANDER SEEDS

5 WHITE PEPPERCORNS

1 BAY LEAF, preferably fresh

Fine SEA SALT and freshly ground BLACK PEPPER

LOBSTERS

2 live LOBSTERS ($1\,1/4$ to $1\,1/2$ pounds each)

3 tablespoons UNSALTED BUTTER

Fine SEA SALT and freshly ground BLACK PEPPER

HORSERADISH SAUCE

$1/2$ cup CRÈME FRAÎCHE

3 tablespoons prepared HORSERADISH

1 teaspoon fresh LEMON JUICE

Fine SEA SALT and freshly ground BLACK PEPPER

MUSHROOMS

1/3 pound BLACK TRUMPET MUSH-
ROOMS, trimmed and halved

4 tablespoons UNSALTED
BUTTER, cold

2 GARLIC CLOVES, smashed

Fine SEA SALT and freshly ground
BLACK PEPPER

2 tablespoons CHICKEN STOCK (see
page 333) or canned low-sodium
chicken broth

2 tablespoons FRESH PARSLEY
LEAVES, sliced into ribbons

SERVES 4 AS A FISH COURSE

5. Meanwhile, place the remaining wine mixture in another saucepan and bring it to a simmer. Toast the coriander seeds in a small dry skillet over medium heat until fragrant, about 2 minutes. Add them, along with the white peppercorns and bay leaf, to the wine. Simmer until the wine is thick enough to coat the back of a spoon (it should have the consistency of heavy cream), about 1 hour. Whisk 1/4 cup of the shallot puree into this sauce, and season with salt and pepper. Cover until ready to use.

6. To cook the lobsters, fill a bowl with water and ice. Bring a large pot of water to a boil and salt it until it tastes like seawater (about 2 teaspoons per quart). To kill the lobsters, insert a thin, sharp knife between their eyes and down through their heads, or briefly hold their heads in the boiling water. Separate the lobster heads from their tails by twisting them off at the abdomen; twist off the claws. (If desired, freeze the heads and use them for a stock or sauce.) Drop the tails and claws into the boiling water and poach until slightly underdone, about 4 1/2 minutes for the tails and 5 minutes for the claws. (To test for doneness, break off the small pincer beneath the claw to expose the meat. The flesh should remain intact, feel somewhat firm to the touch, and be just starting to turn opaque.) Drain and immediately transfer to the ice water.

7. When the lobster is cool, use the back of a large knife or cleaver to smash the claw shells. Remove the claw meat intact. Use a strong set of kitchen shears to cut down the underside of the tail, and remove the tail meat. Rinse the meat and refrigerate it, covered, until ready to use.

8. When you are almost ready to serve the dish, reheat the lobster: Gently melt the butter in a saucepan. Add the cold lobster and allow it to heat through, about 5 minutes. Season with salt and pepper, and keep warm.

DAVID BOULEY There are some flavors that open the palate and some that close it down. The beet here is very sweet, and so is the lobster, and eaten together these can numb the palate after a while. That's why the horserad-ish in the sauce is so important. It wakes up the mouth and offers a diverse range of tastes, countering the sweet-ness and adding an interesting sharpness. Beet and horseradish are a traditional pairing in Austria and farther east into Russia, and this recipe illustrates why those flavors work so beautifully in combination.

9. For the horseradish sauce, combine the crème fraîche, horseradish, and lemon juice in a small saucepan and warm over low heat. Season with salt and pepper, and keep warm.

10. To prepare the mushrooms, swish them in cold water, drain immediately, and pat dry. Heat 2 tablespoons of the butter in a large saucepan, and when it foams, add the garlic and the mushrooms. Season with salt and pepper, and sauté until tender, about 5 minutes. Add the chicken stock and cook for 1 more minute. Sprinkle with the parsley and set aside.

11. Meanwhile bring a large pot of water to a boil, and salt it until it tastes like seawater (about 2 teaspoons per quart).

12. In a small saucepan, bring $1/2$ cup of the red wine sauce to a simmer. Whisk in the remaining 2 tablespoons butter. In a large sauté pan, reheat the remaining red wine sauce.

13. Cook the pasta in the boiling water until al dente, about 1 minute. Drain. Add it to the sauté pan with the red wine sauce, and toss to coat the pasta.

14. To serve, coil the pasta on a fork until you have a portion-size tower. Place one on each plate. Place pieces of lobster on the plate. Garnish with the mushrooms, and drizzle with some of the red wine–butter sauce. Drizzle some horseradish sauce around the plate.

Note: You can buy semolina flour at specialty food shops or mail-order it (see Sources, page 337).

PASTA IN AUSTRIA

Pasta is perhaps not associated as closely with Austria as it is with its southwestern neighbor, Italy, and yet it plays a prominent role in the cuisine. Especially at lunch, pasta is served in many forms, both sweet and savory. In the mountains of Tyrol, Schlutzkrapfen are filled with spinach, and in Carinthia, noodle dough is wrapped around anything from bacon to dried fruit. Austrian pasta dough is always enriched with egg. The dough is formed into a variety of shapes, ranging from little snakes of potato noodles (see Nuss Nudeln, page 124) to broad sheets of pasta that are folded over dollops of meat, cheese, or vegetable filling to create ravioli. Butter and bread crumbs or cheese is a common dressing for savory noodles, while brown butter, sometimes with nuts or poppy seeds, is most often tossed with sweet noodles, which are then blanketed with a generous sprinkling of confectioners' sugar. These dishes are warm and filling, perfect for a midday meal on the ski slopes.

Yellowtail Tuna

WITH SPINACH PUREE, POTATO SALAD, OSETRA CAVIAR, AND VODKA SAUCE

SPINACH PUREE

3 tablespoons UNSALTED BUTTER

3 SHALLOTS, diced

1 teaspoon fine SEA SALT

2 large GARLIC CLOVES, minced

1/2 cup HEAVY CREAM

1 sprig FRESH THYME

3/4 cup VEGETABLE STOCK
(see page 332)

12 ounces (1 bunch) flat-leaf
SPINACH, cleaned, stems removed,
to yield 6 ounces leaves (or use
6 ounces baby spinach)

Freshly ground WHITE PEPPER

CAYENNE PEPPER

Freshly grated NUTMEG

YELLOWTAIL

4 cups CANOLA OIL

8 GARLIC CLOVES, unpeeled

1 sprig FRESH THYME

1 BAY LEAF, preferably fresh

1 pound YELLOWTAIL TUNA FILLET,
cut crosswise into 8 equal slices

Fine SEA SALT and freshly ground
WHITE PEPPER

Poaching fish slowly and gently in oil firms and tightens the flesh without drying it. It's a favorite technique that David learned in Europe over a decade ago and has been perfecting ever since. In this recipe, the buttery fish is served rather simply, with potato salad and a spinach puree that will be by far the best creamed spinach you've ever had. The four-star opulence comes from the vodka-caviar sauce, which can be as decadent as you like, depending upon how much and what kind of caviar you use. David likes to use Belvedere vodka here, but any premium brand will work.

NOTES FROM THE KITCHEN You can skip the potato salad and serve this dish with boiled or steamed potatoes.

1. Prepare the spinach puree: Melt the butter in a wide saucepan or high-sided sauté pan over medium-high heat. Let the butter cook until the white milk solids fall to the bottom and turn nut-brown, about 5 minutes. Add the shallots and 1/2 teaspoon of the salt and cook, stirring, until the shallots begin to soften, 5 minutes. Add the garlic and continue to cook until the garlic and shallots are soft and cooked through, 2 more minutes.

2. Add the cream and thyme, and bring the liquid to a boil. Simmer until reduced by about one third, 3 to 4 minutes. Pour in the vegetable stock and let the liquid return to a boil. Add the spinach and cook gently, stirring and tossing, until it is wilted and tender, about 2 minutes.

3. Remove the thyme. Using a slotted spoon, transfer the spinach and shallots to a blender or food processor, reserving 1/2 cup of the liquid. Puree the spinach and season it with the remaining 1/2 teaspoon salt, white pepper to taste, a pinch of cayenne, and nutmeg to taste. If necessary, add some of the reserved cooking liquid so the puree is just loose enough to pour. Keep warm.

4. To cook the fish, pour the oil into a wide saucepan that is large enough to accommodate the fish in a single layer (or use two pans). The oil should fill the pan halfway. Place a deep-frying thermometer in the pan.

VODKA-CAVIAR SAUCE

1/2 cup CRÈME FRAÎCHE

1 tablespoon plus 2 teaspoons
   VODKA

2 1/2 teaspoons minced SHALLOTS

1 1/4 teaspoons grated ORANGE
   ZEST

1 teaspoon minced FRESH HERBS
   (a mix of chervil, parsley,
   tarragon, and chives)

Fresh LEMON JUICE

SEA SALT and freshly ground
   WHITE PEPPER

2 teaspoons OSETRA CAVIAR, plus
   additional for garnish (see
   page 259)

1/2 recipe POTATO SALAD
   (see page 102)

FRESH CHERVIL, for garnish

SERVES 4 AS A FISH COURSE

5. Add the garlic, thyme, and bay leaf to the oil and heat gently until the thermometer registers 145°F. Gently lay the fish in a single layer on top of the garlic and herbs so that each piece is submerged but does not touch the bottom of the pot. Monitoring the heat to keep the oil at 145°F, cook the fish until it is cooked to medium, 8 to 10 minutes. Drain the fish on a paper towel-lined plate, and season both sides with salt and white pepper.

6. Meanwhile, prepare the vodka-caviar sauce: Bring the crème fraîche to a boil in a small saucepan over medium heat. Let it simmer rapidly until it is reduced almost by half, about 4 minutes. Reduce the heat to low and add the vodka, shallots, orange zest, mixed herbs, lemon juice, and salt and white pepper to taste. Keep warm. Just before serving, stir in the 2 teaspoons caviar.

7. Turn the potato salad onto a large board and chop it with a large knife until the potato pieces are the size of pebbles. Reheat the potato salad in a small pan over low heat.

8. Spoon a wide round of spinach puree onto each plate. Lay 2 thin lines of potato salad across the spinach, and arrange 2 yellowtail fillets on each plate. Spoon the vodka sauce over the fish, and garnish each piece of fish with caviar and chervil.

Roast Chicken
WITH PAPRIKA SAUCE

4 tablespoons UNSALTED BUTTER,
  softened

3 teaspoons SWEET HUNGARIAN
  PAPRIKA (see page 275)

Fine SEA SALT and freshly ground
  BLACK PEPPER

One 3 1/2-pound CHICKEN

10 CIPOLLINI ONIONS, blanched
  and peeled (see Note, page 58)

1 large ONION, cut crosswise into
  1/2-inch-thick slices

1 head GARLIC, cloves separated but
  not peeled

2 BELL PEPPERS (preferably 1 red,
  1 yellow), trimmed, seeded, and
  cut into 1/2-inch slices

1 1/2 ounces (about 6) SHIITAKE
  MUSHROOMS, trimmed

2 sprigs FRESH THYME

1/4 cup DRY WHITE WINE

A good chicken paprikash is a quintessential Austro-Hungarian dish, and there are few chicken dishes that are better. The standard recipe is like a fricassee: Onions and sometimes peppers are slowly cooked until caramelized and meltingly sweet, then spiked with hot and sweet paprika. A cut-up chicken is added and simmered with chicken broth and cream, the whole dish melding into a complex, rusty red–hued stew. This recipe is a little different. In it, the chicken is rubbed generously with butter and paprika, then roasted until the skin crackles and turns a dark mahogany brown. The paprika sauce is made separately and served with the bird. While no Hungarians would recognize this recipe as the paprikash their mothers made, none would likely turn it down, either.

NOTES FROM THE KITCHEN You can serve this dish with boiled potatoes or Quark Spätzle, with or without the cheese (see page 112).

1. Preheat the oven to 450°F.

2. Mix the softened butter with the paprika in a small bowl, and season generously with salt and pepper. Wash and dry the chicken inside and out, and season it generously with salt and pepper. Rub the paprika butter all over the chicken, going under the skin of the breast and trying to stretch your fingers down into the leg so that you can put butter there as well.

3. Lay the cipollini onions, sliced onion, garlic cloves, bell peppers, mushrooms, and thyme sprigs in the bottom of a roasting pan, and place the chicken, breast side down, on top. Drizzle the white wine around the chicken. Roast for 25 minutes. Then baste the chicken with the juices in the pan and turn the chicken over, breast side up. Roast, basting often, until the breast meat feels taut and the internal temperature is 165°F, 25 to 30 minutes. Let the chicken rest for 10 minutes.

PAPRIKA SAUCE

2 tablespoons UNSALTED BUTTER

1 cup chopped ONION

1 GARLIC CLOVE, minced

Fine SEA SALT and freshly ground
WHITE PEPPER

1 tablespoon SWEET PAPRIKA

1/2 teaspoon HOT PAPRIKA

3/4 cup CHICKEN STOCK (see
page 333) or canned low-sodium
chicken broth

1/2 cup HEAVY CREAM

1/4 cup DRY WHITE WINE

2 tablespoons SOUR CREAM

2 tablespoons CRÈME FRAÎCHE
(or use 4 tablespoons sour cream
or crème fraîche instead of
2 tablespoons of each)

Fresh JUICE of 1/2 LEMON

SERVES 4 AS A MAIN COURSE

4. Meanwhile, prepare the paprika sauce: Melt the butter in a saucepan over medium heat. Add the onion and cook, stirring frequently, until it is soft, brown, and caramelized, about 30 minutes. Add the garlic and cook for another minute. Season well with salt and white pepper. Stir in the paprikas, then pour in the chicken stock, heavy cream, and white wine. Cook over medium-low heat until the mixture has reduced by one third, 10 minutes. Add the sour cream and crème fraîche, season to taste with drops of the lemon juice, and add more salt and pepper if needed. Puree the sauce in a blender or with an immersion blender.

5. Serve the chicken with a sauceboat of the paprika sauce alongside.

PAPRIKA Paprika is a predominant feature of Hungarian cuisine, where it became popular as a substitute for pepper during the Napoleonic blockades. Many of the paprika-rich dishes found in Austria stem from the time when both countries were part of the Austro-Hungarian Empire.

But how paprika got to Hungary in the first place remains unclear. The two major theories are related to the Turkish occupation of Hungary in the seventeenth century. It is believed that either the Turks brought pepper seeds and grew them in their gardens in Hungary, or that Balkans, fleeing the Turks, brought the seeds north. Though it is not native to Eastern Europe, the paprika pepper thrives in its hot, dry regions. The Hungarian towns most famed for their paprika are Szeged and Kalocsa, where the peppers are grown, harvested by hand, strung out to dry, then ground with the careful inclusion of some pepper seeds for flavor and spice. The pepper is ground in a closed environment so that the heat of the grinding releases its flavorful, aromatic oils. The lipstick-red powder is then graded to indicate its quality and spiciness.

Different types of paprika vary in terms of texture and taste as well as heat. Some paprika is smoked, rather than dried in the sun—this gives it a more distinct flavor. The varieties commonly found in the U.S. are usually limited to "sweet," which is mild, and "hot," which contains the same fiery chemical, capsaicin, that is found in cayenne, a related spice. The most important thing to look for in either is high quality and freshness. Good paprika should be deep red, with no hint of bitterness, and with a soft, silky-smooth texture that melts into a paste as soon as it's warmed.

In Hungary, dishes based on paprika are divided into four categories: *gulyas, paprikas, porkolt,* and *tokany.* The first two are the ones that have traveled the most beyond Hungary's borders. *Gulyas,* translated as "goulash," is a complex, hearty shepherd's stew that appears in many guises in Austria, often with a prefix indicating the cut of beef it contains. *Paprikas,* or "paprikash," is made of large pieces of meat, often chicken, coated in a thick, creamy paprika sauce. *Porkolt* is a thick stew made with a high proportion of onions. *Tokany* is braised thin strips of meat, usually beef, often mixed with bacon and sausage.

One of the qualities of paprika-based dishes is their simplicity. Generally the base for the hearty, highly flavored stew contains nothing more than onions cooked in oil until they're soft and sweet, garlic, white wine, paprika, and sour cream. It's important to cook paprika carefully, since heat is required to bring out its flavor but scorching will caramelize its sugar, turning it brown and bitter: Add paprika to hot fat, let it bloom for a few seconds, then immediately add liquid. When fresh paprika is cooked gently, it has a full yet delicate flavor and a vegetal sweetness reminiscent of fresh bell peppers. Look for imported paprika, preferably from Szeged or Kalocsa, and buy it from a store with a high turnover to ensure that it isn't stale. Refrigerated, paprika will retain its freshness for up to 1 year. (For mail-order sources for paprika, see Sources, page 337.)

Squab

WITH FOIE GRAS MOUSSE, PARSLEY, AND SCHUPFNUDELN

Squab is a dark-fleshed, assertively flavored bird that is able to stand up to complex preparations. This is one. The squab is covered in a mousse of black truffles, foie gras, and Madeira, then served with salsify, squab *jus*, and an herbaceous parsley puree. All this high-toned elegance is mitigated slightly by the *Schupfnudeln* on the plate. Schupfnudeln, noodles made from a potato dough, are a homey staple at the heart of every Austrian grandmother's repertoire. You can roll the dough into thin noodles as described here, or you can roll it out, cut it into wedges, and deep-fry it. You can shape the dough into gnocchi and boil them, or form them into ropes and sauté them in brown butter, sugar, and nuts for dessert (see Nuss Nudeln, page 124).

1. Place the squab breasts and legs on separate plates, cover with plastic wrap, and refrigerate until ready to use.

2. Prepare the squab *jus:* Heat a large heavy stockpot over high heat for at least 5 minutes. Meanwhile, season the squab bones well with salt and pepper. Add the canola oil to the pot and heat it for 30 seconds. Then add the squab bones and sear well on every side, 15 minutes total. Remove the bones and pour out the oil.

3. Add the butter to the pot and scrape the bottom as the butter foams. Add the celery, carrots, and onion and cook, stirring, for 10 minutes. Reduce the heat to medium-low and cook the vegetables gently, stirring occasionally, until soft, about 30 minutes. Add the garlic and cook for another minute. Add the tomato paste and continue to cook, stirring, until it darkens, 5 minutes. Pour in the Madeira, raise the heat, and bring to a simmer. Cook, stirring, until the liquid is syrupy and reduced, 5 to 7 minutes. Add the squab bones and the chicken and veal stocks, and simmer gently for 1 1/2 hours. Add the bay leaf and thyme sprigs and continue cooking until the liquid is thickened, 1 hour. Strain the sauce and skim excess fat from the surface. Let the *jus* cool, stirring it often. Refrigerate it in a covered container until ready to serve. This can be made 1 day ahead.

5 SQUAB, about 3/4 pound each, trimmed (see Note)

SQUAB *JUS*
Trimmings and bones from 3 SQUAB, about 2 3/4 pounds

Fine SEA SALT and freshly ground BLACK PEPPER

2 tablespoons CANOLA OIL

2 tablespoons UNSALTED BUTTER

3 CELERY STALKS, very roughly chopped

2 CARROTS, sliced into rounds

1 large ONION, very roughly chopped

1 large GARLIC CLOVE, sliced

2 teaspoons TOMATO PASTE

1/2 cup MADEIRA

4 cups CHICKEN STOCK (see page 333) or canned low-sodium chicken broth

1 1/2 cups VEAL STOCK (see page 335)

1 BAY LEAF, preferably fresh

2 sprigs FRESH THYME

FOIE GRAS MOUSSE AND TRUFFLE
1/2 cup MADEIRA

2 teaspoons finely chopped FRESH BLACK TRUFFLE (see page 136)

1/4 cup diced FOIE GRAS, at room temperature (see page 206)

3 ounces BONELESS CHICKEN
BREAST, cut into 1-inch cubes

3/4 cup HEAVY CREAM

Fine SEA SALT and freshly ground
BLACK PEPPER

10 thin slices FRESH BLACK TRUFFLE

SCHUPFNUDELN
3 IDAHO POTATOES

KOSHER SALT

Fine SEA SALT and freshly ground
BLACK PEPPER

Freshly grated NUTMEG

2 teaspoons UNSALTED BUTTER,
softened

1 EGG

1/2 cup ALL-PURPOSE FLOUR, plus
additional for rolling

Fine SEA SALT

1/2 LEMON

4 SALSIFY ROOTS

Freshly ground BLACK PEPPER

5 tablespoons UNSALTED BUTTER

CANOLA OIL

1 teaspoon chopped FRESH PARSLEY

1 recipe PARSLEY PUREE
(see page 329)

Freshly grated NUTMEG

SERVES 5 TO 7 AS A MAIN
COURSE

4. Prepare the mousse: Combine the Madeira and chopped truffle in a small saucepan over medium heat, and bring to a simmer. Cook until the liquid is reduced to a syrup, about 7 minutes. Let cool.

5. Push the foie gras through a sieve into the bowl of a food processor. Slowly, with the motor running, dribble in the reduced Madeira mixture until smooth. Transfer the mixture to a bowl. (If the mixture breaks, or looks curdled, process again at high speed until smooth.)

6. Place the chicken cubes in the food processor and process until chunky. With the motor running, gradually add the cream. Season with salt and pepper. Fold the foie gras mixture into the chicken mousse.

7. Line a baking sheet with aluminum foil, and place the squab breasts at regular intervals on it. (Reserve the squab legs in the refrigerator until ready to use.) Season with salt and pepper, and cover each breast with a truffle slice. Use an offset metal spatula (or a butter knife) to spread a thin, even 1/8-inch-thick layer of mousse over each breast. Wrap the baking sheet in plastic and refrigerate.

8. To prepare the Schupfnudeln, preheat the oven to 350°F.

9. Prick the potatoes all over with a fork. Pour a 1-inch layer of kosher salt into a baking pan and place the potatoes on top. Bake the potatoes until soft, about 1 hour. Let cool on the salt. (Leave the oven on.)

10. As soon as the potatoes are cool enough to handle, scoop out their flesh and push it through a food mill, ricer, or fine-mesh sieve. Place 1 1/2 cups of the sieved potato in a large bowl. Season with salt, pepper, and nutmeg, and place the butter on top. Beat the egg and pour it into the potatoes. Mix gently to combine, then sift in the 1/2 cup flour. Mix gently to form a soft dough.

11. Bring a large pot of water to a boil and salt it until it tastes like seawater (about 2 teaspoons per quart). Roll out 1-inch-thick snakes of dough. Cut the snakes into 1 1/4-inch pieces and then roll each piece into 4-inch-long, 1/2-inch-wide snakes. Cook the noodles in the boiling water until they rise to the surface and are cooked through, 1 to 2 minutes. Drain and set aside.

12. Bring a large pot of water to a boil and salt it until it tastes like seawater (about 2 teaspoons per quart). Squeeze the lemon into a bowl of water. Peel the salsify roots and immediately put them into the acidulated water so they do not brown. Cut the salsify on the diagonal into 3-inch lengths, then blanch them in the boiling water until crisp-tender, 3 to 5 minutes. Drain.

13. Raise the oven heat to 400°F.

14. Unwrap the pan of squab breasts and roast them until medium-rare, 8 to 10 minutes. Let rest for 4 minutes. Season with salt and pepper.

15. Meanwhile, heat 1 tablespoon of the butter in a sauté pan and add the salsify. Cook slowly until the salsify browns, about 10 minutes.

16. Reduce the oven temperature to 350°F. Heat an ovenproof skillet over high heat, and pour in enough canola oil to lightly coat the bottom of the pan. Add the reserved squab legs and sear them on all sides, 5 minutes. Transfer the pan to the oven and roast until the legs feel just firm, 2 to 3 minutes. Add 1 tablespoon of the butter and the chopped parsley to the pan, and baste the legs. Transfer the legs to a plate and let rest.

17. In a saucepan, warm the parsley puree with 1 tablespoon of butter. Season with salt and pepper. Skim the excess fat off the squab *jus* and reheat it.

18. Heat the remaining 2 tablespoons butter in a large skillet and sauté the Schupfnudeln until golden, 3 minutes. Season with salt, pepper, and nutmeg.

19. To serve, spoon some parsley puree onto the center of each plate and spread it into a thin round. Slice the squab breasts at an angle and fan them over the puree. Then place a leg next to the breast meat. Garnish with the salsify and 3 or 4 Schupfnudeln. Spoon the *jus* over the meat.

Note: To prepare the squab, have your butcher separate the breasts and legs from the carcasses, removing the skin from the legs and removing the thigh bone (but leaving the lower bone attached), then roughly chop the bodies and bones. This recipe uses the breasts and legs of all the squab; the trimmings and bones of 3 squab are used to make the jus.

Quark Soufflé

1 cup QUARK CHEESE (see page 14)

Melted UNSALTED BUTTER, for the ramekins

6 tablespoons SUGAR, plus additional for the ramekins

3 large EGGS, separated

1 teaspoon VANILLA EXTRACT

Grated ZEST of 1 LEMON

1/4 teaspoon grated ORANGE ZEST

SERVES 6 AS DESSERT

This creamy yet ethereal soufflé has the tart, milky flavor of Quark, accented with vanilla and citrus. It makes a simple dessert on its own, or you can serve it with a seasonal fruit compote such as rhubarb or strawberries in spring; cherries, apricots, or other stone fruit in summer; plums or pears in fall; or dried fruit in winter.

1. Set a sieve over a bowl, line it with cheesecloth, and place 1/2 cup of the Quark in it. Let the Quark drain in the refrigerator overnight.

2. Preheat the oven to 375°F. Brush six 6-ounce ramekins with melted butter, and sprinkle the insides with sugar.

3. Whisk the egg yolks in a large bowl. Then stir in the drained Quark, the remaining 1/2 cup Quark, the vanilla, and the lemon and orange zests.

4. In a clean bowl of an electric mixer, beat the egg whites until foamy. Add 3 tablespoons of the sugar and beat until soft peaks form; then add the remaining 3 tablespoons sugar and beat until stiff.

5. Stir a little of the egg whites into the Quark mixture to lighten it; then fold in the rest of the whites. Divide the soufflé mixture among the prepared ramekins.

6. Place the ramekins in a 9-by-12-inch glass baking dish and pour in enough very hot water to reach halfway up the sides of the ramekins. Bake until puffed and golden brown, about 16 minutes. Serve warm, in the ramekins, or very carefully unmold before serving.

Passion Fruit–Poached Pears

WITH GRÜNER VELTLINER SABAYON

Most poached pear recipes rely on wine to add flavor and sharpness to the sugary fruit. This recipe uses passion fruit juice, which makes the dessert both tangy and very bright. The sabayon, flavored with Grüner Veltliner, adds richness and balances the acidity. You can also use another aromatic white wine, such as a Riesling or even a Gewürztraminer. If you don't want to make the caramel cage, serve this with some crisp cookies for a bit of crunch.

1. Cut a thin slice off the bottoms of the pears so they can sit upright. In a large saucepan, combine the passion fruit juice, sugar, and lemon zest with 1/4 cup water, and bring to a boil. Add the pears and simmer gently until soft, 8 to 10 minutes. Transfer the pears to a plate to cool.

2. To prepare the sugar basket, upturn a 4-ounce bowl or ladle (or one with at least a 4-inch diameter) over a large sheet of waxed paper. Spray the back of the bowl with nonstick cooking spray or rub it liberally with vegetable oil. If possible, prepare two molds in this way, to form the caramel baskets more quickly.

3. In a small saucepan over low heat, combine the sugar with 1/4 cup water and stir until completely dissolved. Increase the heat to high and bring the liquid to a boil. Cook without stirring until the sugar turns a very light brown caramel color, 6 to 7 minutes (swirl the pan gently if the caramel colors unevenly). Take the pan off the heat and let the caramel cool slightly, without stirring, until the bubbles subside.

4. Working very carefully (the caramel is extremely hot), dip a fork into the pot and swirl the caramel onto the mold in thin strands to form a cross-hatch pattern. Let the caramel basket cool for about 5 minutes, and then twist it to remove it from the bowl. Repeat this process to make 10 baskets, gently reheating the caramel as necessary to keep it liquid. Let the caramel baskets cool completely. They can be made 8 hours ahead and stored at room temperature.

10 FORELLE or small Bosc PEARS, peeled and cored

POACHING LIQUID
1/2 cup PASSION FRUIT JUICE (see Note)
1/2 cup SUGAR
Grated ZEST of 1/2 LEMON

SUGAR BASKETS
Nonstick COOKING SPRAY or vegetable oil, for the mold
1/2 cup plus 2 tablespoons SUGAR

SABAYON
3/4 cup GRÜNER VELTLINER or other dry, aromatic white wine
1/2 cup SUGAR
4 large EGG YOLKS
Grated ZEST of 1 LEMON

SERVES 10 AS DESSERT

5. Prepare the sabayon: Bring a few inches of water to a simmer in the base of a double boiler. In the top of the double boiler, whisk together the wine, sugar, egg yolks, and lemon zest. Place the mixture over the simmering water and whisk constantly until the sabayon is glossy and forms a fat ribbon when dripped from the whisk, about 8 minutes.

6. To serve, place a sugar basket on a plate, stand a poached pear inside it, and top with some of the sabayon.

Note: You can purchase passion fruit juice (also called puree) in gourmet shops, Latin American specialty shops, and some health food stores. Or order it by mail (see Sources, page 337).

Traditional Sweets

AND COFFEEHOUSE FAVORITES

THE COFFEEHOUSE TRADITION As with most important matters of culinary history, the origin of the coffeehouse in Vienna is of great debate. Did the first one open in 1645 or in 1683? Was the beverage brought by the Ottoman Turks, who, according to legend, left behind sacks of coffee beans when fleeing after a defeat in 1683? Or (more likely) was coffee introduced through merchants who had traveled the spice route and developed a taste for the inky, ground-filled beverage they enjoyed in Constantinople?

Finding an answer is never as satisfying as contemplating a question, which is precisely the kind of thing Austrians, and indeed all former members of the Austro-Hungarian Empire, do as they while away the hours in the many coffeehouses that line their cities' streets.

Historically, coffeehouses have been equalizing meeting grounds, like large, gracious salons where people of differing socioeconomic standing could discuss politics, art, or philosophy. Coffeehouses have often served as an extension of the home—many used to stock paper and pens so that writers could set up shop, even having their mail delivered there. During the late nineteenth century, the population growth in Vienna made this "neighborhood" style of living increasingly vital, as people began to spend more and more of their time in public places and less time in their over-crowded apartments.

When entering a coffeehouse, most regulars don't even notice the opulent décor anymore. The marble-topped tables, velvet banquettes (possibly worn, but comfortable nonetheless), grand crystal chandeliers, and gilt-framed mirrors are merely the stage for the real drama: Which of the many coffee beverages should one choose that day? Will it be a Kleiner Schwartzer—a black, thick demitasse? Or perhaps a Kleiner Brauner that same espresso with a dash of milk? One could sample a Maria Theresia (coffee with orange liqueur and whipped cream), named after the eighteenth-century empress who reigned for forty years, or an Eidotter (a glass of coffee with an egg yolk), reputedly a reliable cure for a hangover. The most popular coffee beverage in Vienna is indisputably the Mélange—half hot coffee, half steamed milk, occasionally embellished with a dollop of whipped cream. Of course, true coffeehouse habitués don't even bother ordering. Their beverage of choice is immediately brought over by the apron-clad waiter, who has memorized the preferences of all the regulars.

The 4 p.m. coffee-and-pastry ritual called *Jause* is the busiest time for the coffeehouse. People who should be working somehow make their way through the doors, and then linger over their coffees and pastries for what could be hours. No one is ever rushed out of a coffeehouse. Racks of newspapers line the walls, and after reading stories of politics and gossip, patrons neatly fold the papers and return them to the racks. Some carry chessboards and pass the day in slow, meditative competition. Along with the coffees, waiters always bring glasses of water on their silver trays. The water, constantly refilled, is a symbol of hospitality that was learned from the Ottomans. In fact, the waiters do so much refilling of water glasses that sometimes they might deliver two glasses at once to stave off the next refill just a little longer.

As if the leisurely pace, hospitality, superb coffees, and soaring Old Empire décor weren't enough, the exquisite pastries served at coffeehouses make it even harder to leave. These classics include poppy seed cake, Sachertorte, strudel, Dobos torte, and Gugelhopf. Another excuse to stay just a little bit longer. . .

Apple Strudel

RUM RAISINS

⅓ cup RAISINS

½ cup STROH RUM (see Note, page 298) or dark rum

DOUGH

3⅓ cups ALL-PURPOSE FLOUR, plus additional for the work surface

¼ cup CANOLA OIL, plus additional for the bowl

1 large EGG

1¼ teaspoons SALT

BREAD CRUMBS

3 tablespoons UNSALTED BUTTER

2½ cups BREAD CRUMBS, preferably fresh (see Note, page 107)

APPLE FILLING

6 large (about 3 pounds total) GRANNY SMITH APPLES

¼ cup plus 3 tablespoons SUGAR

2 teaspoons ground CINNAMON

½ cup chopped TOASTED PECANS

8 tablespoons (1 stick) UNSALTED BUTTER, melted and cooled

CONFECTIONERS' SUGAR, for sprinkling

SERVES 15

Unlike so many other pastries Austria is famous for, a good strudel does *not* melt in the mouth. A crisp, crackling, brittle pastry with a crunchy, almost sharp resistance on the tongue is the defining mark of strudel glory, and anything soggy, tough, or wilted need not apply.

While strudel is certainly the beloved child of the former Austro-Hungarian Empire, it is not, as one might think, its rightful offspring. Rather, it was conceived in the Ottoman Empire, where flaky pastries surrounding fillings are a hallmark of the cuisine (think of baklava and borek). Nonetheless, apple strudel is now as Austrian as apple pie is American, and every Austro-Hungarian cook is expected to know how to stretch the dough impossibly thin. In Austria, cooks say that the dough should be so thin you can read a newspaper through it, while the Hungarian saying is that the dough should be large enough to wrap around a hussar and his horse. Americans will say the dough should be as thin as phyllo, which is generally what we use to make our strudels.

And phyllo is a fine substitute for making your own dough. Still, any strudel lover should try making the dough at least once. Stretching strudel dough may seem intimidating, but it's not that much harder than making a pie crust. The key is patience, patience, patience. Don't rush the stretching; it could take you up to an hour the first time you try it, and that is okay. If the dough tears, don't fret. Any mistakes will be covered with more dough when you roll it up. A perfect strudel dough takes practice, but a perfectly acceptable one is much closer at hand.

Making strudel is more fun when it's a two-person job, so rustle up an extra set of hands to help stretch the dough. You should also have ready a large, preferably rectangular, surface that measures approximately 2½ by 6 feet, covered by a tablecloth or bed sheet if possible (any kind will do). To prevent tears, take off your rings and other jewelry before stretching the dough. And roll up your sleeves—cuffs and buttons can slice through strudel dough like knives.

Serve the strudel warm, if possible, on the same day it was made (preferably within 30 minutes of baking). Ice cream and whipped cream make excellent accompaniments.

PEACH STRUDEL FILLING

8 large PEACHES (about 3 pounds), pitted and cut into 1-inch chunks

1/2 cup SUGAR

Grated ZEST and fresh JUICE of 1 LEMON

1 teaspoon grated ORANGE ZEST

1 teaspoon VANILLA EXTRACT

In a large bowl, toss the peaches with the sugar, lemon zest and juice, orange zest, and vanilla extract. Fill and bake as directed in the Apple Strudel recipe.

APRICOT STRUDEL FILLING

15 FRESH APRICOTS (about 3 pounds), pitted and quartered

3/4 cup SUGAR

2 teaspoons fresh LEMON JUICE

Grated ZEST of 1 LEMON

1 teaspoon grated ORANGE ZEST

In a large bowl, toss the apricots with the sugar, lemon juice, and lemon and orange zests. Fill and bake as directed in the Apple Strudel recipe.

1. Place the raisins in a bowl, add the rum, and let soak overnight.

2. Prepare the dough: Place 1 cup plus 2 tablespoons warm water in the bowl of an electric mixer fitted with a dough hook. Add the flour, oil, egg, and salt, and mix at a medium speed for at least 5 minutes. The dough will be soft and slightly moist, but not sticky (when poked it should cling to your finger at first, then pull away, leaving your finger clean). Turn the dough onto a lightly floured surface and knead it for 5 minutes, dusting it with a little more flour if it becomes too sticky.

3. Oil a bowl and place the dough in the bowl, turning to coat it with the oil. Cover the bowl with plastic wrap and let the dough rest at room temperature for 2 hours, or refrigerate it overnight. (This relaxes the gluten in the flour and makes it easier to stretch.) Let the dough return to room temperature before stretching it.

4. Prepare the crumbs: Melt the butter in a sauté pan over medium heat. Add the bread crumbs and cook, tossing, until golden brown, about 5 minutes. Transfer them to a plate to cool.

5. Prepare the filling: Peel and core the apples and slice them into eighths. Cut each slice crosswise into 1/2-inch-wide pieces. In a bowl, toss the apples with the sugar and cinnamon. Drain the rum raisins and stir them, along with the toasted pecans, in with the apples.

6. Preheat the oven to 400°F, and line a baking sheet with parchment paper. You'll need a large, preferably rectangular, surface or table that measures approximately 2 1/2 by 6 feet. If you have a sheet or tablecloth, cover the surface with it.

7. Using the backs of your hands as a support, stretch the dough in a widening circle. As it gets thinner and larger, hook one end on the corner of the table. Continue to stretch the dough, hooking the corners, much as you would make a bed with a fitted sheet. The dough should be so thin that you can see your hands through it (and the pattern on the sheet or tablecloth), and it should hang off the table by at least 3 inches. The gravity of the dough hanging off the table will help you stretch it, so let it fall. You can also use your forearms to help stretch the dough when it gets big enough.

8. Working as quickly as possible, brush the entire expanse of dough with melted butter. Sprinkle the lower 2 inches of the dough on the narrow end of the table with the bread crumbs, then mound the filling over the crumbs, patting it into a log shape. Using your palms, cover the filling with the dough that is hanging over the edge of the table. Then continue rolling the "log" up in the entire length of the dough, trying to keep it relatively tight. Place the strudel on the prepared baking sheet, bending it into a horseshoe shape if necessary for it to fit, and brush the top and sides with butter. Bake until crisp and golden, about 35 minutes. Sprinkle with confectioners' sugar, slice, and serve warm.

Christmas Stollen

When stollen start appearing in the bakeries, all the children take it as a sign that Christmas is nearly here. Stollen is a sweet, spiced yeast bread enriched with butter and studded with rum-soaked raisins and candied fruit. It's the kind of snack that everyone in Austria keeps on hand during the holiday season. You have it for breakfast with coffee, as a snack in the early afternoon to keep you going between lunch and *Jause* (the 4 p.m. coffee break), or as a bedtime treat. Stollen has keeping power and will last for days, if not weeks.

1. Place the raisins in a bowl and cover them with the rum. Let soak overnight.

2. Prepare the sponge: Gently warm the milk in a small saucepan over low heat. When it is just warm (not hot) to the touch, pour it into a large mixing bowl and sprinkle in the yeast. Whisk until the yeast is dissolved; then add the flour and stir with a wooden spoon. Cover the bowl tightly with plastic wrap, and let it rest in a warm place for 30 minutes.

3. Prepare the dough: In the bowl of an electric mixer fitted with the whisk attachment, beat the egg yolks, sugar, corn syrup, and salt together until the mixture is pale yellow and forms a ribbon when the beater is lifted, about 5 minutes. Add the lemon zest, vanilla, cinnamon, and cardamom and mix to combine. Then mix in the sponge. Switch to the dough hook attachment and add the flour and butter. Mix until the dough comes together, about 5 minutes. Transfer it to a lightly oiled bowl.

4. Drain the raisins. Sprinkle the candied orange and lemon peel, hazelnuts, and raisins over the dough, covering all the surface area, and push down slightly to embed the fruit and nuts in the dough. Cover the bowl with plastic wrap and let rise in a warm place for 30 minutes.

RUM RAISINS
2 cups GOLDEN RAISINS

2 1/2 cups STROH RUM (see Note, page 298) or dark rum, to cover

SPONGE
2/3 cup whole milk

2 1/2 teaspoons ACTIVE DRY YEAST

1 1/2 cups ALL-PURPOSE FLOUR

DOUGH
2 large EGG YOLKS

1 tablespoon SUGAR

1 teaspoon LIGHT CORN SYRUP

1/4 teaspoon SALT

Grated ZEST of 1 LEMON

1 teaspoon VANILLA EXTRACT

1 teaspoon ground CINNAMON

1/4 teaspoon ground CARDAMOM

2 1/3 cups ALL-PURPOSE FLOUR

1 cup (2 sticks) UNSALTED BUTTER, cold, cut into small pieces

CANOLA OIL, for the bowl

1 cup diced CANDIED ORANGE PEEL and 1 cup diced CANDIED LEMON PEEL (see Sources, page 337)

1/2 cup HAZELNUTS, toasted, peeled, and chopped (see Note)

Melted UNSALTED BUTTER, for the baking sheet and brushing the stollen

CONFECTIONERS' SUGAR, for sprinkling

MAKES 2 LOAVES

5. Butter a large baking sheet.

6. Turn the dough onto a clean surface and knead it several times, flattening it and folding it over itself to distribute the fruit and nuts evenly. Divide the dough in half, and roll each half into a horseshoe shape. Flatten each cylinder slightly, then fold the edges under. Place the stollen, seam side down, on the prepared baking sheet. Cover the loaves with plastic wrap and let them rest at room temperature for 45 minutes.

7. Meanwhile, preheat the oven to 350°F.

8. Place the baking sheet in the oven and spray the oven floor with water to create steam. Bake until the loaves are brown and sound hollow when tapped on the bottom, about 45 minutes. Let them cool on wire racks.

9. Liberally brush the cooled loaves with melted butter, and sprinkle them with a thick layer of confectioners' sugar. Let the stollen sit for at least 4 hours, and then sprinkle them heavily with more confectioners' sugar. Stollen is best eaten at least a day after baking.

Note: To remove the astringent, papery brown skin from hazelnuts, spread them out in a single layer on a baking sheet and bake at 350°F, stirring once, until they are brown and fragrant, 8 to 10 minutes. Immediately transfer the nuts to a mesh sieve and use a kitchen towel to rub off their skins while still warm. Place the nuts on a plate to cool.

Rum Raisin Gugelhopf

RUM RAISINS

1 cup GOLDEN RAISINS

1 1/4 cups STROH RUM (see Note) or
  dark rum, to cover

Melted UNSALTED BUTTER,
  for the pan

1/2 cup SLIVERED ALMONDS

1 1/4 cups (2 1/2 sticks) UNSALTED
  BUTTER, softened

2 cups CONFECTIONERS' SUGAR

1/2 cup CORNSTARCH

1 tablespoon STROH RUM (see Note)
  or dark rum

2 teaspoons VANILLA EXTRACT

Grated ZEST of 1/2 LEMON

7 large EGG YOLKS

6 large EGG WHITES

Pinch of SALT

3/4 cup SUGAR

2 1/4 cups ALL-PURPOSE FLOUR

SERVES 10

Another rum raisin- and nut-filled yeast bread, this one is molded in a decorative pan. Unlike stollen, which is a Christmas cake, Gugelhopf is enjoyed year-round, and in fact has been for centuries—though how many is, of course, a topic for endless coffeehouse debate. It is known that the sweet-toothed Emperor Franz Joseph loved it, which gives this pastry the status of a cake fit for royalty. Gugelhopf, unlike stollen, is best eaten within a day or two of baking. Keep it wrapped in plastic to preserve the moist texture.

1. Place the raisins in a dish, cover with rum, and let soak overnight.
2. Preheat the oven to 325°F. Brush the inside of a 6-cup tube or bundt pan with melted butter, and sprinkle it with the slivered almonds.
3. In the bowl of an electric mixer fitted with the paddle attachment, cream the butter with the confectioners' sugar and cornstarch until pale and creamy, 4 to 5 minutes.
4. Add the rum, vanilla extract, and lemon zest. Beat in the egg yolks one at a time.
5. Place the egg whites in a clean bowl of an electric mixer fitted with the whisk attachment, and beat until foamy. Add the salt and gradually pour in the sugar, whipping until soft peaks form.
6. Drain the raisins. Using a rubber spatula, fold the flour into the butter-and-egg-yolk mixture, in three additions. Gently fold in the egg whites, working slowly to avoid deflating them. Fold in the raisins.
7. Pour the batter into the prepared mold, and use a wide rubber spatula to sweep the batter to the edges, so that the cake looks slightly concave (this will prevent it from rising too much in the center). Bake until a cake tester inserted into the center of the cake comes out clean and dry, 60 to 70 minutes. Let cool on a wire rack before unmolding.

Note: Most Austrian desserts are made with a dark, highly aromatic rum called Stroh rum. While it's hard to find here (see Sources, page 337), it's nearly ubiquitous in Austria, where it has the somewhat dubious reputation of being the rum of choice for both pastry cooks' baking projects and college-age kids' drinking binges. You can substitute dark rum instead.

Linzertorte

There are many different types of Linzertorte. Some are more like tarts, with crisp and buttery cookie-like crusts. Others, like this one, are softer and more cakelike. But all the recipes share two elements, namely a nutted pastry redolent with spices and a thick, sweet filling of jam, usually raspberry or red currant. This version also has almonds on top to give the cake a little crunch. As the name indicates, the pastry hails from the city of Linz, which is justly famous for its desserts. It's also the home of Linzer Augen, which are often made with leftover dough from a Linzertorte (see recipe, page 324).

1. Preheat the oven to 375°F. Butter and flour a 10-inch cake pan.

2. In the bowl of an electric mixer fitted with the paddle attachment, cream the butter and confectioners' sugar until smooth. Add the whole eggs one at a time, scraping down the bowl between additions. Then add the yolks, lemon zest, cinnamon, vanilla, cloves, and salt. Beat at medium-high speed until very light and fluffy, about 5 minutes.

3. Meanwhile, place the hazelnuts in a food processor. Sprinkle the 1 tablespoon flour over the nuts and pulse until the mixture is ground to a fine meal. Transfer the hazelnut meal to a large bowl and whisk in the remaining 1 cup flour and the cake crumbs.

4. Use a large rubber spatula to fold the dry ingredients into the butter mixture. Spread a 1 1/2-inch layer of batter in the prepared cake pan. Spread the jam over the batter. Then spoon the rest of the batter into a pastry bag, or a resealable plastic bag with one corner cut off, and pipe out a lattice pattern on top. Sprinkle with the slivered almonds and bake until golden, about 40 minutes. Let cool in the pan completely before serving.

Note: With typical frugality, European pastry makers often turn leftover cake and brioche into flavorful crumbs that form the basis of many desserts. It works best with slightly stale, dry bread or cake, but if you have a fresh, moist cake or brioche, you can dry it out a little in the oven before grinding it into crumbs in a food processor. The crumbs needn't be totally dry, just enough so they don't turn to mush.

1 cup (2 sticks) plus 5 tablespoons UNSALTED BUTTER, softened, plus additional for the pan

1 cup plus 1 tablespoon ALL-PURPOSE FLOUR, plus additional for the pan

2 1/3 cups CONFECTIONERS' SUGAR

4 large EGGS

2 large EGG YOLKS

Grated ZEST of 1 LEMON

1 tablespoon ground CINNAMON

1 teaspoon VANILLA EXTRACT

1/4 teaspoon ground CLOVES

Pinch of SALT

2 1/2 cups (10 1/2 ounces) whole HAZELNUTS, toasted and peeled (see Note, page 297)

5 cups (1 pound) PLAIN CAKE or brioche CRUMBS (see Note)

1 cup SEEDLESS RASPBERRY JAM or red currant jam

3 tablespoons SLIVERED ALMONDS

SERVES 12

Sachertorte

CHOCOLATE CAKE

¹/₂ cup (1 stick) plus 2 tablespoons UNSALTED BUTTER, at room temperature, plus additional for the pans

1¹/₄ cups sifted ALL-PURPOSE FLOUR, plus additional for the pans

5 ounces BITTERSWEET CHOCOLATE, chopped

¹/₂ cup CONFECTIONERS' SUGAR

¹/₂ VANILLA BEAN, split lengthwise, seeds scraped out with a knife

6 large EGGS, separated

³/₄ cup plus 2 tablespoons SUGAR

2 cups APRICOT JAM

CHOCOLATE GLAZE

³/₄ cup plus 2 tablespoons SUGAR

5 ounces BITTERSWEET CHOCO-LATE, chopped

SERVES 6 TO 8

Another of Austria's illustrious cakes, this one has a long, somewhat fraught history. Who invented the original cake and where is a matter of such heated debate that there was even a lawsuit to settle the dispute that lasted for seven years. Now only the Hotel Sacher in Vienna has the right to call their torte "the Original." Other recipes do abound, however. What they all have in common is a dense chocolate cake either filled with or topped by apricot jam, and a somewhat sticky, thick chocolate glaze. Serve this with plenty of whipped cream—and coffee, of course.

1. Preheat the oven to 400°F. Butter and flour two 6-inch cake pans, then line the bottoms with parchment paper.

2. In the bottom of a double boiler, bring a few inches of water to just below simmering (or use a saucepan with a clean bowl suspended over the water). Place the chopped chocolate in the top of the double boiler (or in the bowl) and set it over, not in, the barely simmering water. Melt the chocolate, stirring a few times when it is glossy to be sure all the bits are melted. (Alternatively, melt the chocolate in a microwavable dish on medium-low power, microwaving for 30 seconds at a time and stirring each time.)

3. In the bowl of an electric mixer fitted with the paddle attachment, beat the butter with the confectioners' sugar until creamed and fluffy, 4 to 5 minutes. Add the vanilla seeds, then beat in the egg yolks one at a time. Stir in the melted chocolate and set aside.

4. In a clean bowl of an electric mixer fitted with the whisk attachment, beat the egg whites until they are foamy. Gradually add the sugar, and beat until the whites form soft peaks.

5. Stir a little of the egg whites into the chocolate mixture to lighten it. Use a rubber spatula to gently fold in the remaining whites, working slowly to avoid deflating them. Fold in the sifted flour.

6. Pour the batter into the prepared pans, and use a wide rubber spatula to scrape the batter from the center to the edges of the pans, so that the cakes look slightly concave (this will prevent them from rising too much in the center). Bake for 20 minutes. Then reduce the oven temperature to 325°F and bake until the center is set and a cake tester inserted into the middle of the cake comes out clean, about another 20 minutes.

7. Slide a knife around the cakes to loosen them, and immediately turn them out onto a wire rack to cool.

8. Place the apricot jam in a small saucepan over medium heat and bring it to a simmer. Cook until the jam is slightly thickened, 1 to 2 minutes. Let cool.

9. When the cakes are cool, split each layer in half so that you have 4 layers. Cut a stiff piece of cardboard into a round slightly smaller than the diameter of the cakes (or use a 6-inch purchased cardboard cake round). Place a layer of cake on the cardboard. Set a wire rack over a rimmed baking sheet (to catch excess glaze), and place the layer with the cardboard on the rack.

10. Spread a layer of jam over the cake. Place another layer on top and repeat the process, using all the layers of cake. Finish by spreading a thin layer of jam over the top and sides of the cake.

11. To prepare the glaze, you'll need a clean metal or marble surface to pour the hot glaze out on (if you don't have an appropriate countertop or marble slab, use a large overturned metal baking sheet). Place the sugar in a saucepan with 1/3 cup water and bring to a boil, stirring until the sugar is dissolved. Stir in the chopped chocolate and boil until the temperature reaches 350°F on a candy thermometer.

12. Strain the liquid through a fine-mesh strainer set over a bowl. Immediately pour about 1 cup of the glaze onto a metal or marble surface. Stir the remaining chocolate in the bowl. Use a long metal spatula to move the chocolate around on the work surface until it cools slightly (it should not become hard). Scrape up the chocolate and stir it back into the chocolate in the bowl. Pour another cup of glaze out onto your work surface and repeat the process. It is important to keep all the chocolate moving and to work quickly. You want to lower the temperature and thicken the glaze. Repeat one more time if necessary, until the glaze is sticky and slightly thickened. Immediately pour the glaze evenly over the cake. Let it cool until the chocolate hardens.

Poppy Seed Cake

This is a simple, homey, plain cake that can be dressed up in myriad ways. You can split the layers and sandwich them with a thick filling of apricot or raspberry jam. You can fill and ice the cake with whipped cream or chocolate frosting. You can toast slices and serve them with a pat of melting butter on the top. But even eaten on its own with a cup of tea or coffee, this is a fine-textured, moist cake with excellent flavor.

1. Preheat the oven to 350°F. Butter two 8-inch cake pans and line them with parchment paper.

2. Place 1 tablespoon of the confectioners' sugar in a coffee grinder or spice mill with one quarter of the poppy seeds. Pulse until the poppy seeds are finely ground and the texture of sand, about 20 seconds (avoid over-processing—they should not become a paste). Transfer the ground poppy seeds to a bowl. Repeat this three more times with the remaining poppy seeds and 3 more tablespoons of the sugar.

3. Place the walnuts in a food processor (using the smallest work bowl you have). Add $1/4$ cup of the confectioners' sugar and pulse until the nuts are airy, with the consistency of fine bread crumbs, about 40 seconds. Whisk the ground nuts into the poppy seed mixture and set aside.

4. In a small bowl, whisk together the flour, cinnamon, and baking powder, and set it aside. Using a hand grater or a food processor, grate the apple and set it aside.

5. In the bowl of an electric mixer, combine the egg yolks with the remaining $1 1/2$ cups confectioners' sugar, and beat until light and very fluffy, about 2 minutes.

6. In a clean bowl of an electric mixer fitted with the whisk attachment, beat the egg whites on high speed until they are very foamy, about 2 minutes. Add the honey and salt. Continue to beat on high speed until the whites are stiff but not dry and form glossy peaks. Add a little of the white mixture to the yolk mixture and stir to combine. Gently fold the remaining whites into the yolk mixture.

UNSALTED BUTTER, for the cake pans

2 cups CONFECTIONERS' SUGAR

1 cup plus 1 tablespoon POPPY SEEDS

$1 1/3$ cups roughly chopped WALNUTS

5 tablespoons plus 1 teaspoon ALL-PURPOSE FLOUR

$2 1/4$ teaspoons ground CINNAMON

$1 1/4$ teaspoons BAKING POWDER

1 small GRANNY SMITH or other tart green APPLE, peeled and cored

6 large EGG YOLKS

7 large EGG WHITES

2 tablespoons plus 1 teaspoon HONEY

Pinch of SALT

SERVES 10

7. Working slowly so the batter does not deflate, fold the flour mixture and then the nuts and poppy seeds into the batter. Combine gently until the mixture is almost smooth. Fold in the grated apple. Divide the batter between the prepared pans, and using a wide spatula, gently scrape the batter from the center to the edges of the pans, so that the cakes look slightly concave (this will prevent them from rising too much in the center).

8. Bake until a cake tester inserted into the middle of the cake comes out clean and the tops are golden, about 30 minutes. When the cakes are done, run a knife around the sides of the pan to loosen them. Invert the pans over a wire cooling rack and peel the parchment paper off the bottoms. Let cool thoroughly.

POPPY SEEDS

Poppy seeds are ubiquitous in Austria. They are sprinkled on top of buns and pastries, used ground in sweetened fillings, and tossed into pasta, potato, and egg dishes. Poppy seed oil is used for cooking and dressing salads.

Since they contain a high percentage of oil, poppy seeds can go rancid if they are not used fairly soon after purchase. If you can, taste a seed when buying them to make sure it isn't bitter or stale. Don't buy much more than you plan to use, and store extra poppy seeds in the refrigerator or freezer to keep them fresh.

Most Austrian kitchens are equipped with a poppy seed grinder, a hand-cranked metal tool that resembles a small meat grinder. These are available at specialty cookware stores (or see Sources, page 337), although the results can be approximated by grinding the seeds with sugar or flour in an electric coffee bean or spice grinder.

Malakoff

LADYFINGERS

¹/₄ cup SLICED ALMONDS or hazelnuts, skinned and toasted

¹/₂ cup SUGAR

1 cup ALL-PURPOSE FLOUR

3 tablespoons CORNSTARCH

6 large EGGS, separated

1 teaspoon VANILLA EXTRACT

¹/₈ teaspoon SALT

CREAM

3 large EGGS, separated

6 tablespoons SUGAR

1 ¹/₂ teaspoons powdered UNFLA-
  VORED GELATIN

2 ¹/₂ cups HEAVY CREAM

5 tablespoons COINTREAU or Grand
  Marnier

SOAKING SYRUP

1 cup SUGAR

1 cup fresh ORANGE JUICE

5 tablespoons COINTREAU or
  Grand Marnier

1 cup HEAVY CREAM

1 tablespoon SUGAR

1 cup SLIVERED ALMONDS, toasted
  (see Note)

SERVES 10 TO 12

This rather froufrou dessert is an elaborate confection of layered home-made ladyfingers, orange liqueur-flavored custard and syrup, and whipped cream. It is simultaneously light and very rich, which makes it possible to eat more of it at one sitting than anyone practicing modera-tion might like. It's a special cake that takes some time to prepare, but none of the steps are particularly difficult. What *is* difficult is limiting yourself to one slice.

1. Preheat the oven to 375°F. Line two baking sheets with parchment paper.
2. Prepare the ladyfingers: In a food processor, pulse the nuts with 1 table-spoon of the sugar until finely ground. Set aside. In a small bowl, whisk together the flour and cornstarch. Set it aside.
3. In the bowl of an electric mixer fitted with a paddle attachment, beat the egg yolks with 3 tablespoons of the sugar, the vanilla extract, and the salt until the mixture is pale yellow and a ribbon forms when the paddle is lifted, about 5 minutes.
4. In a clean bowl of an electric mixer fitted with the whisk attachment, whip the egg whites until foamy. Then gradually add the remaining ¹/₄ cup sugar and beat until soft, glossy peaks form.
5. Stir a little of the egg white mixture into the yolk mixture to lighten it, then use a rubber spatula to gently fold in the rest of the whites. Work slowly to avoid deflating them. Fold the flour mixture into the batter.
6. Transfer the batter to a pastry bag fitted with a plain tip (or use a reseal-able plastic bag with one corner snipped off). Pipe out 12 small ladyfingers (2-inch-long ovals—they will be slightly peanut shaped) on one of the pre-pared baking sheets, and sprinkle them with the ground nuts. Pipe the rest of the batter into larger ladyfingers (3 inches long) on the second sheet. Bake for 10 minutes. Cool on wire racks.

7. Prepare the cream: Bring a few inches of water to a gentle simmer in the bottom of a double boiler (or use a saucepan with a metal bowl suspended over it). In the top of the double boiler (or in the bowl), whisk together the egg yolks and 3 tablespoons of the sugar. Place the yolks over (not in) the simmering water and whisk constantly until the mixture is thick and glossy, about 6 minutes. Transfer the mixture to the bowl of an electric mixer fitted with the whisk attachment, and beat at medium speed until completely cool.

8. Pour 1/4 cup cold water into a bowl and sprinkle the gelatin over it. Let sit for 10 minutes. Whip the cream and set it aside.

9. In a clean bowl of an electric mixer fitted with a (clean) whisk attachment, beat the egg whites until foamy. Then sprinkle in the remaining 3 tablespoons sugar and beat until the whites form soft peaks.

10. Transfer the gelatin mixture to a small saucepan and add the Cointreau. Cook over low heat, stirring constantly, until the gelatin dissolves completely.

11. Whisk the gelatin mixture into the egg yolk mixture. Stir a little of the egg whites into the yolk mixture to lighten it. Then use a rubber spatula to gently fold in the rest of the whites. Work slowly to avoid deflating them. Fold the whipped cream into the batter.

MARIO, SWEET TALKING . . . Cakes are popular throughout the year and we eat them in the afternoon, maybe with some coffee. But cookies are for Christmas. During the Christmas season, we eat cookies all day long—cookies in the morning, cookies in the afternoon, before lunch, after lunch, or with lunch, even. Cookies at night . . .

In the mornings before Christmas day, we wake up to the smell of cookies baking. This is what everyone's grandmother does: She bakes hundreds of cookies. Then she gives them out to all her friends, and they give her their cookies, and it always seems that you end up with more cookies than you started with. But you always like the ones your grandmother made the best.

When you get invited somewhere during the holidays, you bring cookies. Even if you don't bake them yourself, you go to the bakery and buy special Christmas cookies. Everyone knows which bakery makes the best of a certain type, so you might go one place for one kind and another place for another kind. It can be a lot of work, Christmas.

12. Prepare the soaking syrup: Combine the sugar with 1 cup water in a saucepan over medium heat and bring to a boil, stirring until the sugar dissolves. Transfer to a bowl and stir in the orange juice and Cointreau.

13. Set aside all the small ladyfingers and 20 of the large ladyfingers. Have ready a deep 10-inch springform pan (or use a cake ring). Drop the remaining large ladyfingers into the syrup one at a time, soaking each for 10 seconds, then taking it out of the syrup and gently squeezing the excess syrup back into the bowl. Lay the soaked ladyfingers on a plate.

14. To assemble the dessert, place as many of the large unsoaked ladyfingers as you can fit in a single layer in the springform pan, all facing the same direction. Spread a $1/2$-inch-deep layer of the cream over them, filling all the spaces and leveling the top of the cream. Next, use the soaked ladyfingers to create a layer in the same way, but arranging the cookies in the other direction, so they are perpendicular to the cookies in the layer below. Spread another layer of cream over this, to fill the spaces and cover the ladyfingers by at least $1/4$ inch. Continue this process, alternating dry and soaked ladyfingers, until the pan is full. Be sure to spread the final layer of cream so that no ladyfingers show through. Refrigerate for 3 hours.

15. To finish, lightly whip the cream with the sugar. Cut out a round of stiff cardboard that is slightly smaller than the diameter of the cake (or use a purchased cardboard or metal cake bottom). Unmold the cake and place it on the cake round. Spread a layer of whipped cream over the whole cake. Score the cream on the top of the cake to mark off 12 equal portions. Transfer the remaining whipped cream to a pastry bag fitted with a star tip, and pipe a small rosette of whipped cream at the edge of each of the 12 portions. Place a small ladyfinger in each of the rosettes. Holding the cake from beneath, press the toasted almonds onto the sides. Serve lightly chilled.

Note: To toast the slivered almonds, spread them on a rimmed baking sheet and bake them in a 325°F oven, stirring once, until golden and fragrant, about 6 minutes.

Hazelnut-Jam Sandwiches, Dotterbusserl, Vanilla Butter Crescents, Anise Cookies, Neros, Eisenbahner

Hazelnut-Jam Sandwiches

1 cup (2 sticks) plus 2 tablespoons UNSALTED BUTTER, plus additional for the baking sheets

2 1/4 cups ALL-PURPOSE FLOUR, plus additional for the baking sheets

1/4 cup WHOLE HAZELNUTS, toasted and peeled (see Note, page 297)

Pinch of SALT

3/4 cup CONFECTIONERS' SUGAR

3 large EGG YOLKS

2 tablespoons WHOLE MILK

1/3 cup SEEDLESS RASPBERRY JAM

1/3 pound BITTERSWEET CHOCOLATE, chopped

MAKES ABOUT 15 COOKIES

Another Christmas specialty, this variation on the jam-filled nut cookie theme consists of two hazelnut cookies sandwiched with raspberry jam and dipped halfway in bittersweet chocolate.

1. Preheat the oven to 325°F. Butter and flour two baking sheets, or line them with nonstick liners.

2. Place the hazelnuts in a food processor and add 1 tablespoon of the flour. Pulse until they are ground to a fine meal. Add the remaining flour and the salt, and pulse a few times to combine.

3. In the bowl of an electric mixer fitted with the paddle attachment, beat the butter and confectioners' sugar until light and fluffy, 3 minutes. Add the egg yolks and beat to incorporate. Alternating, add the flour mixture in three additions and the milk in two additions; mix until just combined.

4. Scoop the batter into a pastry bag fitted with a 1/2-inch star tip and pipe crescents, or other shapes, onto the prepared baking sheets, leaving 1 inch between cookies. Bake until golden brown around the edges, 15 to 17 minutes. Let cool on wire racks.

5. Spread a teaspoonful of the jam on the bottom of each cooled cookie, and press another cookie over it to make a sandwich.

6. Melt the chocolate in the top of a double boiler set over barely simmering water (or in the microwave on medium-low power, stirring every 30 seconds). Dip the cookies halfway into the chocolate, then lay them on parchment-lined baking sheets to dry and set, about 4 hours. Or refrigerate them for 30 minutes to set the chocolate. These cookies keep for 3 days, stored airtight at room temperature.

Dotterbusserl

EGG YOLK KISSES

Once you start eating these sugary, apricot jam—filled little morsels, you'll find it hard to stop. The chocolate coating is optional, but divine.

1. Preheat the oven to 350°F. Line a baking sheet with parchment paper or a nonstick liner.

2. In the bowl of an electric mixer fitted with the whisk attachment, beat the eggs, sugar, and vanilla extract until the mixture is light yellow and forms a ribbon when the beater is lifted, 5 minutes. Use a rubber spatula to gently fold in the flour.

3. Transfer the batter to a pastry bag fitted with a plain tip (or use a resealable plastic bag with one corner cut off), and pipe 1-inch spheres onto the prepared pan. Bake until light golden in color, about 8 minutes. Let cool on wire racks.

4. Spread about 1 teaspoon of the jam onto the bottom of a cookie, then press another cookie onto the jam to form a sandwich. Repeat until all the cookies are sandwiched.

5. If you want to dip the cookies in chocolate, melt the chocolate in the top of a double boiler set over barely simmering water (or in the microwave on medium-low power, stirring every 30 seconds). Dip the cookies halfway into the chocolate, then lay them on parchment-lined baking sheets to dry and set, about 4 hours. Or refrigerate them for 30 minutes to set the chocolate. These cookies keep for 1 day stored airtight at room temperature.

4 large EGGS

1/2 cup SUGAR

1 teaspoon VANILLA EXTRACT

1 1/4 cups ALL-PURPOSE FLOUR

1/2 cup APRICOT JAM

1/2 pound BITTERSWEET CHOCO-LATE, chopped (optional)

MAKES 2 DOZEN COOKIES

Vanilla Butter Crescents

½ cup WHOLE HAZELNUTS, toasted and peeled (see Note, page 297)

1 cup ALL-PURPOSE FLOUR, plus additional for the baking sheets

1¼ cups CONFECTIONERS' SUGAR

Pinch of fine SEA SALT

8 tablespoons (1 stick) UNSALTED BUTTER, chilled and cut into small cubes

1 VANILLA BEAN, split lengthwise, seeds scraped out with a knife, or 1 teaspoon vanilla extract

UNSALTED BUTTER, for the baking sheets

MAKES 2 DOZEN COOKIES

These buttery shortbread-type cookies are made with ground nuts, which give them an especially tender texture. This is compounded by the confectioners' sugar shower they get while they are still warm, which sinks in and softens them even further. Be careful if you're wearing black clothes when you eat these . . .

1. Place the hazelnuts in a food processor and add 3 tablespoons of the flour. Pulse until the mixture is ground to a fine meal.

2. In a bowl, whisk the remaining flour with ¼ cup of the confectioners' sugar and the salt. Add this to the hazelnut mixture and pulse to combine. Add the butter and pulse until the dough begins to come together. Add the vanilla seeds and pulse until a smooth dough forms. Wrap the dough in plastic and refrigerate for at least 30 minutes or as long as 3 days.

3. Preheat the oven to 325°F. Butter and flour two baking sheets, or line them with nonstick liners.

4. Form the dough into 1-inch balls; then roll each ball out to form a 3-inch-long snake, and curve it like a horseshoe. Place the cookies on the prepared baking sheets and bake until light golden brown, 8 to 10 minutes. Transfer the baking sheets to wire racks. Generously sift some of the remaining 1 cup confectioners' sugar over them while they are still warm, and then again when they are cool. Store in an airtight container for up to 2 weeks.

Anise Cookies

These buttery, brittle cookies are like French *tuiles*, or tile-shaped cookies, but with an anise flavor. They are perfect to serve after dinner, with coffee or liqueurs.

1. Preheat the oven to 350°F. Butter a baking sheet, or use a nonstick liner.
2. In the bowl of an electric mixer fitted with the paddle attachment, whip the eggs and sugar for 4 minutes. Use a rubber spatula to gently fold in the flour.
3. Spread 2-inch circles—they don't have to be perfectly round—onto the prepared baking sheet. Sprinkle each cookie with about 8 anise seeds. Bake until light golden brown, 6 to 8 minutes. Immediately lift the cookies with a thin spatula and drape them over a rolling pin or a bottle. Let the cookies cool on the rolling pin, to develop their characteristic curved shape. The cookies will keep for 2 days stored airtight at room temperature.

UNSALTED BUTTER, for the baking sheet

2 large EGGS

1/4 cup SUGAR

1/4 cup ALL-PURPOSE FLOUR

ANISE SEEDS, for sprinkling

MAKES ABOUT 3 DOZEN COOKIES

Neros

COOKIES

1 cup plus 2 tablespoons UNSALTED BUTTER, softened

1/2 cup plus 3 tablespoons SUGAR

2 large EGGS

1 large EGG YOLK

1 teaspoon VANILLA EXTRACT

Pinch of SALT

1 1/3 cups ALL-PURPOSE FLOUR

1/2 cup plus 1 tablespoon UNSWEET-ENED COCOA POWDER

FILLING

3/4 cup HEAVY CREAM

6 ounces BITTERSWEET CHOCO-LATE, chopped

MAKES 32 COOKIES

These moist, fudgy little cookies are Austria's answer to the brownie. In fact, with their melt-on-the-tongue texture and ridiculously decadent whipped chocolate ganache filling, they may be even better. Be careful not to overbake these—you want them to be soft and spongy.

1. Preheat the oven to 325°F, and line several baking sheets with parchment paper or nonstick liners.

2. In the bowl of a mixer fitted with the paddle attachment, cream the butter with the sugar and beat on medium-high speed until light and fluffy, 3 minutes. Add the eggs and yolk one by one, waiting until each is incorporated before adding the next. Add the vanilla extract and salt.

3. Whisk the flour and cocoa powder together in a small bowl. Using a rubber spatula, fold this mixture into the butter mixture. Spoon the batter into a pastry bag or a resealable plastic bag with one corner cut off. Pipe chestnut-size (1 1/2-inch) balls of dough onto the prepared baking sheets. Bake until just firm to the touch, 7 to 8 minutes. Let cool on wire racks.

4. To prepare the filling, bring the cream to a simmer in a medium saucepan. Add the chocolate and remove from the heat. After the chocolate has melted, stir to combine. Scrape the chocolate into the bowl of an electric mixer fitted with the whisk attachment, and whip until it is cool, light, and fluffy, about 12 minutes.

5. Spoon heaping teaspoons of filling onto the underside of each cookie, and sandwich it with another cookie. The cookies will keep in an airtight container for 2 to 3 days.

OBERLAA One of the best places to get a pastry in Vienna these days is Oberlaa. This boutique chain of artisan bakeries is considered by some to have the finest, lightest, most inventive pastries in the city. It's a particular favorite of David's, and he stops at one or another of the shops on every trip he makes to Vienna. He never leaves without sampling at least five or six sweets—even when he is alone.

Eisenbahner

RASPBERRY ALMOND COOKIE "RAILS"

These chewy almond cookies look like train tracks, hence the name. You can fill them with any kind of jam you like, though a red one such as raspberry, strawberry, or currant gives the most dramatic look.

1. In the bowl of an electric mixer fitted with the paddle attachment, beat the confectioners' sugar and butter until smooth and fluffy, about 3 minutes. Beat in the egg yolk, vanilla, and lemon zest. Scrape down the sides of the bowl, and add the flour and salt. Mix just until the ingredients form a smooth dough.

2. Form the dough into a disk, wrap it in plastic, and refrigerate it for at least 30 minutes or as long as 3 days.

3. Preheat the oven to 325°F. Line a baking sheet with parchment paper or a nonstick liner.

4. Lightly flour a work surface and roll the dough out to form a 6- by 12-inch rectangle, 1/8 inch thick. Slice the dough into four long rectangles, each 1 1/2 by 12 inches—the size of a ruler. Carefully lay the rectangles on the prepared baking sheet, and bake until golden brown, 16 to 18 minutes. Cool on baking sheets.

5. When the cookies are cool, spread 1/4 cup of the raspberry jam on each of two cookies, and sandwich them with the remaining two. Return the sandwiched cookies to the baking sheet.

6. Preheat the oven to 500°F.

7. Prepare the macaroon batter: Beat the almond paste, egg, confectioners' sugar, and butter together in a bowl until smooth. Transfer the batter to a pastry bag fitted with a star tip (or use a resealable plastic bag with one corner cut off—this will pipe plain strips instead of stars) and pipe a thin edge, like a frame, all the way around the perimeter of each sandwich cookie. Bake until the macaroon batter is golden, about 5 minutes.

8. Place the remaining 1 1/2 cups raspberry jam in a saucepan and bring to a simmer over medium heat. Simmer until the jam is sticky and reduced by one third, about 5 minutes. Pour a thin layer of the warm jam onto each sandwiched cookie, spreading it to fill the macaroon "frame." Let cool, then slice the rectangles on the diagonal to create 1-inch cookies.

COOKIES

1 cup CONFECTIONERS' SUGAR

1 cup (2 sticks) UNSALTED BUTTER, at room temperature

1 large EGG YOLK

2 teaspoons VANILLA EXTRACT

1 teaspoon GRATED LEMON ZEST

2 1/2 cups ALL-PURPOSE FLOUR

1/8 teaspoon SALT

2 cups SEEDLESS RASPBERRY JAM

MACAROON BATTER

1/4 cup ALMOND PASTE

1 large EGG

2 tablespoons CONFECTIONERS' SUGAR

1 tablespoon UNSALTED BUTTER

MAKES 2 DOZEN COOKIES

Cinnamon Sablés, Linzer Augen

Cinnamon Sablés

These buttery cinnamon cookies are David's all-time favorite. Make them and you'll see why.

1. In the bowl of an electric mixer fitted with the paddle attachment, or in a food processor, beat the butter and brown sugar until smooth. Then add one of the eggs and mix to combine. Add the flour, cinnamon, and salt, and beat or pulse to form a dough. Roll the dough to form one or two long cylinders about 2 inches in diameter, wrap them in plastic, and refrigerate for at least 30 minutes or as long as 3 days.

2. Preheat the oven to 325°F. Line several baking sheets with parchment paper or nonstick liners.

3. Beat the remaining egg in a bowl. Pour about $\frac{1}{4}$ inch of granulated sugar into a shallow dish. Brush the outside of the dough log with the beaten egg, then roll the log in the sugar to coat it. Slice $\frac{1}{4}$-inch coins of cookie dough from the log, and arrange them on the prepared baking sheets.

4. Bake until lightly browned around the edges and firm, about 15 minutes. Let cool on the baking sheets. These cookies will keep for 1 week, stored airtight at room temperature.

$1\frac{1}{2}$ cups plus 6 tablespoons ($3\frac{3}{4}$ sticks) UNSALTED BUTTER

$\frac{3}{4}$ cup plus 1 tablespoon LIGHT BROWN SUGAR

2 large EGGS

$3\frac{2}{3}$ cups ALL-PURPOSE FLOUR

2 tablespoons ground CINNAMON

$\frac{1}{2}$ teaspoon SALT

GRANULATED SUGAR, for rolling the cookies

MAKES 7 DOZEN COOKIES

Linzer Augen

JAM-FILLED BUTTER RINGS

2 cups ALL-PURPOSE FLOUR, plus additional for the baking sheets

3/4 cup plus 2 tablespoons CONFECTIONERS' SUGAR, plus additional for sprinkling

1 teaspoon GRATED LEMON ZEST

Pinch of SALT

3/4 cup (1 1/2 sticks) plus 2 tablespoons UNSALTED BUTTER, cut into cubes, plus additional for the baking sheets

3 large EGG YOLKS

1 teaspoon VANILLA EXTRACT

1/3 cup SEEDLESS RASPBERRY or apricot JAM

MAKES ABOUT 30 COOKIES

Making homemade jam in the summer, when there is plenty of ripe fruit, is an Austrian tradition. While you certainly can buy excellent Austrian preserves, the best ones are made at home, preferably with fruit from a nearby orchard. And everyone has a favorite recipe. In this cookie, named for the city of Linz, an "eye" of jam peeks through a crumbly shortbread round. This is one of the most popular cookies in Austria, possibly because it goes so perfectly with coffee.

1. Place the flour, confectioners' sugar, lemon zest, and salt in the bowl of an electric mixer fitted with the paddle attachment, and stir to combine. Add the butter and beat until smooth, scraping down the sides of the bowl with a rubber spatula as needed. Add the egg yolks and vanilla, and beat until just combined. Wrap the dough in plastic wrap and refrigerate for at least 30 minutes or as long as 3 days.

2. Preheat the oven to 350°F. Butter and flour several baking sheets, or line them with nonstick liners.

3. Divide the dough in half. Working with one piece of dough at a time, roll the dough out on a lightly floured surface to 1/8-inch thickness. Using a round or fluted round cookie cutter, preferably 2 1/2 inches in diameter, cut out rounds of dough. Using a smaller (maximum 1-inch) cookie cutter, or the reverse end of a pastry tip, cut rounds from the middle of half the cookies. (Don't reroll these scraps. Instead, bake the cut-out holes and make tiny sandwich cookies out of them, using more jam, if desired.) Place the cookies on the prepared baking sheets and bake until very light brown, about 8 minutes. Transfer the cookies to wire racks to cool.

4. When the cookies are cool, sift confectioners' sugar over the ring-shaped ones. Drop teaspoonfuls of jam in the center of each round cookie. Place the ring over the jam; the filling should peek through the hole.

Pantry

Oil-Cured Salmon

KOSHER SALT to cover (about 4 cups)
One 3/4-pound SALMON FILLET
4 cups CANOLA OIL
2 BAY LEAVES, preferably fresh
2 whole STAR ANISE
One 1-inch-long slice FRESH GINGER
1 teaspoon freshly ground BLACK PEPPER

MAKES 12 OUNCES CURED SALMON

1. Select a wide, shallow pan that is large enough to comfortably hold the salmon, and cover the bottom with a thick layer of kosher salt. Lay the salmon on the salt and cover it with more kosher salt, patting it on so that no salmon shows through. Refrigerate until the salmon feels firmer at the thickest part, 3 to 4 hours.
2. Combine the canola oil, bay leaves, star anise, ginger, and pepper in a saucepan and heat until the oil just begins to steam. Remove from the heat and let cool.
3. Rinse the cured salmon thoroughly and pat it dry. Place the salmon in a shallow dish, and pour the oil and seasonings over it. Cover and refrigerate for at least 24 hours or as long as 1 week.

Egg Pasta Dough

1 1/4 cups ALL-PURPOSE FLOUR, plus additional for rolling the pasta
1/2 teaspoon fine SEA SALT
4 large EGG YOLKS
1 large EGG
2 teaspoons EXTRA-VIRGIN OLIVE OIL

MAKES ABOUT 1 POUND

1. *To prepare the pasta dough by hand:* Stir the flour and salt together and mound the mixture on a clean surface. Make a wide well in the center. Beat the egg yolks, whole egg, and oil in a bowl, and pour the mixture into the well. With a fork, swirl the eggs, picking up flour as you go. Continue to incorporate more flour until the dough is stiff. Move the dough to a clean part of your work surface, lightly flour, and knead for 15 minutes, until it is completely smooth and not at all sticky. Cover with plastic wrap and let rest for 30 minutes before rolling out.
To prepare the pasta dough in a stand mixer fitted with a dough hook: Place the flour and salt in the bowl and mix to combine. Beat the yolks and egg together in a bowl, and then pour them into the mixer bowl. Add the oil. Mix on medium speed, scraping down the sides of the bowl several times, until the dough comes together and is smooth, about 5 minutes. Transfer the dough to the counter and knead a few times. Cover with plastic wrap and let rest for 30 minutes before rolling out.
2. Divide the dough into 4 pieces and roll each piece out to form a small rectangle, using a rolling pin. Beginning on the thickest setting, crank the dough through a pasta machine. Lightly sprinkle the dough with flour, then fold it in thirds and put it through the pasta machine again. Repeat this process once more on the thickest setting. Then make the setting one size smaller, and roll the pasta through. Repeat, reducing the setting by one size at a time until you reach the thinnest setting. Lightly dust the sheets with flour and cut as desired. Wrap in plastic and refrigerate for up to 24 hours.

Tomato Water

2 1/2 pounds PLUM TOMATOES, cored and chopped
1/4 cup CHAMPAGNE VINEGAR
2 large FRESH BASIL LEAVES
1 tablespoon fine SEA SALT
2 teaspoons CORIANDER SEEDS
1 teaspoon WHITE PEPPERCORNS

MAKES 1 1/2 CUPS

1. Combine all the ingredients in a large bowl and let marinate at room temperature for 1 hour.
2. Working in two batches, puree the tomato mixture in a blender until frothy and pink.
3. Soak a large clean dish towel in water, and wring it out. Place the towel in a sieve suspended over a large bowl.
4. Pour the tomato mixture into the dish towel-lined sieve, and cover the top with plastic wrap. Place the bowl in the refrigerator, and let the mixture drip for 12 hours.
5. Carefully remove the sieve from over the bowl, and discard the tomato pulp. Refrigerate the tomato water, tightly sealed, for up to 4 days.

Parsley Puree

Fine SEA SALT
2 cups packed FRESH FLAT-LEAF PARSLEY LEAVES
Freshly ground BLACK PEPPER

MAKES 1 1/4 CUPS

1. Fill a bowl with water and ice. Bring a pot of water to a boil and salt it until it tastes like seawater (about 2 teaspoons per quart). Blanch the parsley in the boiling water until it is tender but still bright green, about 1 minute. Drain, and transfer immediately to the ice water to cool. Use a slotted spoon to remove the cooled parsley, reserving the ice water. Squeeze the parsley dry in a clean dish towel.
2. Immediately place the parsley in a blender with 1/4 cup of the ice and water. Season with salt and pepper, and puree. Add more water and ice as needed to make a smooth puree. Refrigerate, tightly covered, for up to 4 days.

Chive Oil

1 1/4 cups very roughly chopped FRESH CHIVES
   (1-inch lengths)
1/2 cup GRAPESEED or CANOLA OIL

MAKES 1/2 CUP

Place the chives in a blender and cover with a few table-spoons of the oil. Process until the oil is green. With the motor running, slowly drizzle in the rest of the oil. Do not strain. Store in a covered container in the refrigerator for up to 1 week.

Basil Oil

1 cup packed BASIL LEAVES
3/4 cup GRAPESEED or CANOLA OIL, chilled

MAKES 3/4 CUP

Combine the basil and 1/2 cup of the cold oil in a blender or food processor, and puree until very smooth. With the blender running, drizzle in the remaining 1/4 cup oil. Blend until smooth. Then push the puree through a fine-mesh strainer into a bowl, discarding the solids. Cover and refrigerate for up to 4 days.

Garlic Oil

1 head GARLIC, cloves separated but not peeled
1 cup CANOLA OIL

MAKES 1 CUP

Place the garlic cloves and the oil in a saucepan over medium-low heat, and simmer for 1 hour. Remove from the heat and let cool. Strain, discarding the garlic (or reserve it for a garlic puree). The oil can be refrigerated for up to 3 days.

Vegetable Stock

1 ONION, coarsely chopped

4 CELERY STALKS, coarsely chopped

3 CARROTS, coarsely chopped

5 FRESH PARSLEY STEMS

2 sprigs FRESH THYME

1 BAY LEAF, preferably fresh

1 1/2 teaspoons BLACK PEPPERCORNS

1 teaspoon fine SEA SALT

MAKES 5 CUPS

Combine all the ingredients in a large stockpot and add 7 cups water. Bring the liquid to a boil over medium-high heat, and then simmer over medium-low heat, uncovered, for 1 hour. Strain the stock through a fine-mesh strainer, discarding the solids. Let it cool completely, and then refrigerate for up to 3 days.

Note: All the stocks can be frozen for up to 3 months.

Mushroom Stock

2 1/2 pounds FRESH MUSHROOMS, wiped clean and trimmed

Fine SEA SALT

MAKES 3 CUPS

1. Place 1 1/2 pounds of the mushrooms in a stockpot with water to cover (about 5 cups). Bring to a boil, lower the heat to medium-low, and simmer for 2 hours. Strain the broth, discarding the mushrooms, and return the liquid to the pot. Add the remaining mushrooms, bring to a boil, and simmer for another 1 1/2 hours. Strain the broth, discarding the mushrooms.

2. Pour the stock into a saucepan, bring it to a boil, and then simmer until it is reduced to about 3 cups and is the color of a dark cup of coffee. Season with salt. Let cool, cover, and refrigerate for up to 3 days.

Chicken Stock

5 pounds CHICKEN BONES, trimmed of fat
   and skin, roughly chopped

1 LEEK, roughly chopped

1 CARROT, roughly chopped

1 CELERY STALK, roughly chopped

1/2 head GARLIC

1 SHALLOT, chopped

4 sprigs FRESH PARSLEY

1 sprig FRESH THYME

1/2 teaspoon WHITE PEPPERCORNS

1 BAY LEAF, preferably fresh

Fine SEA SALT, to taste

MAKES ABOUT 2 QUARTS

1. Rinse the chicken bones well and place them in a stockpot with cold water to cover (about 2 1/2 quarts). Bring the liquid to a simmer and skim the surface.

2. Add the remaining ingredients, and cook at a gentle simmer for 2 1/2 hours, skimming off the foam from time to time. Strain the stock through a fine-mesh sieve, discarding the solids, and let it cool completely. Cover and refrigerate for up to 4 days. Skim off the congealed fat before using.

White Beef Stock

2 pounds MEATY BEEF BONES, rinsed and roughly
   chopped

1 ONION, roughly chopped

1 CARROT, roughly chopped

1 CELERY STALK, roughly chopped

4 sprigs FRESH PARSLEY

1 sprig FRESH THYME

1/2 teaspoon BLACK PEPPERCORNS

2 WHOLE CLOVES

1 BAY LEAF, preferably fresh

Fine SEA SALT, to taste

MAKES 2 QUARTS

1. Place all the ingredients except the salt in a stockpot with cold water to cover (about 2 1/2 quarts). Bring the liquid to a simmer, partially cover, and keep the liquid barely simmering for 2 1/2 hours.

2. Season the stock with salt. Then strain it through a fine-mesh sieve, discarding the solids, and let it cool completely. Cover, and refrigerate for up to 4 days. Skim off the congealed fat before using.

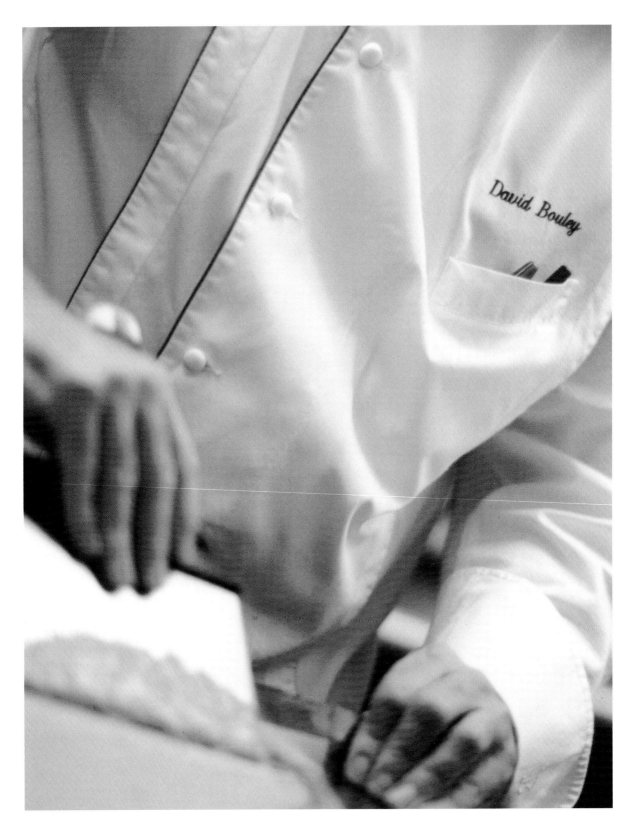

Veal Stock

3 pounds VEAL BONES, roughly chopped (you can have your butcher chop them) and rinsed

1 pound BEEF (use trimmings, if desired)

1 cup DRY RED WINE

1 ONION, roughly chopped

1 CARROT, roughly chopped

1 CELERY STALK, roughly chopped

1/2 cup roughly chopped MUSHROOMS (use mushroom stems, if desired)

1/2 head GARLIC

4 sprigs FRESH PARSLEY

1 sprig FRESH THYME

1/2 teaspoon BLACK PEPPERCORNS

1 BAY LEAF, preferably fresh

Fine SEA SALT

MAKES 2 QUARTS

1. Preheat the oven to 400°F.

2. Place the veal bones and the beef in a large, heavy, heatproof enameled pot and roast for 30 minutes, turning several times so they brown evenly.

3. Transfer the pot to the stovetop and pour off the fat. Add the wine and stir to scrape up the cooked-on juices.

4. Add cold water to cover (about 2 1/2 quarts), bring the liquid to a simmer, and skim the surface.

5. Add all the vegetables, herbs, and spices, and cook at a gentle simmer for 3 hours, skimming off the foam from time to time. Season the stock with salt. Then strain it through a fine-mesh sieve, discarding the solids, and let it cool completely. Cover, and refrigerate for up to 4 days. Skim off the congealed fat before using.

How to Render Poultry Fat

Poultry fat (skin on), cut into 1-inch cubes

Cook the poultry pieces in a heavy pan over medium heat, turning them occasionally, until they begin to lose some of their fat to the pan. Raise the heat slightly and continue to cook until the fat is clear and liquid and the skin is browned and crisp. Strain the fat and let it cool. Refrigerate, covered, for up to 1 month. (Serve the crisped skin, salted, as a snack, if desired.)

Wine Notes

TERMS YOU MIGHT SEE ON THE LABEL

Alte Reben: old vines

Ried: vineyard

Trocken: bone dry

Spätlese: not really sweet, but made from fruity, very ripe grapes

Beerenauslese: medium sweetness, usually affected by botrytis

Ausbruch: historical term used for dessert wines made from grapes affected by botrytis, from the town of Rust

Trockenbeerenauslese: full-throttle sweetness, always affected by botrytis

Eiswein: from grapes shriveled by freezing, a succulent wine with brilliant acidity

Qualitätswein: some sugar might be added, but still fairly dry

Kabinett: no added sugar is allowed, but chaptalization is allowed

Since the late 1990s Austrian wines have been critically noted and ardently sought out. The stony soil along the Danube gives grapes character. In addition to the must-drink Rieslings is Grüner Veltliner (Grüner to its growing number of fans), once a mindless thirst-quencher and now being produced as an increasingly dry, serious wine.

Some of the best whites originate within fifty miles of Vienna. The Wachau is the most well known (and expensive) area. There, winemakers have developed labeling laws that indicate the ripeness of the grapes (as opposed to the sugar content), which is reflected in the weight and richness of the wine. (From the least ripe grapes and lightest wines to the ripest and heaviest, these are: Steinfeder, Federspiel, and Smaragd.) Other notable white wine regions along Austria's Danube are Kamptal, Kremstal, and Wien (Vienna).

Grüner counts for about two thirds of the white production. Like the other Austrian white wines, it is very dry. The wine is produced in various styles and weights, from lean and mean (Steinfeder) to lush and sensual (Smaragd). The Steinfeder can have almost a chlorophyll-like greenness. At its friendliest, it has edgy, smoky, spicy, and green apple elements, sometimes with the citrus-peel quality of a fine Riesling.

Harder to grow and rarer, Austrian Rieslings are gorgeous and bone dry, and they can taste and smell of hefty doses of lime and grapefruit zest. With age, they can develop characteristic petrolish weight and mineral complexity.

Other expressive whites are Pinot Blanc (Weissburgunder); Pinot Gris (Grauburgunder); Gewürztraminer (Traminer); and Scheurebe (usually seen in Germany). Austria also produces Chardonnay, called Morillon, and in the tiny area of Styria, Sauvignon Blanc is gaining a reputation for its intensity.

Though less common, Austrian reds can be a joy. The best come from the south, along the Hungarian border. Burgenland, Austria's warmest region, produces the country's finest reds and dessert wines. Its long growing season is great for late-ripening red grapes, and its swampy lake, the Neusiedlersee, provides the humidity conducive to noble rot, which can create world-class dessert wines.

Among Austria's unique reds is Blaufränkisch (also known as Lemberger), which can show anywhere from as light and fruity as Gamay to as hefty and robust as Syrah. Pinot Noir (called Blauburgunder) tends to have a gentle, wild berry-like quality. Blauer Portugieser and Zweigelt (a St. Laurent-Lemberger hybrid) are usually spicy and lightweight, with Beaujolais-like easy drinking.

—Alice Feiring

Sources

THE BAKER'S CATALOGUE: Sheet gelatin; Callebaut chocolate; poppy seed grinder; candied orange and lemon peel
(800)827-6836
www.kingarthurflour.com

DARTAGNAN: Wild mushrooms; truffles and truffle products; foie gras and foie gras terrine; venison
(800)327-8246
www.dartagnan.com

FAR AWAY FOODS: D'Arbo Fine Plum Conserve (Powidl); semolina flour; hot and sweet paprika (Szeged); elderflower syrup
(650)344-1013
www.farawayfoods.com

THE GRILL STORE & MORE: Wood chips (for smoking)
(877)743-2269
www.grillingaccessories.com

INTERNET WINES AND SPIRITS: Stroh rum
(877)624-1982
www.internetwines.com

KALUSTYAN'S: Passion fruit puree; hot and sweet paprika (Szeged); black sesame seeds
(212)685-3451
www.kalustyans.com

HUDSON VALLEY FOIE GRAS: Foie gras
(845)292-2500
www.hudsonvalleyfoiegras.com

MURRAY'S CHEESE SHOP: Hoch Ybrig; Brin d'Amour; Quark
(888)692-4339
www.murrayscheese.com

SPICE TRADERS NORTHWEST: Sausage casings
(509)624-1490
www.spicetradersnw.com

SUTTONS BAY TRADING COMPANY, INC.: Poppy seeds; sausage casings; carob powder
(888)747-7423
www.suttonsbaytrading.com

URBANI: Frozen, peeled chestnuts; truffles and truffle products
(800)281-2330
www.urbani.com

VERMONT BUTTER & CHEESE COMPANY: Quark
(800)884-6287
www.vtbutterandcheeseco.com

Index

agnolotti, chestnut, with fresh white truffles, 36-38

almond-crusted halibut with asparagus, porcini, and kohlrabi puree, 252-54

almond paste, in raspberry almond cookie "rails," 321

anise cookies, 319

apple:

    in big apple (cocktail), 229

    gelée, Kumamoto oysters with, 18

    horseradish sauce, boiled beef with spinach puree, baby vegetables and, 50-53

    rosemary puree, in gently heated salmon with a julienne of Styrian Wurzelgemüse and chive-horseradish sauce, 40-42

    salad, hot-smoked salmon with salmon caviar, sherry dressing and, 21-23

    strudel, 290-92

apricot:

    filling, for strudel, 292

    jam, in sachertorte, 302-4

    jam, marmalade palatschinken with, 170

asparagus:

    almond-crusted halibut with porcini, kohlrabi puree and, 252-54

    white, warm rabbit salad with foie gras, tarragon-Riesling sauce and, 155-57

Austrian:

    cheese ravioli with harvest corn and smoked mushrooms (schlutzkrapfen), 243-47

    crescent potatoes, wiener schnitzel with cucumbers, lingonberries and, 102-7

    potato salad with fresh black truffles, 78-81

avocado:

    dumplings, crab-filled, 131

    mousse, salmon ravioli with, 184

baby lettuce, in mache salad with bacon and quail eggs, 132

baby squid, sea scallops, and crabmeat, with Paradeiser, coriander, and lemon thyme sauce, 249-50

bacon, mache salad with quail eggs and, 132

basil oil, 330

bass, striped, roasted prosciutto-wrapped, with Szegediner sauerkraut, 93-95

beef:

    boiled, with spinach puree, apple horseradish sauce, and baby vegetables, 50-53

    cheek goulash with potato puree, 96-99

    cheeks, wine-braised, with chanterelle goulash, 158-61

    shanks, in goulash soup, 100

    stock, white, 333

beet(s):

    -fennel salad, cured mahimahi with blood orange vinaigrette and, 83-85

    juice, in red beet fettuccine, 263

    salad with caraway seeds and walnut oil, 240

    sorbet, oysters with sour cream and, 230

bell peppers, red, Liptauer-stuffed, 16

bibb lettuce-and-cucumber vinaigrette, mackerel "herring style" with, 188

big apple (cocktail), 229

bittersweet chocolate:

    for egg yolk kisses, 317

    in hazelnut-jam sandwiches, 316

    in neros, 320

    in passion fruit parfait, 116-18

    in sachertorte, 302-4

black truffles:

    Austrian potato salad with, 78-81

    in Bouley's truffle martini, 224

    leaf spinach with poached egg and, 134-36

    marinated sea scallops with passion fruit and, 233-35

    in squab with foie gras mousse, parsley, and schupfnudeln, 277-79

black trumpet mushrooms, Maine lobster with red beet fettuccine and, 263-65

blood orange vinaigrette, cured mahimahi with beet-fennel salad and, 83-85

blueberry martini, 224

Bohemian plum pancakes, 64-66

boiled beef with spinach puree, apple horseradish sauce and baby vegetables (kavalierspitz), 50-53

bone marrow dumplings, oxtail consommé with, 74-76

Bouley's truffle martini, 224

braised veal shank with porcini risotto, 212-14

brandteigkrapfen (swan-shaped cream puffs), 166-68

bread:

    Christmas stollen, 295-97

    pudding, chocolate, 122

    rum raisin Gugelhopf, 298

Brussels sprouts, venison strudel with plum jam, chestnuts and, 109-10

butter, browned, homemade noodles with nuts and, 124

buttermilk, and rhubarb parfait, 163-65